P9-DGT-931

THE COMPETITION
PARADIGM

THE COMPETITION PARADIGM

America's Romance with Conflict, Contest, and Commerce

Pauline Vaillancourt Rosenau

ROWMAN & LITTLEFIELD PUBLISHERS, INC.
Lanham • Boulder • New York • Oxford

ROWMAN & LITTLEFIELD PUBLISHERS, INC.

Published in the United States of America
by Rowman & Littlefield Publishers, Inc.
A Member of the Rowman & Littlefield Publishing Group
4501 Forbes Boulevard, Suite 200, Lanham, Maryland 20706
www.rowmanlittlefield.com

PO Box 317, Oxford OX2 9RU, United Kingdom

Copyright © 2003 by Rowman & Littlefield Publishers, Inc.

All rights reserved. No part of this publication may be reproduced, stored in a
retrieval system, or transmitted in any form or by any means, electronic, mechanical,
photocopying, recording, or otherwise, without the prior permission of the publisher.

British Library Cataloguing in Publication Information Available

Library of Congress Cataloging-in-Publication Data

Vaillancourt Rosenau, Pauline.
  The competition paradigm : America's romance with conflict, contest,
and commerce / Pauline Vaillancourt Rosenau.
    p. cm.
Includes bibliographical references and index.
  ISBN 0-7425-2037-4 (cloth : alk. paper) — ISBN 0-7425-2038-2 (pbk. : alk. paper)
  1. Competition (Psychology) 2. Competition—United States. I. Title.
BF637. C47 V36 2003
320' .14—dc21

                                                                      2002015744

♾™ The paper used in this publication meets the minimum requirements of American
National Standard for Information Sciences—Permanence of Paper for Printed Library
Materials, ANSI/NISO Z39.48-1992.

This book is dedicated to Véronique Vaillancourt, my remarkable daughter, with the profound hope that hers will be a world where competition takes on softer, kinder, gentler forms that permit all to be truly productive, to find life fulfilling, and to make a contribution to society.

Contents

Preface

READERS HAVE A DISTINCT ADVANTAGE over authors—that of time relevance. Writers are stuck, confined and defined by the concrete imprinting of ideas on paper. Readers are forever current if they choose, and able to take recent events into account. They are empowered by the possibility of reassessing the written word in light of new material that can never be anticipated by the writer. It is in this context of a time-bound presentation that setting out to write about a topic such as competition is intimidating.

Broad consideration of a topic such as competition is presumptuous and audacious. It requires a commitment to an interdisciplinary approach to scholarship, an unusual set of personal life experiences, an intellectual passion for a topic, and a foolish optimism regarding how much time is involved. *The Competition Paradigm* comes from my having studied and received academic degrees in both the social sciences and the health sciences. It is also the result of my changing and broadening my academic specialization over the years from sociology, to psychology, to political science, to philosophy, and now to public health. Living outside the United States for decades cultivated cultural skepticism. It meant becoming marginal enough to question what is taken for granted by most Americans. But of greatest importance is the fact that repeatedly, in so many life circumstances and academic encounters, the data just do not support the theory, the philosophy, and the basic assumptions about the competition paradigm, and it seems to be time that someone says so.

The message of this book is that not all forms of competition are the same. Some are benign or even beneficial, and others are destructive. *The Competition Paradigm* involves synthesis, integration, and analysis. It takes the isolated results of already existing research, dispersed across fields and disciplines, and brings them together. The goal is a unique contribution to knowledge that goes beyond any single study because the weight of the evidence, taken together, is compelling and cannot be dismissed as an exception to the rule, an outlier, or simply a fluke. If successful, the whole is greater than the sum of its parts.

My approach is basically inductive, though those who read the book from front to back may not notice this. I proceed point by point, study by study. The strength of such an approach is that it is comprehensive, meticulous, and thorough. The weakness is that it can be quite tedious because the overall conclusion is postponed to the end. The risk, then, is that the importance of the conclusion may be overshadowed by the weight of detail that supports it. The compromise employed here is to begin with an overview and then move on to examine the evidence. This, too, has disadvantages: The order of presentation is opposite that of the logic of discovery—it appears to be deductive when it is in fact inductive. In addition, it seems repetitive because the argument is first stated and then developed. The impression of repetition is compounded because each chapter or subsection of a chapter starts with a brief summary. This course seems advisable in a world where time constraints on so many readers mean that a quick read is all that is likely. Presentation is a trade-off, and I believe that the presentation chosen here is the better of several approaches to the order of argument, none of which is perfect.

Initial reactions to *The Competition Paradigm* suggest to me that fundamental issues are at stake here. One reader of an early version of the manuscript for this book indicated that the cultural change required to modify the competition paradigm was simply insurmountable. He argued that America's real problem, in any case, is a failure of government. There is certainly a crisis of leadership in America today. But an overcommitment to destructive forms of competition is also central to America's predicament. I do not agree that one explanation need be the only reasonable account or that these two are in some way incompatible. As Sir Michael Marmot states it so nicely, "It is a common tendency in science to argue that in order for my pet hypothesis to be correct yours has to be wrong. Indeed, it is somewhat unsatisfying for both yours and mine to be right at the same time."[1] In a complex world, multiple accounts are often the most reasonable.

Individual chapters of this book have been presented at professional conferences—none has been published elsewhere. I am indebted to the many anonymous reviewers that read the manuscript and spent so much time commenting on it. A few agreed to reveal their identity, and this makes it possible for me to thank Florence Denmark, past president of the American Psychological Association and currently the Robert Scott Pace Distinguished Professor and chair of psychology at Pace University in New York City for a careful reading of chapter 3 and for providing helpful feedback. Olga Favreau, professor of psychology at the University of Montreal in Quebec, Canada, did the same. John Ribble, M.D., professor emeritus and former dean of the University of Texas Medical School, reviewed chapter 2. Robert Lineberry, professor of political science at the University of Houston, offered constructive criticism on the entire manuscript. I would like to acknowledge the support, tolerance, and friendship of my colleagues at the University of Texas School of Public Health (UT-SPH), most especially Stephen Linder. Professor Richard Wilkinson, Division of Public Health Sciences, University of Nottingham Medical School, Nottingham, United Kingdom, held a visiting appointment at the Center for Society and Population Health at the UT-SPH. He gave generously of his time to educate and advise. His input made this a better book.

The production of the manuscript would not have been possible without the patience, hard work, and conscientious attention to detail on the part of three research assistants: Jennifer Bennett, Malorie Gist, and Jessica Speer Neal. Each was a student in the joint University of Texas and University of Houston law and public health degree program at the time she acted as my research assistant—all are amazing women destined to distinguished and ethically exemplary careers in their chosen field. A special thanks also goes to my students in Public Health 3998, "Competition and Public Health" (summer 2002), who read the manuscript: Christina Daw and Karen McClure were especially helpful. I am responsible for the errors that remain.

"The Juggler" by Michael Parkes appears on the cover of this book because it symbolizes the extent to which the competition paradigm involves a similar precarious balancing act. I argue that the competition paradigm is blind to the world and to its consequences as the juggler on the cover is blindfolded—oblivious to his plight. The child on the side represents, for me, innocence—the vulnerable populations of our society and the poverty-stricken nations that watch the dance of competition being played out on the tenuous tightrope. Their participation is limited and they are largely left on the sidelines. The juggler is handsome and this reflects the idea that so many admire and seek to imitate the paradigm. This little kitten on the rope represents the absurd, and perhaps insincere, attempts to "balance" the excesses of the competition paradigm. For example, tiny amounts of foreign aid are offered to assist the developing countries. The fragility of the competition paradigm is reflected by the fact that the tightrope is suspended in midair. I argue that the competition paradigm may appear to be a success but that in the long term it fails us all. That juggler is in for a terrible tumble and this may also be the plight of the competition paradigm.

Note

1. Marmot, M. Aetiology of Coronary Heart Disease. *British Medical Journal* 2001;323:1261–62.

1

Introducing the Competition Paradigm

IT SEEMS SO INTUITIVE—COMPETITION is the key to success for individuals, groups, organizations, and nations. Advanced Micro Devices, Inc., a giant microprocessor company, is a good example. Competition may not be much fun, but at AMD it is never questioned. "Competition is a lot like cod liver oil. First it makes you sick. Then it makes you better. . . . At AMD we believe that competition is good. It's how products get better, faster, cheaper. It's how companies stay hungry, nimble, focused. . . . A funny thing happens when competition gives people a choice. Everybody gets better."[1, p. 7] But is it true? Perhaps not.

There is a large gap between word and deed. Archer Daniels Midland, for example, does not win by embracing competition. It wins by competing in a fraudulent, illegal manner. Strong accusations, but three of its executives were fined and sentenced to prison for the part they played "in a world wide scheme to fix prices of a feed additive manufactured by the company. . . . The company pleaded guilty to price fixing and paid a $100 million fine."[2, p. C1, 3] Accusations of collusion and rigging bids on global products continue to plague this company.[4] And it is not alone.[5] Enron is another example of a corporate citizen that preached the virtues of competition and then gamed the process to avoid competing. For many of us, as with Enron, what we say about competition and how we act are two different things. But the bottom line is that America's commitment to competition, as a way of life, is too pervasive and too important to go unexamined.

Reconsidering America's taken-for-granted enchantment with competition from a critical, evidence-oriented perspective, is a little like saying, "Let's take another look at motherhood and apple pie." The United States is committed to competition. It is central to our belief system, consistent with our individualism. Our economists suggest that competition maximizes societal well-being by eliminating less competitive players from the field. It is efficient, making the most goods available at the least price.[6, 7] Experts in business and commerce argue for investing only in countries with a high competitiveness rating. Competition is assumed to yield the best, meanest, leanest systems of production with the least waste, whether it is among individuals, groups, organizations, corporations, or nations.[8, 9]

There is much intuitive evidence and economic theory to buttress these assumptions. American financial success, global prestige, and military supremacy support those who argue that commitment to competition translates into social, political, and economic policy superiority across the board. Competition has been praised for increasing productivity, rewarding innovation, encouraging each individual to perform to his or her utmost, wringing out excess market capacity, lowering costs, increasing organizational efficiency, raising standards, distributing what a society produces more adequately, protecting the public from government bureaucracy, promoting learning, and stimulating advancement in science and education.[10–13] It "promises more for less; it will generate more and better services for less money."[14, p. 397] It is thought to bring about needed change and to end bureaucratic rigidity.[6] Competition is even said to build character and improve interpersonal relations.[15] Polls suggest that 68 percent of Americans believe in competition and the free market.[16] Ninety percent of Americans say they have great respect for entrepreneurs.[17] Experts attribute the competitive success of the United States to open labor markets, low levels of bureaucracy, and the philosophy that accompanies an entrepreneurial spirit. It is all part of the same package.

In the United States, children are taught to compete at an early age. They learn it in preschool and in the Little League sandlot. Schools compete with each other to see which ones achieve the best statewide student test scores. Television programs aimed at youngsters directly, subtly, and repeatedly instruct on the importance of winning and the costs of losing. Video games designed for children reinforce America's cultural orientations regarding competition.

Competition is said to be in some way unqualifiedly superior to other forms of social motivation. It makes demands of self-discipline, toughness, courage, and sacrifice. For example, it requires "shutting down or selling off troubled companies, boosting competitiveness, getting rid of unneeded workers and stopping banks from propping up industrial companies that otherwise would go bust." Successful countries have "sold off most state-owned companies, imposed strict bankruptcy laws, and scrubbed the economy of thousands of money losers."[18, p. A1] There is little worry about the possibility that competition can be too intense or even destructive.

If many Americans view competition as fundamental to their personal and common self-definition, it is also something that should be shared with others who seek to be like the United States.[19, 20] If whatever good comes to the United States is a result of a strong commitment to competition, then whatever misfortune befalls America's enemies must be because they failed to embrace its discipline. The message is "act more like us and you'll perform more like us."[21, p. A10] The United States therefore urges other nations, regardless of level of development, history, or culture, to become more competitive and to embrace higher levels of uncertainty and risk.[22, 23] They are advised to pursue economic policies that generate investor confidence even if economic theory indicates a different policy would be better.

Those countries that adopt these recommendations end up with less and less control over their fiscal policies. This is because being competitive requires relinquishing protection of domestic markets, reducing government spending, lowering taxes, and deregulating. It means losing the ability to determine their own currency, banking regulations, privatization policies, exchange rates, and export and import priorities.[17, 24-26] Little disagreement is tolerated regarding an open competitive market policy.[27] There is some evidence that developing countries that reject such externally imposed fiscal policies do better than those that accept them.[28-30] But such studies go against the predominant view; they receive little attention in the media and are frequently dismissed by scholars.

Today, many nations look with envy at the United States. They worry about their own competitiveness compared to that of other countries. Private businesses have developed to gather data and sell information to governments about relative national competitiveness. Consultants charge substantial fees to advise political leaders on how to improve their country's competitiveness rating.[31] Government ministries and highly placed trade officials take to the airways to praise or criticize publicized assessments of their country's competitiveness rankings.[32]

The Competition Paradigm: What Is It?

Competition has taken on such a broad importance that it constitutes a paradigm today. A paradigm is a "constellation of concepts, values, perceptions and practices shared by a community, which forms a particular vision of reality that is the basis of the way the community organizes itself."[33, p. 11] In short, it is a global worldview, a value-laden ideology, a meta-narrative, or a philosophy that goes relatively unquestioned. Paradigms are adopted in the first place because they successfully solve a problem of importance to the community. They are useful because they constitute a fundamental set of assumptions, permitting the group or community to proceed with discussion, communication, work, or play without having to always review and reconsider the essentials. Over time, a paradigm actually moves beyond definition as it limits the range of topics considered and restricts the admissible solutions to new problems that arise.

Paradigms are tenacious, once established, and they take on a life of their own. A community expends enormous energy to protect a paradigm, even in the face of contradictory information. The path to change is deeply painful to all concerned. This is perhaps why paradigms are hardly ever revised or discarded altogether until an enormous amount of information contradicts them, until the anomalies that they cannot explain abound, and until this situation is obvious to the vast majority of the community. It is hard to overcome the inertia of a good idea. Over time, many people come to have a stake in the continued existence of an established paradigm. The intellectual retooling required by the passing of time is extremely costly, involving crisis and turmoil. But paradigms must be challenged because, while initially useful, in the long run they encourage rigidity, limit vision, and discourage innovation.

America's competition paradigm is driven by politics, values, and philosophy as well as by economics.[34] It is grounded on normative assumptions about the nature of humankind that are far from flattering; people are regarded as fundamentally and primarily self-interested and hedonistic. Sigmund Freud, Thomas Hobbes, Adam Smith, Charles Darwin, and Niccolò Machiavelli all held such beliefs.[35] Individual satisfaction becomes the chief goal in life. The private and self-interested behavior of individuals, groups, organizations, enterprises, and societies leads to the best possible outcome and maximizes the general welfare.

Philosophical individualism, personal responsibility, liberty, autonomy, and the competition paradigm seem to go together. Since the last half of the twentieth century, the rights and interests of the individual have become more central than the obligations to community.[36] Personal effort is understood to fully explain success or failure.[37, p. 416] Struggling to get ahead without regard to others is viewed as positive and is rewarded. It is part of American culture. "The United States is very likely the world's most individualistic society, placing less emphasis on group solidarity and more on individual freedom, competitiveness and rights than the other industrialized democracies."[38, p. 393] The competition paradigm reduces the social world to an association of autonomous individuals and at the same time loosens restraints on what would usually be described as unacceptable social behavior.[39]

Market fundamentalism is part of the competition paradigm with its belief that everything can be left to the free-enterprise system. Rivalry, striving, contention, opposition, and the market are the natural order of things.[40] The market forces of creative destruction give rise to new opportunities.[41] Intervention designed to moderate the pain associated with the normal play of the market mechanism, such as protecting jobs, will only short-circuit innovation and ultimately reduce the number of jobs available.[42] Implicit in the competition paradigm is the view that competition is the most important way of putting a value on something; there is an assumption that value is equal to price, that money is a primary criterion.

The virtues of the private sector are emphasized, and ownership is defined as essentially private. Public ownership is discouraged, and private not-for-profits are increasingly ignored. The paradigm implies that "the private sector has become good, the public sector bad, and the cooperatively owned and non-owned irrelevant."[43, p. 76] Government and public institutions, from the perspective of the competition paradigm, should have minimal responsibilities.[44] At the same time, they should be supportive of the private sector.[45] The result has been deregulation, the outsourcing of public sector responsibilities,[46] the privatization of government education and welfare functions, and the transfer of public wealth to private ownership.[47] Government's role "should be minimized apart from creating competitive conditions for enterprises. Governments should however provide macroeconomic and social conditions that are predictable and thus minimize the external risks for economic enterprise."[48]

The competition paradigm has become such an obsession that it overrides political preference. It is a master-code for America, at once both Democrat and Republican, left wing and right wing, liberal and conservative. Governments of both the right and the left agree when it comes to forging national industrial competitiveness policies.[49, p. 236] It is supported across the ideological spectrum, from the most right wing of Latin American dictators and East Asian autocracies[50, p. 28] to Marxists[51, 52] and socialists.[53, 54]

The competition paradigm takes on an almost moral stance in America today. If some competition is good, more competition is better. Winning is not just valued, it is a virtue. Competition becomes a builder of character, "a test of personal worth, and a powerful stimulus to individual achievement that ultimately produces the maximum economic value for society."[37, p. 416] Losers are expected "to exit quietly having lost; to protest is at best bad form, at worst blasphemy."[55, p. x]

A Spiral of Destructive Competition: An Overview

A self-reinforcing spiral of too much competition of the most destructive type at once sustains the competition paradigm and undermines it. Winning and losing at each level, be it the individual, the group, the organization, the corporate entity, or the nation, is not random.[56] Under conditions of intense competition, results are predictable. This is because at the outset, competitors seldom start at a point of equality. Some have more resources, attributes, and wealth than others. Even those attesting to the virtue of the magic of the invisible hand suggest that "one cannot explain the pattern of output or results in any market system by pointing exclusively to market transactions, for the pattern is always a result of both the transactions and the prior determinations taken together."[57, p. 171] The most destructive forms of competition increase these differences and sustain a spiral of winning or losing, thus generating even greater levels of inequality. Eventually, and in the absence of any outside interventions, as the process moves along over time, it leads to big winners and continual losers. Healthy forms of competition are less and less viable. To the extent that competition continues, the winners, often at the expense of the losers in previous competitive encounters, influence the terms of play. Repeated losers, be they individuals, organizations, or societies, make for lower overall societal productivity. In the end, everyone is worse off because when productivity suffers, the quality of life is compromised for all.

Competition is specifically designed to separate out winners and losers. Professional and amateur sports pit winner against winner in elimination-type tournaments. Social structures do the same in a slightly more subtle fashion at the societal level. Of course, in both sports and daily life there are the exceptions, those that come from behind and surprise us all. But the specter of repeated, hard-core losers is more common. It is generally assumed to be inevitable, even in the richest of societies. "Winners get the best education, the most desirable jobs, the most sought-after mates, the highest quality health care, and so on."[58, p. 4] The worry is that the situation will get worse in the future at every level, from the individual to the society.

At the individual level, people become discouraged when they repeatedly lose.[59, 60, p. 11] The intrinsic motivation to try to put forth one's best effort is reduced by losing over and over again.[61] At the biological level, competition-generated anxiety and stress reactions disturb normal hormonal processes, especially regarding those who lose. If pushed to the extreme limits, biological self-correction mechanisms are overridden. Hormonal imbalances persist on an almost permanent basis. This reduces the ability to do well in future competitive situations.[62] Stress, high anxiety, distraction, and low concentration all diminish the probability of winning even more. At the same time, winning increases the desire to compete again. All these processes contribute to the self-reinforcing spiral of destructive competition.

At the level of the organization and the corporation, a similar spiral of self-reinforcing competition is at play. Markets and contracts require a high degree of trust and reciprocal obligation. Destructive forms of competition may generate distrust that undermines the market.[63] The degree of cooperation and collective responsibility necessary for commerce is increasingly difficult to sustain in the presence of intense competition.[64, p. 246] Once the spiral of distrust is set in motion, reciprocal bonds of trust are very difficult to reestablish. For organizations, the spiral of self-reinforcing intense competition may end abruptly with bankruptcy, or it might make for concentration through mergers, consolidations, and acquisitions. Losers in the corporate world simply disappear and no longer exist as separate entities. In the end, fewer organizations remain to compete. The worry then becomes that too much cooperation in the form of monopoly and oligopoly might encourage collusion. The mechanisms that ensure equilibrium in the market fail in the face of destructive competition.

The dynamics of the spiral of competition at the national and international levels are, again, quite well known. A variety of mechanisms and self-reinforcing social processes appear to be at work. The competitive process reduces the probability of investment in the poorest nations, especially if uncertainty and future political unrest threaten. Less investment increases the likelihood of greater social and political uncertainty over time. The result is that within many countries, the difference between the rich and the poor is increasing. Inequality between the rich and the poor countries is also becoming greater.

In the long run and over time, if allowed to proceed without constraint, the spiral of destructive competition leads to an excessive concentration of wealth that, ironically, undercuts the legitimacy of market competition itself at the same time that it reinforces the competition paradigm.[65, p. 383, 66] To be efficient, societies must be inclusive in the sense of bringing everyone in, offering incentives to all to do their best. The same is true of the global community of nations. If the world were shrunk to a village with one hundred people, 75 percent of the community's wealth would be concentrated in the portfolios of just twenty citizens.[67] Without a better distribution of wealth, society (and humankind in general) will be burdened by the failures generated by competition, be they individuals, groups, or nations, or it will have to spend enormous resources containing unrest and social disruption. To assume that there is no downside to overly intense competition is shortsighted. Lee Kuan Yew, senior minister of Singapore, worries about market competition's losers. "Capitalism naturally rewards the winners, whether they be entrepreneurs, managers, artists, craftsmen, top sportsmen or pop stars, and rewards them unduly. Unless the losers also share in the gains made by their contribution, there will be acute divisions both between and within societies."[68, p. R25] After the September 11, 2001, terrorist attacks in the United States, world leaders fretted that the underclass in the poor countries would be a source of terrorist activism that would spread across the globe in the future.[69]

In the United States, where the competition paradigm is taken so very seriously, the Department of Justice reports that 6.3 million adults are either in jail, on probation, or on parole. By some estimates, this is 3.1 percent of the adult population.[70, 71, p. 5] While the percentage of the U.S. population in jail may have reached a peak, it is still five times that of the European Union and six times that of Canada and Australia.[72, 73] Constructing prisons has been a growth industry in the United States in recent years.[74] Is this because too much competition makes for higher levels of the population being defined as losers who simply give up on the system?

All Forms of Competition Are Not the Same: Defining Competition

Efforts to define competition and to distinguish among its various forms are few. This is commonly the case for a strong and convincing paradigm. It may be that meaning is so broadly agreed on that no further effort at definition seems needed. But definition is critical regarding competition—to neglect it constitutes a significant loss of information. Appreciating the distinctions regarding various forms of competition is also the key to revising the competition paradigm, something that is discussed in the last chapter of this book.

Defining "competition" is difficult not just because it is multidimensional and complex. Any definition of use here must apply across many levels of analysis and several disciplines, from psychology and biology to international relations. The common element across all these levels is that one entity is evaluated against another regarding some dimension of performance. Competition refers to the process by which contest or rivalry yields rankings, results, or relative excellence.[75] The related term, "competitiveness," is also of interest here. It is attributed to one entity rather than another based on a set of characteristics that is assumed to result in a greater likelihood of success in entity-to-entity comparative evaluations.

As the title of this book suggests, competition is understood in the broadest sense. It is "contest" in that some are rewarded relative to others across every level of human social structure. Children in school are rewarded with good grades, sports teams with pennants and trophies, employees with bonuses, corporations with profits, nations with greater foreign investment, and societies with a higher standard of living. It is about commerce, too. The *Oxford English Dictionary* takes "commerce" and "competition" to be synonyms.[75] Competition as conflict is also considered, though in this case conflict is defined in its narrower dictionary definition as psychological conflict or perceived interentity differences grounded in discordant values, beliefs, and perceptions. Morton Deutsch used the term "conflict" in this same sense, pointing out that "although competition produces conflict, not all instances of conflict reflect competition."[76, p. 10] But this book is not about conflict as war or personal aggression.

Competition is not the unitary phenomenon the competition paradigm suggests, nor do all forms of competition play out in the same way. For example, competition can be intense or moderate. Intense competition has drawbacks that may not apply to forms that are more reasonable. Some argue that, to be effective, competition should be of the middle range, that both high and low levels of competition result in lower productivity than do middle levels.[77, 78] Others contend that periods of intense competition may not be inherently bad if they are regularly balanced by periods of stability, consolidation, and coexistence.[13] At the same time very intense competition may be organized to avoid some of its most negative effects.

Competition can be structured in various ways, and each has significant but different consequences. Goal-oriented competition encourages each player, each person, to do his or her best and to work with others to achieve an objective. An example is how the World Health Organization encourages each country to set time-specific national goals for improving population health and then strive to attain those goals. Each country is competing with itself to reach national health objectives.[79, 80] Interpersonal competitiveness is not so benign because it emphasizes doing better than others, winning over others for its own sake.[81] Johnson and Johnson suggest that there are important differences as well between zero-sum competition and appropriate competition.[82–84] Zero-sum competition involves the distribution of rewards on a "winner-take-all" basis. This means that I win, you lose. A bet between two people on the outcome of a soccer game is an example—one person wins all the money.

Quite a lot is known about the effect of structuring competition one way or another.[85] Appropriate competition seeks to maximize personal well-being, improve overall societal productivity, and advance global community. But it might hardly be recognized as competition at all within the terms of the competition paradigm. Appropriate competition is associated with four characteristics. First, winning must not be so important that it generates the extreme anxiety that interferes with performance. Second, all participants in the competition must see themselves as having a reasonable chance to win and thus remain motivated to give it an honest try, their best effort. Third, the rules of the competition need to be clear and fair as to procedures and criteria for winning. Finally, those competing should be able to monitor how they are doing compared to others. This feedback may, in fact, be more important than actually winning.[82]

Competition can also be described as either constructive or destructive, though such descriptions do not constitute a definition.[86] To define competition solely in terms of its effects would constitute circular reasoning. The terms "destructive" and "constructive" are adjectives, not nouns. They are employed here to help distinguish the negative aspects of competition from its positive dimensions, not as mere post facto labels.

The research reviewed in the chapters to follow indicates that when competition is constructive, it involves competing at efficiency in controlled circumstances. Destructive, excessive, or unfettered competition seems to be associated with serious, negative, though sometimes unintentional side effects. Examples of destructive competition include cutting costs by polluting the environment, competing by reducing worker safety and protection measures, and competing at socially irresponsible, damaging financial speculation. Destructive competition drives out constructive competition. For example, "Firms will not be able to compete at the skillful management of the production process if they are undersold by firms that are competing at evading waste-treatment costs."[82, pp. 32–33] Groups, individuals, and countries practice destructive competition when they win by cheating on the rules or when they cheat more than their competitors. In the business world, destructive competition is about price wars that benefit those who have the resources to outlast others, some of whom may be more efficient than the survivors.[87] Destructive competition involves undercutting standards and manipulating or exploiting others. Examples include securities confidence games, stock market manipulation, tricky accounting mechanisms, confusing fares and fee schedules, deceptive advertising, marketing ploys, less-than-truthful sales promotions or nonexistent sweepstakes, and exploitation of vulnerable populations who may be too trusting or who simply lack alternatives.[86, pp. 27–28] Destructive competition is also apparent in our civic life when candidates for political office win by being better than other candidates at negative publicity. Discussion of the relative merits of candidates' policy proposals in the public sphere is subsequently neglected, and democracy suffers.

Certainly, most people enjoy competition at some level, be it card games or basketball. These forms of competition do not do much harm if they are not taken too seriously. Constructive competition is as essential for commerce as it is for international relations. While enthusiastic about competition in principle, few of us take pleasure in destructive competition or do well under its pressure.

Reconsidering the Competition Paradigm

The competition paradigm has been broadly and uncritically adopted, with relatively little serious attempt at evidence-based assessment or critical reflection. There seems to be something almost religious or magical about competition, especially in the marketplace, that is so evident that it does not need to be subjected to inquiry. But sometimes excessive enthusiasm for a paradigm engenders overgeneralization and the view that one cannot have too much of a good thing. More competition is assumed to be better than less, no matter what the circumstances or the type of competition involved. Qualifiers are forgotten, counterevidence is neglected, and the existence of a spiral of destructive competition is ignored.

The competition paradigm has been the basis of the American policy revolution since the last quarter of the twentieth century. Policymakers concluded that there was no reason to proceed with caution regarding competition even in the absence of evidence. As Robert D. Reischauer, former director of the U.S. Congressional Budget Office puts it, "Uncertainty should not become an excuse for not realizing the full potential of a competitive structure."[88, p. 5] In most areas of life, uncertainty gives pause. To proceed anyway, to embrace the competition paradigm in the presence of such ambiguity, is an act of either courage or pure folly on the part of the United States.

Paradigms have a life of their own beyond evidence. Reconsidering such assumed truth, even in the presence of substantial inadequacy, is a difficult task at best. But such a reconsideration is the goal here because while the intuitive basis for the competition paradigm is strong, the evidentiary grounding is weak. The competition paradigm is in trouble. On balance, data-based research, case studies, and expert opinion concur that overly intense, destructive competition generates substantial problems.

The overall goal of this book is also to help one gain a more comprehensive understanding of competition, ranging from its consequences at the biological level to its impact on society as a whole and to how it plays out within the process of globalization. Casting the net broadly means relating microphenomena to macrotopics, moving through them step by step with reference to already existing research wherever possible. The analysis begins with the most fundamental aspects of competition at the biological and molecular levels. Groups and individuals are considered next. Analysis then moves to organizations, largely commercial in character, because of the relevance of competition for these types of enterprises. Beliefs about competition and actual organizational behavior are compared and found to differ substantially. If action speaks louder than words, then this discrepancy may reflect doubt about beliefs regarding competition. A discussion of competition at the societal level follows.

While each of these levels of analysis from biology to society is treated separately, in fact they are all interrelated. Societies are made up of groups, organizations, and individuals. It is difficult to discuss the consequences of competition at the organizational level without referring to individuals and groups within that organization. Some overlap is inevitable.

Information brought to bear on the competition paradigm comes from a wide variety of disciplines, fields of study, and time frames. Economists dominate discussions about competition. But a fair assessment must go beyond economic theory. Therefore, biology and medicine inform this assessment of how competition influences human performance at the most fundamental level. Knowledge about competition's impact on groups and individual social interaction draws on psychology, sports (human performance), education, and sociology. For example, research carried out over the past one hundred years in schools and in the workplace, some of it forgotten in the wave of enthusiasm for competition, is brought to bear on the topic of interest. What is known about competition and organizations also comes from research in sociology and from the fields of business and commerce. At the societal level, research from political science, international relations, anthropology, and economics is considered.

A comprehensive approach is proposed, and a broad-ranging examination is essential. Data at the biological level are more solidly grounded in scientific inquiry and less contestable than those from the social sciences and the humanities. It suffices here to indicate a strategy. Evidence and research, when they exist, are given priority over less grounded forms of discourse. In one case involving societal level competition (chapter 6), new data are presented that shed light on the link between national competitiveness and inequality. When evidence-based research cannot be obtained, other methods and approaches are required (see appendix 2). For example, in the study of organizations and societies, evidence becomes more controversial. More formal, rigorous methods are seldom applied because it is so difficult to carry out truly scientific studies involving randomization and experimental manipulation at those levels. Inquiry is more qualitative, and relevant research is necessarily based on case studies, expert opinion, and investigative journalism, or it is logical and analytical in nature.

Certainly, any single piece of information that contradicts a paradigm is relatively unimportant. Isolated disagreements from time to time are irrelevant in the larger scheme of things. In everyday life, we hear all the time that "the exception proves the rule." But exceptions, when they are too numerous, undermine paradigms, wearing them away little by little. Today, a surprising weight of evidence across so many disciplines and levels of analysis challenges the competition paradigm.

Notes

1. Advanced Micro Devices Inc. Advertisement. *Wall Street Journal* (March 20, 1996) A7.

2. Eichenwald, K. Three Sentenced in Archer Daniels Midland Case. *New York Times* (July 10, 1999) C1.

3. Eichenwald, K. *The Informant: A True Story.* New York: Broadway Books; 2000.

4. Simpson, GR. ADM Used European Wine for Ethanol. *Wall Street Journal* (April 25, 2002) A4.

5. Labaton, S. The World Gets Tough on Price Fixers: With Consumers Pinched at Every Turn, U.S. Leads a Crackdown. *New York Times* (June 3, 2001) sec. 3, p. 1, 7.

6. Osborne, D, Gaebler T. *Reinventing Government: How the Entrepreneurial Spirit Is Transforming the Public Sector.* New York: Addison-Wesley Publishing Company; 1992.

7. Scherer, FM. *Competition Policies for an Integrated World Economy.* Washington, DC: Brookings Institution Press; 1994.

8. Van Hooff, JARAM. Intergroup Competition and Conflict in Animals and Man. In: Van Der Dennen J, Falger V, editors. *Sociobiology and Conflict.* New York: Chapman & Hall; 1991. p. 23+.

9. FitzRoy, FR, Acs ZJ, Gerlowski DA. *Management and Economics of Organization.* London: Prentice Hall Europe; 1998.

10. Rich, JM, De Vitis JL. *Competition in Education.* Springfield, IL: Charles C. Thomas Publisher; 1992.

11. Cronbach, LJ. *Educational Psychology.* New York: Harcourt, Brace & World; 1963.

12. Horowitz, IL. *Professing Sociology.* Chicago: Aldine; 1968.

13. Bengtsson, M. *Climates of Competition.* Amsterdam: Harwood Academic Publishers; 1998.

14. Freeman, R. Competition in Context: The Politics of Health Care Reform in Europe. *International Journal for Quality in Health Care* 1998;10(5):395–401.

15. Shaw, ME. Some Motivational Factors in Cooperation and Competition. *Journal of Personality* 1958;26:155–69.

16. Duff, C. Rich May Be Different, but Few of Us Either Envy or Resent Their Wealth. *Wall Street Journal* (March 3, 1998) A10.

17. Wysocki, B. Where We Stand: Capitalism May Appear to Have Won the Global Ideological War, but Plenty of Battles Remain. *Wall Street Journal* (September 27, 1999) R5.

18. Frank, R. Czech Republic Is Free, Fun to Visit and Rich, but Only Superficially: Large Businesses Still Are Run Much as the Communists Ran Them, Inefficiently. *Wall Street Journal* (July 15, 1997) A1, A8.

19. Porter, ME. *On Competition.* Cambridge, MA: Harvard Business School Publishing; 1998.

20. Sanger, DE. The Invisible Hand's New Strong Arm. *New York Times* (September 13, 1998) sec. 4, p. 1, 3.

21. Phillips, MM. Summers Urges EU and Japan to Take Steps He Says Will Boost Economies. *Wall Street Journal* (January 17, 2000) A10.

22. Garelli, S. The Fundamentals of World Competitiveness. *World Competitiveness Yearbook 1996.* Lausanne, Switzerland: International Institute for Management Development; 1996. p. 10–17.

23. *The Economist.* China and the WTO: Ready for the Competition? *The Economist* (September 15, 2001) 35–36.

24. Sachs, JD. Ten Trends in Global Competitiveness in 1998. Geneva, Switzerland: World Economic Forum; 1999.

25. Gilpin, R, Gilpin JMG. *The Challenge of Global Capitalism: The World Economy in the 21st Century.* Princeton, NJ: Princeton University Press; 2000.

26. Stiglitz, JE. *Globalization and Its Discontents.* New York: W. W. Norton & Company; 2002.

27. Stevenson, RW. Outspoken Chief Economist Leaving World Bank. *New York Times* (November 25, 1999) B1, B2.

28. Wessel, D, Davis B. Less Cash Flow: Currency Controls Gain a Hearing as Crisis in Asia Takes Its Toll. *Wall Street Journal* (September 4, 1998) A1, A2.

29. Cohen, R. Redrawing the Free Market: Amid a Global Financial Crisis, Calls for Regulation Spread. *New York Times* (November 14, 1998) A17, A19.

30. Smith, SC. *Industrial Policy in Developing Countries.* Washington, DC: Economic Policy Institute; 1991.

31. World Economic Forum. *The Global Competitiveness Report 1998.* Geneva, Switzerland: World Economic Forum; 1998.

32. Maiden, M. Nation Ranking System Blasted. *The Age* (September 12, 2000) A8.

33. Capra, F. The Concept of Paradigm and Paradigm Shift. *ReVISION* 1986;9(1):11.

34. Cohen, R. Earning Power: Global Forces Batter Politics. *Wall Street Journal* (November 17, 1996) C2, C10.

35. Edwards, J. Co-operation and Competition: Two Sides of the Same Coin? *The Irish Journal of Psychology* 1991;12(1):76–82.

36. Janowitz, M. *The Reconstruction of Patriotism: Education for Civic Consciousness.* Chicago: University of Chicago Press; 1983.

37. Coleman, JW. Toward an Integrated Theory of White-Collar Crime. *American Journal of Sociology* 1987;93(2):406–39.

38. Yankelovich, D. A Conversation about Our Public Priorities. *National Civic Review* 1994;83(4):389–99.

39. Coleman, JW. Crime and Money: Motivation and Opportunity in a Monetarized Economy. *American Behavioral Scientist* 1992;35(6):827–36.

40. Pink, DH. *Free Agent Nation: How America's New Independent Workers Are Transforming the Way We Live.* New York: Warner Books; 2001.

41. Schumpeter, JA. *Capitalism, Socialism, and Democracy.* New York: HarperCollins; 1984.

42. Cox, WM, Alm R. *The Churn: The Paradox of Progress.* Dallas: Federal Reserve Bank of Dallas; 1992.

43. Mintzberg, H. Managing Government, Governing Management. *Harvard Business Review* 1996;74:75–83.

44. Stiglitz, JE. The Role of Government in the Contemporary World. In: Tanzi V, Chu K-y, editors. *Income Distribution and High-Quality Growth.* Cambridge, MA: MIT Press; 1998. p. 21–53.

45. Kirby, P. World Bank Analyses Infrastructure. *The Irish Times* (June 20, 1994) 16, Business and Finance.

46. Savas, ES. *Privatization: The Key to Better Government.* Chatham, NJ: Chatham House Publishers; 1987.

47. Silk, L, Silk M. *Making Capitalism Work.* New York: New York University Press; 1996.

48. International Institute for Management Development. *The World Competitiveness Yearbook: Executive Summary.* Lausanne, Switzerland: International Institute for Management Development; 1999.

49. Sandholtz, W. Cooperating to Compete: The European Experiment. In: Rapkin DP, Avery WP, editors. *National Competitiveness in a Global Economy.* Boulder, CO: Lynne Rienner Publishers; 1995.

50. Kuttner, R. *Everything for Sale: The Virtues and Limits of Markets.* New York: Alfred A. Knopf; 1997.

51. Roemer, J. Socialism's Future: An Interview with John Roemer. *Imprints* 1998;3(1):4–24.

52. Roemer, JE. Egalitarian Strategies. *Dissent* 1999:64–74.

53. Krugman, P. Competitiveness: A Dangerous Obsession. *Foreign Affairs* 1994;73(2):28–44.

54. *The Economist.* Beyond Left and Right. *The Economist* 346 (May 2, 1998) 52–53.

55. Burke, T, Genn-Bash A, Haines B. *Competition in Theory and Practice.* London: Routledge; 1991.

56. Gorney, R. *The Human Agenda.* New York: Simon & Schuster; 1972.

57. Lindblom, CE. *The Market System: What It Is, How It Works, and What to Make of It.* New Haven, CT: Yale University Press; 2001.

58. Frank, RH. *Choosing the Right Pond: Human Behavior and the Quest for Status.* Oxford: Oxford University Press; 1985.

59. Campbell, DJ. Determinants of Choice of Goal Difficulty Level: A Review of Situational and Personality Influences. *Journal of Occupational Psychology* 1982;5:79–95.

60. Drucker, PF. The Next Society. *The Economist* (November 3, 2001) 3–20.

61. Deci, EL, Ryan RM. *Intrinsic Motivation and Self-Determination in Human Behavior.* New York: Plenum Press; 1985.

62. Campbell, DJ, Furrer DM. Goal Setting and Competition as Determinants of Task Performance. *Journal of Organizational Behavior* 1995;16(4):377–89.

63. Fox, A. *Beyond Contract.* London: Faber & Faber; 1974.

64. Hudson, B. Joint Commissioning. *Policy and Politics* 1995;23(3):233–49.

65. Yergin, D, Stanislaw J. *The Commanding Heights: The Battle between Government and the Marketplace That Is Remaking the Modern World.* New York: Simon & Schuster; 1998.

66. Marks, GW, Lipset SM. *It Didn't Happen Here: Why Socialism Failed in the United States.* New York: W. W. Norton & Company; 2000.

67. Meadows, DH. If the World Were a Village. *The Independent* (October 20, 1996) 4.

68. Hofheinz, P. What Now? That's What We Asked Economics, Business Executives and Others. Here's What They Said. *Wall Street Journal* (September 27, 1999) R25, R27.

69. Kahn, J, Weiner T. World Leaders Rethinking Strategy on Aid to Poor. *New York Times* (March 18, 2002) A3.

70. Henneberg, MA. Bureau of Justice Statistics 2000: At a Glance. Washington, DC: U.S. Department of Justice, Office of Justice Programs, and Bureau of Justice Statistics; 2000.

71. Freeman, RB, Cohen J, Rogers J. *The New Inequality: Creating Solutions for Poor America (The New Democracy Forum)*. Boston: Beacon Press; 1999.

72. U.S. Department of Justice. Americans Behind Bars: U.S. and International Use of Incarceration. Washington, DC: The Sentencing Project Publications; 1995.

73. Butterfield, F. Number of People in State Prisons Declines Slightly. *New York Times* (August 13, 2001) A1, A14.

74. Hallinan, JT. *Going up the River: Travels in a Prison Nation*. New York: Random House; 2001.

75. Simpson, JA, Weiner ES. *The Oxford English Dictionary, Set*. 2nd ed. Oxford: Oxford University Press; 1989.

76. Deutsch, M. *The Resolution of Conflict: Constructive and Destructive Processes*. New Haven, CT: Yale University Press; 1973.

77. Lambert, R. Cooperation et Competition Dans Des Petits Groupes (Cooperation and Competition in Small Groups). *Revue Française de Sociologie* 1960;1(1):61–72.

78. Rocha, RF, Rogers RW. Ares and Babbitt in the Classroom: Effects of Competition and Reward on Children's Aggression. *Journal of Personality and Social Psychology* 1976;33(5):588–93.

79. U.S. Department of Health and Human Services, editor. *Healthy People 2000: National Health Promotion and Disease Prevention Objectives Full Report, with Commentary*. Boston: Jones & Bartlett Publishers; 1992.

80. U.S. Department of Health and Human Services, editor. *Healthy People 2010*. Vols. 1 and 2. McLean, VA: International Medical Publishing; 2001.

81. Morey, N, Gerber GL. Two Types of Competitiveness: Their Impact on the Perceived Interpersonal Attractiveness of Women and Men. *Journal of Applied Social Psychology* 1995;25(February 1):210–22.

82. Johnson, DW, Johnson RT. *Cooperation and Competition: Theory and Research*. Edina, MN: Interaction Book Company; 1989.

83. Johnson, DW, Johnson RT. *Learning Together and Alone: Cooperative, Competitive, and Individualistic Learning*. 4th ed. Boston: Allyn & Bacon; 1994.

84. Stanne, MB, Johnson DW, Johnson RT. Does Competition Enhance or Inhibit Motor Performance: A Meta-Analysis. *Psychological Bulletin* 1999;125(1):133–54.

85. Johnson, DW, Johnson, RT. Instructional Goal Structure: Cooperative, Competitive or Individualistic. *Review of Educational Research* 1974;4(2):213–40.

86. Culbertson, JM. *Competition, Constructive and Destructive*. Madison, WI: Twenty-First Century Press; 1985.

87. Swisher, K. Why Is Jeff Bezos Still Smiling? *Wall Street Journal* (April 24, 2000) B1, B10.

88. Reischauer, RD. Testimony: Medicare Restructuring. Washington, DC: U.S. Senate Committee on Finance; 2000.

2

The Biology of Competition, Stress, and Individual Health Status

A very large group of illnesses are psychologically determined . . . by the stress of competitive society.[1, p. 28]

COMPETITION HAS DIRECT AND INDIRECT effects on the health of the individual that are largely negative. But the evidence about competition's health effects is dispersed across the various subdisciplines of medicine and biology, and its public health importance has not received the attention it deserves. Accumulating evidence links destructive competition to stress and, in turn, to ill health. While stress can sometimes enhance performance, much of the time this is not the case. Many forms of stress appear to increase the risk for disease and death. At the molecular level, stress effects have been closely studied in the past fifty years. They can be devastating. The link between competition and stress is of more recent interest and not nearly as well documented in the research literature. Still, it appears that the cumulative and repeated effects of competition-generated stress come to constitute a negative, self-reinforcing spiral at the biological level.

Competition Increases Stress

Animal research first drew attention to the association between competition and stress. Stress is defined and measured at the biological level in terms of changes in hormone levels. Competition is one important, though not the only, source of stress in the wild. The effects of competition between male baboons fighting for status and access to females have been closely studied. Those that lose out in this type of competition are found to be extremely vulnerable to stress.[2–8] Lizards have been studied too, and similarly competition increases their stress hormone levels.[9] Animals that reside in groups with stable hierarchies where competition is minimized are not as susceptible to the ravages of stress hormones as those that live in unstable hierarchical groups where competition for position is relentless. Stress hormones are highest where competition for rank is greatest.[3, 4] Until recently, the assumption that people suffer from competition-driven biological stress effects was convincing only if one accepted that the animal model could be generalized to humans.[10]

Exactly how stressful social processes such as competition affect humans at the biological, molecular level is not fully understood, though promising hypotheses abound.[11] Learning more about the precise chemistry of the wear and tear on the body's cells and the acceleration of the aging process is central to this research topic. Social stress is thought to upset the equilibrium of the neurological, endocrine, and immune systems.[12–15] The independent regulation of these systems and their joint interaction are disturbed by too much stress. Stress interferes with the autonomic nervous system and its huge network of intricate activities, including heart rate and breathing, that are all so carefully coordinated in normal circumstances. The hypothalamic–pituitary–adrenal (HPA) axis of the endocrine system is similarly affected. In short, stress plays havoc with our hormones.

Competition-related stress effects in humans inhibit performance on the sports field.[16] The relationship is well established regarding athletic competition. The outcome of competitive sports events affects the biology of mood, self-esteem, and behavior, whether individuals participate or just watch.[17–20] The effects of stress are greater when the competitive pressure is increased and are higher in actual competitive conditions than in training sessions. Intense competition leads to acute abnormal elevation of heart rate and blood pressure.[21] The consequences are also greater in the demanding, higher-ability competition situations of professional sports.[22]

It is the competition aspect of sports that generates stress, not physical exercise itself. In fact, regular noncompetitive physical exercise has been found to counteract stress and facilitate positive psychological health.[23] It is recommended for those who want to improve health and have a better overall quality of life. Some believe that exercise actually increases longevity, though the evidence for this benefit is far from certain.

Competition-related stress also has negative effects in the workplace[24–27] and in educational settings.[28] Highly competitive educational situations generate stress effects on individuals. Twelve percent of medical students experience stress, attributable in good part to competition, to the point of psychiatric disorder.[29] For many individuals, stress increases with a variety of other educational experiences, including classroom presentations followed by formal evaluation.[30]

Stress Has Consequences for Health Status: How It Works

Almost all antecedents of stress that affect health outcomes do so in a complex fashion,[31] and competition is no exception. But no matter what the source of the stress, directly and indirectly, it affects health status. Biological research indicates that when destructive competition increases stress, it leads to hormonal changes that affect metabolic and physiological processes that in turn influence health. While historically important for survival, today acute stress responses in the form of "fight or flight" reactions are not needed to ensure the continued existence of the human species. For example, a supervisor under intense pressure from a new competitor in her geographic region gets angry and shouts at her employee, whose body produces too much cortisol, which makes his heart beat faster. The rapid heart rate that results may continue long after the "danger" has passed. The employee's body acts like it is being chased by a tiger. This helps him run faster, and this was useful for our ancestors in the distant past. But such biological reactions can be dysfunctional today because the tiger is not really there. A calm brain rather than fast feet may best address the genuine danger this employee faces.

Stress can protect and restore the body, but it can also damage it, with severe consequences in certain cases.[32, 33] Some individuals are more susceptible to negative stress effects than others. Some employees are more likely than others to exhibit exaggerated biological reactions to the boss' unpleasant eruptions, whether these outbursts are because of stress from competitive pressure or the result of other events. However, at higher levels of stress, such as those associated with destructive competition, almost everyone suffers some harm. Mild levels of stress may improve performance, encourage creativity, and promote innovation. But prolonged, unremitting stress is likely to be dysfunctional.[34, 35, p. 396, 36, 37] Psychologists have known about this since early in the twentieth century.[38]

Biological, physical reactions to stress are normal and healthy. But a rapid return to baseline is essential if disease is to be avoided.[12] Stress, if it is positive, increases cardiovascular and catecholamine hormone responses but only temporarily raises cortisol levels. The supervisor in the company that is under new pressure from a competitor hollers about a needed report. The employee rushes around and gets the report completed quickly. Things quiet down, and everyone is happy. Stress is negative if it is due to intense fear and distress or if it persists over a prolonged period of time and becomes chronic. To illustrate, suppose the supervisor continually takes it out on the employee. This is the type of situation where overproduction of cortisol may not subside, and the employee's health may be the worse for it.[39][p. 73]

The most destructive forms of competition may cause the sympathoadrenal pathway or the HPA axis to overreact.[12] Normally, the autonomic nervous systems, the HPA axis, the cardiovascular system, the organs involved in metabolism, and the immune system function together to protect the body from excess stress.[32, 40] These are extremely sensitive systems, with elaborate mechanisms that activate them and shut them down when they are not needed and when the "danger" has passed. This is what happens when the supervisor stops shouting at her employee or when she takes a coffee break and cools down a bit. These biological stress systems have broad boundaries, and people are generally pretty adaptable. But sometimes, for certain individuals, through repeated overstimulation, the inactivation mechanisms become inefficient. This has serious health consequences.[7, 32, 41] In the extreme, the health effects of very high levels of stress may include muscle wastage, hypertension, impaired immunity,[15] and even infertility.[4, p. 120, 42] Lower stress levels have fewer negative health effects on the immune system and endocrine system, but people vary a great deal in terms of their reactions.[43]

Most doctors and scientists are notoriously cautious about stating their findings, and this means that the health effects of competition-driven stress that trickle up from the biological to the social level are probably underestimated. What is known ends up being formulated very carefully and is often meticulously qualified. To keep a scientific audience comfortable, only the following type of presentation is acceptable: On balance, stress appears to lead to hormonal changes that in turn negatively affect health and well-being.[44, 45] Stress raises cortisol levels, which may damage the hippocampus. Stress-related increases in cortisol and beta-endorphins are probably associated with poor self-esteem and affective instability.[46] In some humans, the stress that causes psychological problems is directly linked to competition.[27] This suggests that "individual differences in basal HPA-function are associated with individual differences in psychological functioning following stress."[46, p. 591, 47] Stress-generated serotonin deficiencies appear to be correlated with increased irritability, insomnia, and depression.[48] Stress-generated endocrinological changes can increase or decrease the tendency to be impulsive, aggressive, or even violent.[49]

But there are occasions when competition-generated stress effects are more certain. Here members of the medical community are ready to state their findings more decisively. In these cases, statements such as the following are common: Increased cortisol is associated with nervousness,[50, 51] depression,[52–54] and impaired memory function.[55] Disruptions of hypothalamic regulatory function increase with elevated blood pressure for older patients.[56]

In many cases, the physical pathways and biological mechanisms that underlie the relationship between competition, stress, and health are only beginning to be understood.[32, 57] Coronary problems are an example. The role of stress in heart disease appears to be as great as that of hypertension and high cholesterol.[58, 59] But why? Specific cells are now identified that may be the connection between too much competition, high levels of stress, and heart attacks. Activated mast cells strategically placed throughout the body help protect against environmental threats. But they are also likely to precipitate a blocked artery (thrombotic coronary occlusion) because they are directly involved in hypersensitivity reactions, perhaps part of the inflammatory process, at the molecular level.[60] Or another example, the human body is less efficient at controlling virus infections during periods of stress.[61–63]

Stress makes already existing health problems, such as Parkinson's disease, much worse. But how? Overall, and on the most general level, it is clear that too much stress generates chemical changes in the body that also influence the biological antecedents of disease and give rise to specific cognitive processes, behaviors, general physical functioning, morbidity (illness), and mortality (death). Research on the exact linkages is under way. In some cases, the connections are so obvious that one wonders why medical science is so slow to come to a conclusion about the relationships. It seems intuitive that stress gives us a headache. The employee who gets screamed at often keeps aspirin in his desk for a good reason.

The caution experienced by the scientific community is, after all is said and done, a wise thing. The link between stress and health is very complicated, and even the direction of causality is not necessarily one way. Stress causes illness, but illness may also cause stress.[64] Acute and chronic stress induces coronary artery disease through mechanisms that involve excessive sympathetic nervous system activation. But whether stress initiates the process or merely makes it worse once it has begun is not entirely clear. The best evidence suggests that it plays both roles, that the negative effects move in both directions.

A causal relationship is presumed likely in cases where research establishes a temporal priority between stressful life events and subsequent health consequences.[65] Observations of the same individuals over several years, across many points in time, indicate that stress leads to an increased probability of hypertension, cardiovascular disease, diabetes,[66] heart disease,[67] depression,[68] and mortality.[69] Laboratory experiments involving closely controlled temporal relations have established a causal link between stress and reduced immunity.[30, 70, 71] Stress makes individuals more susceptible to colds[37, 72–74] and herpes.[75] The same type of time-limited data show that stressed subjects exhibit higher levels of cortisol. Increases in cortisol over a two- or three-year period were correlated with declines in cognitive functioning for women but not men.[76]

While scientists are very cautious about concluding that stress and competition tend to go together, it is increasingly clear that this is the case. Medical research is moving toward the conclusion that high levels of stress, including those that result from too much competition, are noxious for those who are stress sensitive. For these individuals, medical advice may be that stress and extreme competition are best avoided in the same way that other negative health exposures should be discouraged, such as too much saturated fat and cigarette smoking. Courses to improve stress-coping ability are already widely available and reimbursed by some health insurance plans in the United States. Health providers are being trained to identify individuals most at risk.

Losing in a competitive situation has documented consequences for health and future performance, and stress plays a role. An employee who just lost out in a competition with a colleague for a job promotion could speak to this issue. Stress resulting from sports competition involves an athlete's anxiety over "self-presentation" during competition and his or her worry about how other people will judge them.[11] Losing produces a negative self-evaluation.[77] This also lowers immune responses.[78] Losing may even lead to social isolation, and this in turn is associated with negative health effects.[79] Social isolation has been linked to increased cortisol levels in animal studies.[80] In humans, it reduces longevity, slows recovery from illness and injury, and is correlated with increased severity of illness.[81, p. 130] Much the same is true of the hostility, cynicism, mistrust, and anger that result from competition-generated psychological stress.[39, 82, 83]

Social support can reduce, to some extent, the negative biological impact of competition, stress, and losing.[84] When the supervisor explodes at the employee, it helps if the employee receives sympathy from fellow workers, friends, and family. Such support diminishes the negative health effects that the highly motivated, driven, type A personalities experience under stress.[85, 86] It moderates the neuroendocrine reaction to stress,[87] especially for women.[88] Research indicates that competition between groups attenuates some of the negative individual psychological effects of losing, probably because being a member of a group reduces the often-demoralizing aspects of failure.[89]

Competition, of course, is not always stressful, and stress is not entirely negative for everyone in all circumstances. But where it is detrimental, social support moderates the biological effects of stress, and cooperation rather than competition might protect against excess hormone-related stress consequences. Cooperative settings and benign forms of competition encourage positive human interaction in ways that destructive competition do not.[90]

Individual Differences to Stress Reactions

Individual hormonal reactions to competition and stress vary across the population, with some people being highly susceptible and others not, for a variety of reasons.[39, 44, 91] It seems clear that while for some individuals stress causes manageable anxiety, in others the same level of stress results in uncontrollable fear, depression, or despair. Animal studies indicate that these differences are a combination of genetics and life experiences. In some individuals, stress can cause anger or uncontrollable rage.[92] There seems to be a clustering effect of stress in the sense that some people bear a greater burden across a range of psychosocial dimensions.[58, 93] This compounds the problem. In humans, known characteristics are associated with stress sensitivity. These factors include early life experiences, personality, gender, marital status, age, occupation, and work environment.

Life Experience

It seems amazing, but it appears that early life experiences can have both an immediate and a long-term effect on humans and animals. How babies are cared for has an impact on brain development. "Neuroscientists are finding that a strong, secure attachment to a nurturing caregiver can have a protective biological function, helping a growing child understand (and, indeed, learn from) the ordinary stresses of daily life."[94, p. x] Even life in the womb may disturb fetal growth and development. Pre- and postnatal maternal stress is an example. High stress levels are not good for a pregnant woman or her unborn child.[65, 95–97] After birth, the immune systems of infant monkeys born to mothers who had experienced high stress during pregnancy were significantly different from those born to mothers with less stress during pregnancy.[98] Some early life experiences also influence later life hormonal responses to intense stress.[99] These early life hormonal effects may increase or decrease, for example, stress-induced damage to specific, already identified parts of the primate brain, especially the hippocampus.[5, pp. 312–15]

Stressful experiences during infancy lead to increased lifetime health vulnerability. The resulting organ malfunctions and adverse changes are made worse if the already-at-risk adult smokes or is overweight.[97, p. 47] These lifestyle considerations, such as smoking and alcohol abuse, also affect the relationship between stress and the endocrine response, though they do not influence cortisol elevation.[100] But positive effects of early life experience are also possible. Human handling of laboratory animals (stroking) early in life reduces the animals' negative biological reaction to stress later in life.[101] No one has studied whether the employee who experiences a highly competitive work environment all day comes home less prepared to interact calmly and reassuringly with an infant. The long-term consequences for the infant's reaction to stress later in life would be even more difficult to study. But such connections are possible.

Personality and Perception

Personality type influences how individuals react to stress generated under conditions of intense competition.[34, 102, 103] For example, a competitive type A personality responds to stress in ways that can be directly measured, such as blood pressure. Individuals who are not comfortable in a highly competitive situation and also have a high need to avoid social conflict are more likely than others, with different personality profiles, to develop hypertension as a result of exposure to high levels of stress.[104, p. 260] Those with high personal coping skills suffer fewer effects from stress.[39] Being an optimist or a pessimist also affects how one responds to stress-generated competition.

Perception—how one views a stressful situation—plays a role in how individuals respond to competition, either increasing or decreasing the body's reaction to this source of stress.[4, 105] For one employee, the loud, offensive supervisor is viewed as bluffing, while for another the supervisor's behavior is understood to be a serious threat. It is the same supervisor, the same outpouring of emotion. But how the supervisor's message is perceived can vary substantially. Still, the fact that some individuals manifest stress-induced hormonal changes during surgery, even when they are not fully conscious, indicates that stress reactions are not entirely psychological or solely a function of perceptions.[5, pp. 296, 312–15]

Gender

Gender differences in biological and hormonal reactions to stress, both acute and chronic, are significant.[93, p. 664] But the exact biology underlying these gender differences is not known. Women are more susceptible than men to hormonal changes linked to stress. Some women experience a measurable decline in memory due to stress.[76, p. 175] Because of role conflicts, women are at greater risk for psychophysiological disturbances both at work and at home.[106, p. 117] For example, women who work and have children at home are found to excrete greater amounts of cortisol than do those without young children at home to worry about.[107, p. 352] Still, women are less likely than men to show elevation of epinephrine (a hormone secreted by the adrenal glands), which is a good indicator of on-the-job stress demands.[108, 109] On the other hand, women's higher estrogen levels are believed to enhance the action of oxytocin, which has a calming effect during stress exposure.[88, 110] The fact that women experience greater chronic stress is thought to explain why women have higher levels of mental health problems compared to men.[91]

Context: Work Environment

Work environments differ, and the most competitive ones have the greatest biological effects resulting in serious health consequences. Competition is a source of stress in a wide range of workplace settings in the United States as well as in other countries.[111] The precise aspects of the competitive workplace that contribute to the stress that in turn results in negative health effects are just beginning to be understood.[112] It appears that workplace conditions are directly or indirectly associated with higher levels of heart disease and other cardiovascular risks, especially for workers of a lower social class background.[113, pp. 672–73] Biological and social effects are intertwined. Work-related stress, including psychosocial stress, correlates with a whole host of negative biological processes, including "hyperinsulinemia, hyperglycemia, dyslipidemia, hypertension, increased abdominal obesity, and plasminogen activation inhibitor-1 (PAI-1) antigen comprising the IRS (insulin resistance syndrome)."[66, p. 1533, 114, p. 697]

A competitive and stressful work environment has indirect health consequences that are sometimes counterintuitive. While it might seem logical that the most successful people would be the most competitive and the most stressed at work because they have the most demanding careers (high levels of responsibility and long hours), this is not always the case.[115] These powerful, high-status individuals have the ability to personally control the stress they encounter in life. The opposite is true for those who hold lower-level jobs. Here the individual has little autonomy and must live with a high level of stressful uncertainty and competition.[116] The absence of job-decision latitude, a characteristic of low-paid positions, is similarly correlated with higher health risks.[117]

At least two different scenarios offer possible explanations for this unexpected result. Both involve the biology of stress, and both are intertwined with competition for monetary reward or personal recognition, though competition is unlikely to be the only cause of this stress. First, individuals in the lower ranks may work very hard and yet receive few rewards for their efforts. There is an absence of appropriate reward for effort. Second, they may have little control over the work they do, how it is planned, and how it is carried out. In both instances, stress increases, and health consequences follow.[118, 119] In fact, "subjects experiencing high effort and low reward conditions and subjects with low job control had higher risks of new coronary heart disease than their counterparts in less adverse psycho-social work environments."[120, p. 71] Over the course of a lifetime, mortality is 43 percent higher for those working in low-control jobs.[121]

Competition in the workplace is often about status. The impact of status in the British civil service has been studied, and the health consequences were found to be substantial, especially for those at the bottom of the hierarchy.[84, 122, 123] Research suggests that higher socioeconomic status makes for greater life control, lower stress, and lower mortality.[124, 125] High job demands and high competition for status are less likely to be associated with negative stress effects, however, if the individual has control of the work situation.[27, 32, 126, 127] If employees feel that they must violate their own personal and moral ethical norms to be successful on the job, emotional conflict may increase stress. This is even more the case if the behavior involved is not entirely voluntary and if the employee is pressured to lie, cheat, or steal on the job.[128, p. 152]

Macroeconomic trends that lead to job loss have been found to have biological effects resulting in ill health. During times of economic boom, stress is lower than during economic slowdowns because layoffs are far more common during periods of economic contraction.[129] Close to fifty studies completed in the 1980s and 1990s confirm a strong association between unemployment and increased risk of morbidity (physical and mental illness) and mortality.[130] The direction of causation has been studied; it is more likely that job loss causes ill health and mortality than vice versa.[131] Even merely anticipating job loss has been found to have negative consequences for health.[118, 132] Competition-generated unemployment, as with unemployment in general, is often involuntary. It is related to increased stress levels, loss of confidence, reduced self-esteem, and increases in mental health problems, anxiety, and depression.[133-135] The feeling of hopelessness that accompanies unemployment may in turn also lead to serious negative health effects, such as arteriosclerosis.[13] It results in higher suicide rates.[136]

Individuals are less stressed and healthier if they are working than if they are not. Biology favors the individual with a good job more than it does an individual with a bad job, defined on the basis of income, high meaningfulness, and low physical hazard. Stable employment is better than multiple jobs. Careers with employable skills and upward mobility help, too.[137]

Why It Matters: Biology and a Spiral of Competition

There is a biology of winning and losing that may mean that some people repeatedly gain and others repeatedly lose out. The hormonal changes and negative health effects that follow exposure to intense competition compound and even amplify dysfunctional stress reactions in some people. This in turn reduces an individual's competitive performance. A negative self-reinforcing spiral of competition is evident, even at this most fundamental biological level. Stress causes hormonal reactions that may, in many people, increase stress even more. Prolonged exposure to stress leads to physiological changes that increase vulnerability to stress. The overall effect reduces the physiological mechanism that turns off the body's response to stress and thus increases the likelihood of further damage.[90, p. 174, 138] The response to stress is potentially damaging, even if the stress is entirely perceived rather than a result of real experience, because the mind has such a powerful effect on the body's production of hormones.[139]

Competition, even potential competition, has a different biological effect on winners and losers. Competition-generated anxiety interferes with performance for many people.[140–143] Winners have higher testosterone levels than do losers across a range of situations.[19, 51, p. 569, 144, 145] Among single men, competition for women and other scarce resources leads to an increase in testosterone that sets in motion a spiral of responses: higher testosterone, increased dominance behavior, challenges, more competitiveness behavior, higher testosterone, and so on.[144] Men feel more sexually attractive[18] because winning raises testosterone levels. Testosterone levels influence behavior, and behavior affects testosterone.[146] Sports research indicates that the persistently heightened testosterone levels that result from victory add momentum to a winning streak, while depressed testosterone functions in the opposite direction.[51]

Expectations may play a role in the spiral of competition. Anticipating winning or losing appears to have an impact on the outcome of competition. Biological measures and mood prior to sports competition often predict winning and losing.[19] Those with the greatest fear of losing prior to an actual competition have an increased probability of failure.[147] In a precompetition test, those who later turned out to be the winners ranked higher on scales named Vigor, Anger, and Self-Confidence. Losers scored higher on scales designed to measure tension, depression, fatigue, and confusion.[148] In a target-shooting competition, positive and negative anticipation about success was extremely important in determining results.[149]

While individual studies may be disputed, overall trends are clear. The spiral of competition and the resulting negative biological health effects, often due to increased stress, have significant consequences. At the biological level, the immediate costs of stress and ill health resulting from competition may appear to be borne primarily by the individual rather than the organization or society. For example, an individual may become unemployed if she or he becomes ill or disabled because of stress or stress-related disease. The costs of this negative spiral of competition are not always evident on the corporate accounting sheet. But when competition generates stress, the consequential health-related illness leads to absenteeism and higher job turnover; it increases the cost of health services to the individual and to the employer who sponsors health insurance. A large majority of doctor visits are thought to be stress related, according to the Center for Corporate Health at Beth Israel Deaconess Medical Center. Employees who report greater on-the-job stress have health expenditures that are 46 percent higher than those of other workers. This was much more than the increased health expenditures attributable to tobacco use (14 percent) and high blood pressure (12 percent).[150] Based on estimates from the 1980s, job stress costs $2,770 per employee per year.[151]

In this chapter, the biological-level dynamics of destructive competition were examined. Competition was found to lead to stress and stress to exacerbate specific kinds of disease and illness. While the consequences of competition-related stress vary from individual to individual, the overall pattern remains much the same. We all pay a price for our collective commitment to the competition paradigm. "The invisible hand conjures ill health along with wealth."[152, pp. 1607-8] We now turn to the individual and the group, where the situation regarding destructive competition is much the same.

Notes

1. Black, DAK. *The Logic of Medicine.* Edinburgh: Oliver & Boyd; 1968.

2. McGuire, M, Raleigh M, Brammer G. Sociopharmacology. *Annual Review of Pharmacological Toxicology* 1982;22:643–61.

3. Sapolsky, RM. Stress, Social Status, and Reproductive Physiology in Free-Living Baboons. In: Crews D, editor. *Psychobiology of Reproductive Behavior: An Evolutionary Perspective.* Upper Saddle River, NJ: Prentice Hall; 1987.

4. Sapolsky, RM. Stress in the Wild. *Scientific American* 1990:116–23.

5. Sapolsky, RM. *Stress, the Aging Brain, and the Mechanisms of Neuron Death.* Cambridge, MA: MIT Press; 1992.

6. Sapolsky, RM. Endocrinology Alfresco: Psychoendocrine Studies of Wild Baboons. *Recent Progress in Hormone Research* 1993;48:437–68.

7. Syvalahti, E. Endocrine and Immune Adaptation in Stress. *Annals of Clinical Research* 1987;19(2):70–77.

8. Deutsch, J, Lee P. Dominance and Feeding Competition in Captive Rhesus Monkeys. *International Journal of Primatology* 1991;12(6):615–28.

9. Matt, K, Moore M, Knapp R, Moore I. Sympathetic Mediation of Stress and Aggressive Competition—Plasma-Catecholamines in Free-Living Male Tree Lizards. *Physiology & Behavior* 1997;61(5):639–47.

10. Gilbert, P. *Human Nature and Suffering.* Hillsdale, NJ: Lawrence Erlbaum Associates; 1989.

11. Wilkinson, R. *Mind the Gap.* New Haven, CT: Yale University Press; 2001.

12. Brunner, E, Marmot M. Social Organization, Stress, and Health. In: Marmot M, Wilkinson RG, editors. *Social Determinants of Health.* Oxford: Oxford University Press; 1999.

13. Everson, SA, Kaplan GA, Goldberg DE, Salonen R, Salonen JT. Hopelessness and 4-Year Progression of Carotid Atherosclerosis: The Kuopio Ischemic Heart Disease Risk Factor Study. *Arteriosclerosis, Thrombosis and Vascular Biology* 1997;17(8):1490–95.

14. Sapolsky, RM. Why Stress Is Bad for Your Brain. *Science* 1996;273(5276):749–50.

15. Marshall, GD, Agarwal SK, Lloyd C, Cohen L, Henninger EM, Morris GJ. Cytokine Dysregulation Associated with Exam Stress in Healthy Medical Students. *Brain Behavior and Immunity* 1998;12:297–307.

16. Kugler, J, Reintjes F, Tewes V, Schedlowski M. Competition Stress in Soccer Coaches Increases Salivary—Immunoglobin-A and Salivary Cortisol Concentrations. *Journal of Sports Medicine and Physical Fitness* 1996;36(2):117–20.

17. Bernhardt, PC, Dabbs JMJ, Fielden JA, Lutter CD. Testosterone Changes during Vicarious Experiences of Winning and Losing among Fans at Sporting Events. *Physiology & Behavior* 1998;65(1):59–62.

18. Hirt, ER, Zillmann D, Erickson GA, Kennedy C. Costs and Benefits of Allegiance: Changes in Fans' Self-Ascribed Competencies after Team Victory versus Defeat. *Journal of Personality and Social Psychology* 1992;63(5):724–38.

19. Mazur, A, Booth A, Dabbs JM. Testosterone and Chess Competition. *Social Psychology Quarterly* 1992;55(1):70–77.

20. Hillman, CH, Cuthbert JC, Cauraugh J, Schupp HT, Bradley MM, Lang PJ. Psychophysiological Responses of Sport Fans. *Motivation and Emotion* 2000;24:13–28.

21. Fenici, R, Ruggieri MP, Brisinda D, Fenici P. Cardiovascular Adaptation during Action Pistol Shooting. *Journal of Sports Medicine & Physical Fitness* 1999; 39(3):259–66.

22. Kerr, J, Pos E. Psychological Mood in Competitive Gymnastics—An Exploratory Field Study. *Journal of Human Movement Studies* 1994;26(4):175–85.

23. Wankel, L. The Importance of Enjoyment to Adherence and Psychological Benefits from Physical-Activity. *International Journal of Sport Psychology* 1993; 24(2):151–69.

24. Hanna, E. The Psychodynamically Oriented Clinical Social-Worker as Sports Consultant—A Preliminary Report. *Clinical Social Work Journal* 1993;21(3):283–300.

25. Bloom, G, Durandbush N, Salmela J. Precompetition and Postcompetition Routines of Expert Coaches of Team Sports. *Sports Psychologist* 1997;11(2):127–41.

26. Cote, J, Salmela J, Russell S. The Knowledge of High Performance Gymnastic Coaches—Competition and Training. *Sport Psychologist* 1995;9(1):76–95.

27. Short, JD. Psychological Effects of Stress from Restructuring and Reorganization: Assessment, Intervention, and Prevention Strategies. *AAOHN Journal (American Association of Occupational Health Nurses)* 1997;45(11):597–606.

28. Schwartz, A, Black E, Goldstein M, Jozefowicz R, Emmings F. Levels and Causes of Stress among Residents. *Journal of Medical Education* 1987;62(9):744–53.

29. Liu, X, Oda S, Peng X, Asai K. Life Events and Anxiety in Chinese Medical Students. *Social Psychiatry and Psychiatric Epidemiology* 1997;32(2):63–67.

30. Bristow, M, Hucklebridge FH, Clow A, Evans PD. Modulation of Secretory Immunoglobulin-A in Saliva in Relation to an Acute Episode of Stress and Arousal. *Journal of Psychophysiology* 1997;11(3):248–55.

31. Staw, BM. Organizational Behavior: A Review and Reformulation of the Field's Outcome Variables. *Annual Review of Psychology* 1984;35:627–66.

32. McEwen, BS. Protective and Damaging Effects of Stress Mediators. *New England Journal of Medicine* 1998;338(3):171–77.

33. McEwen, BS, Stellar E. Stress and the Individual: Mechanisms Leading to Disease. *Archives of Internal Medicine* 1993;153:2093–101.

34. Welford, AT. Stress and Achievement. *Australian Journal of Psychology* 1965;17(1):1–11.

35. Anonymous. *The Merck Manual of Medical Information Home Edition*. Whitehouse Station, NJ: Merck Research Laboratories; 1997.

36. Gordon, JR. *A Diagnostic Approach to Organizational Behavior*. 3rd ed. Boston: Allyn & Bacon; 1991.

37. Herbert, TB, Cohen S. Stress and Immunity in Humans: A Meta-Analytic Review. *Psychosomatic Medicine* 1993;55(4):364–79.

38. Yerkes, RM, Dodson JD. The Relation of Strength of Stimulus to Rapidity of Habit-Formation. *Journal of Comparative Neurology and Psychology* 1908;18:459–82.

39. Lovallo, WR. *Stress & Health: Biological and Psychological Interactions*. Thousand Oaks, CA: Sage Publications; 1997.

40. Gaillard, RC, Al-Damluji S. Stress and the Pituitary-Adrenal Axis. *Baillieres Clinical Endocrinology & Metabolism* 1987;1(2):319–54.

41. Bremner, JD, Licinio J, Darnell A, Krystal JH, Owens MJ, Southwick SM, et al. Elevated CSF Corticotropin-Releasing Factor Concentrations in Posttraumatic-Stress-Disorder. *American Journal of Psychiatry* 1997;154(5):624–29.

42. Lacour, C, Consoli S. Psychological and Behavioral Characteristics Predicting Blood-Pressure Reactivity to Mental Stress. *Archives des Maladies du Coeur et des Vaisseaux* 1993;86(8):1177–80.

43. Wilkinson, R. *Unhealthy Societies: The Afflictions of Inequality*. London: Routledge; 1996.

44. Frost, RO, Morgenthau JE, Riessman CK, Whalen M. Somatic Response to Stress, Physical Symptoms and Health Service Use. *Behaviour Research & Therapy* 1986:569–76.

45. van Eck, M, Berkhof H, Nicolson N, Sulon J. The Effects of Perceived Stress, Traits, Mood States, and Stressful Daily Events on Salivary Cortisol. *Psychosomatic Medicine* 1996;58(5):447–58.

46. Zorilla, EP, DeRubeis RJ, Redei E. High Self-Esteem, Hardiness and Affective Stability Are Associated with Higher Basal Pituitary-Adrenal Hormone Levels. *Psychoneuroendocrinology* 1995;20(6):591–601.

47. File, SE. Recent Developments in Anxiety, Stress, and Depression. *Pharmacology, Biochemistry & Behavior* 1996;54(1):3–12.

48. Coppen, A. The Role of Serotonin in Affective Disorders. In: Barchas J, Usdin E, editors. *Serotonin and Behavior*. New York: Academic Press; 1973.

49. Megargee, EI. Aggression and Violence. In: Sutker PB, Adams HE, editors. *Comprehensive Handbook of Psychopathology.* 2nd ed. New York: Plenum Press; 1993. p. 617–44.

50. Mazur, A. Do Cortisol and Thyroxin Correlate with Nervousness and Depression among Male Army Veterans? *Biological Psychology* 1994;37(3):259–63.

51. Booth, A, Shelley G, Mazur A, Tharp G, Kittok R. Testosterone, and Winning and Losing in Human Competition. *Hormones & Behavior* 1989;23(4):556–71.

52. Peeters, B, Broekkamp C. Involvement of Corticosteroids in the Processing of Stressful Life-Events: A Possible Implication for the Development of Depression. *Journal of Steroid Biochemistry & Molecular Biology* 1994;49(4-6):417–27.

53. Chodzko-Zajko, WJ, O'Connor PJ. Plasma Cortisol, the Dexamethasone Suppression Test and Depression in Normal Adult Males. *Journal of Psychosomatic Research* 1986;30(3):313–20.

54. Loosen, PT. Pituitary Responses to Thyrotropin Releasing Hormone in Depressed Patients: A Review. *Pharmacology, Biochemistry & Behavior* 1976;5(Suppl. 1):95–101.

55. de Quervain, DJ-F, Roozendaal B, Nitsch RM, McGaugh JL, Hock C. Acute Cortisone Administration Impairs Retrieval of Long-Term Declarative Memory in Humans. *Nature Neuroscience* 2000;3(4):313–14.

56. Gotthardt, U, Schweiger U, Fahrenberg J, Lauer CJ, Holsboer F, Heuser I. Cortisol, ACTH, and Cardiovascular Response to a Cognitive Challenge Paradigm in Aging and Depression. *American Journal of Physiology* 1995;268(4, Pt. 2):R865–73.

57. Uchino, BN, Cacioppo JT, Malarkey W, Glaser R. Individual Differences in Cardiac Sympathetic Control Predict Endocrine and Immune Responses to Acute Psychological Stress. *Journal of Personality and Social Psychology* 1995;69(4):736–43.

58. Rozanski, A, Blumenthal JA, Kaplan J. Impact of Psychological Factors on the Pathogenesis of Cardiovascular Disease and Implications for Therapy. *Circulation* 1999;99(16):2192–217.

59. Langer, RD, Criqui MH, Feigelson HS, McCann TJ, Hamburger RN. IgE Predicts Future Nonfatal Myocardial Infarction in Men. *Journal of Clinical Epidemiology* 1996;49(2):203–9.

60. Kovanen, PT, Kaartinen M, Paavonen T. Infiltrates of Activated Mast Cells at the Site of Coronary Atheromatous Erosion or Rupture in Myocardial Infarction. *Circulation* 1995;92(5):1084–88.

61. Glaser, R, Rice J, Sheridan J, Fertel R, Stout J, Speicher C, et al. Stress-Related Immune Suppression: Health Implications. *Brain, Behavior, & Immunity* 1987; 1(1):7–20.

62. Kiecolt-Glaser, JK, Garner W, Speicher C, Penn GM, Holliday J, Glaser R. Psychosocial Modifiers of Immunocompetence in Medical Students. *Psychosomatic Medicine* 1984;46(1):7–14.

63. Kiecolt-Glaser, JK, Glaser R. Psychological Stress and Wound Healing: Kiecolt-Glaser et al. (1995). *Advances in Mind–Body Medicine* 2001;17(1):15–16.

64. Rawson, HE, Bloomer K, Kendall A. Stress, Anxiety, Depression, and Physical Illness in College Students. *Journal of Genetic Psychology* 1994;155(3):321–30.

65. Blane, D. The Life Course, the Social Gradient, and Health. In: Marmot M, Wilkinson RG, editors. *Social Determinants of Health.* Oxford: Oxford University Press; 1999.

66. Raikkonen, K, Keltikangas-Jarvinen L, Adlercreutz H, Hautenen A. Psychosocial Stress and the Insulin Resistance Syndrome. *Metabolism: Clinical and Experimental* 1996;45(12):1533–38.

67. Moyer, AE, Rodin J, Grilo CM, Cummings N, Larson LM, Rebuffe-Scrive J. Stress-Induced Cortisol Response and Fat Distribution in Women. *Obesity Research* 1994;2:255–61.

68. Vanpraag, HM. Faulty Cortisol/Serotonin Interplay—Psychopathological and Biological Characterization of a New, Hypothetical Depression Subtype. *Psychiatry Research* 1996;65(3):143–57.

69. Phillips, DP, Liu GC, Kwok K, Jarvinen JR, Zhang W, Abramson IS. The *Hound of the Baskervilles* Effect: Natural Experiment on the Influence of Psychological Stress on Timing of Death. *British Medical Journal* 2001;323:1443–46.

70. Glaser, R, Sheridan J, Malarkey WB, MacCallum RC, Kiecolt-Glaser JK. Chronic Stress Modulates the Immune Response to a Pneumococcal Pneumonia Vaccine. *Psychosomatic Medicine* 2000;62:804–7.

71. Kennedy, S, Kiecolt-Glaser JK, Glaser R. Immunological Consequences of Acute and Chronic Stressors: Mediating Role of Interpersonal Relationships. *British Medical Journal Psychology* 1988;61:77–85.

72. Cohen, S, Tyrrell DA, Smith AP. Psychological Stress and Susceptibility to the Common Cold. *New England Journal of Medicine* 1991;325(9):606–12.

73. Cohen, S, Frank E, Doyle WJ, Skoner DP, Rabin BS, Gwaltney JM, Jr. Types of Stressors That Increase Susceptibility to the Common Cold in Healthy Adults. *Health Psychology* 1998;17(3):214–23.

74. Cohen, S, Doyle WJ, Skoner DP, Rabin BS, Gwaltney JM, Jr. Social Ties and Susceptibility to the Common Cold. *Journal of the American Medical Association* 1997;277(4):1940–44.

75. Glaser, R, Friedman SB, Smyth J, Ader R, Bijur P, Brunell P, et al. The Differential Impact of Training Stress and Final Examination Stress on Herpes Virus Latency at the United States Military Academy at West Point. *Brain Behavior and Immunity* 1999;13(3):240–51.

76. Seeman, TE, McEwen BS, Singer BH, Albert MS, Rowe JW. Increase in Urinary Cortisol Excretion and Memory Declines. *Journal of Clinical Endocrinology and Metabolism* 1997;82:2458–65.

77. Meeker, BF. Cooperation, Competition, and Self-Esteem: Aspects of Winning and Losing. *Human Relations* 1990;43(3):205–19.

78. Strauman, T, Lemieux A, Coe C. Self-Discrepancy and Natural Killer Cell Activity: Immunological Consequences of Negative Self-Evaluation. *Journal of Personality and Social Psychology* 1993;64(6):1042–52.

79. Coplan, JD, Pine DS, Papp LA, Gorman JM. A View on Noradrenergic, Hypothalamic-Pituitary-Adrenal Axis and Extrahypothalmic Corticotropin-Releasing Factor Function in Anxiety and Affective Disorders. *Psychopharmacology Bulletin* 1997;33(2):193–204.

80. Levine, S, Lyons DM, Schatzberg AF. Psychobiological Consequences of Social Relationships. *Annals of the New York Academy of Sciences* 1997;807:210–18.

81. Johnson, DW, Johnson RT. *Cooperation and Competition: Theory and Research.* Edina, MN: Interaction Book Company; 1989.

82. Barefoot, JC, Dahlstrom WG, Williams RB. Hostility, CHd Incidence, and Total Mortality: A 25-Year Follow-Up Study of 255 Physicians. *Psychosomatic Medicine* 1983;45(1):59–63.

83. Barefoot, JC, Siegler IC, Nowlin JB, Peterson BL, Haney TL, Williams RB. Suspiciousness, Health, and Mortality. *Psychosomatic Medicine* 1987;49(5):450–57.

84. Evans, RG, Barer ML, Marmor TR, editors. *Why Are Some People Healthy and Others Not? The Determinants of Health of Populations.* Hawthorne, NY: Aldine De Gruyter; 1994.

85. Blumenthal, JA, Burg MM, Barefoot J, Williams RB, Haney T, Zimet G. Social Support, Type A Behavior, and Coronary Artery Disease. *Psychosomatic Medicine* 1987;49(4):331–40.

86. Brummett, BH, Babyak MA, Barefoot JC, Bosworth HB, Clapp-Channing NE, Siegler IC, et al. Social Support and Hostility as Predictors of Depressive Symptoms in Cardiac Patients One Month after Hospitalization: A Prospective Study. *Psychosomatic Medicine* 1998;60(6):707–13.

87. Seeman, TE, McEwen BS. Impact of Social Environment Characteristics on Neuroendocrine Regulation. *Psychosomatic Medicine* 1996;58:459–71.

88. Taylor, SE, Klein LC, Lewis BP, Gruenewald TL, Gurung RAR, Updegraff JA. Biobehavioral Responses to Stress in Females: Tend-and-Befriend, Not Fight-or-Flight. *Psychological Review* 2000;107(3):411–29.

89. Fiedler, FE. The Effect of Inter-Group Competition on Group Member Adjustment. *Psychology* 1967;20(1):33–44.

90. Evans, RG, Hodge M, Pless IB. If Not Genetics, Then What? Biological Pathways and Population Health. In: Evans RG, Barer ML, Marmor TR, editors. *Why Are Some People Healthy and Others Not? The Determinants of Health of Populations.* Hawthorne, NY: Aldine De Gruyter; 1994. p. 161–88.

91. Turner, RJ, Wheaton B, Lloyd DA. The Epidemiology of Social Stress. *American Sociological Review* 1995;60(February):104–25.

92. Suomi, SJ. A Biobehavioral Perspective on Developmental Psychopathology: Excessive Aggression and Serotonergic Dysfunction in Monkeys. In: Sameroff AJ, Lewis M, Miller S, editors. *Handbook of Developmental Psychopathology.* New York: Plenum Press; 2000. p. 237–56.

93. Cacioppo, JT, Berntson GG, Malarkey WB, Kiecolt-Glaser JK, Sheridan JF, Poehlmann KM, et al. Autonomic, Neuroendocrine, and Immune Responses to Psychological Stress: The Reactivity Hypothesis. *Annals of the New York Academy of Sciences* 1998;840:664–73.

94. Shore, R. *Rethinking the Brain: New Insights into Early Development.* New York: Families and Work Institute; 1997.

95. Rini, CK, Dunkel-Schetter C, Wadhwa PD, Sandman CA. Psychological Adaptation and Birth Outcomes: The Role of Personal Resources, Stress, and Sociocultural Context in Pregnancy. *Health Psychology* 1999;18(4):333–45.

96. Hobel, CJ, Dunkel-Schetter C, Roesch SC, Castro LC, Arora CP. Maternal Plasma Corticotropin-Releasing Hormone Associated with Stress at 20 Weeks' Gestation in Pregnancies Ending in Preterm Delivery. *American Journal of Obstetrics & Gynecology* 1999;180(1):S257–63.

97. Wadsworth, M. Early Life. In: Marmot M, Wilkinson RG, editors. *Social Determinants of Health*. Oxford: Oxford University Press; 1999. p. 44–63.

98. Coe, CL, Lubach GR, Karaszewski JW. Prenatal Stress and Immune Recognition of Self and Nonself in the Primate Neonate. *Biology of the Neonate* 1999;76(5):301–10.

99. Barker, DJP. *Mothers, Babies and Disease in Later Life*. London: BMJ Publishing Group; 1994.

100. Vingerhoets, A, Ratliff-Crain J, Jabaaij L, Tilders F, Moleman P, Menges L. Self-Reported Stressors, Symptom Complaints and Psychobiological Functioning—II: Psychoneuroendocrine Variables. *Journal of Psychosomatic Research* 1996;40(2):191–203.

101. Meaney, MJ, Aitken DH, van Berkel C, Bhatnagar S, Sapolsky RM. Effect of Neonatal Handling on Age-Related Impairments Associated with the Hippocampus. *Science* 1988;239:766–68.

102. Prapavessis, H, Grove JR. Personality Variables as Antecedents of Precompetitive Mood States. *International Journal of Sports Psychology* 1994;25:81–99.

103. Mitchell, JL. Stress in Life and Work: Part 2: Stress in the Workplace. *Occupational Health* 1990(November):315–16.

104. Boekaerts, M. Competitive Drive, Coping and Math Achievement: What's So Detrimental about Avoidance Behavior? In: Hagtvet KA, Johnsen TB, editors. *Advances in Test Anxiety Research*. Amsterdam: Swets & Zeitinger; 1992.

105. Mechanic, D. Adolescent Health and Illness Behavior: Review of the Literature and a New Hypothesis for the Study of Stress. *Journal of Human Stress* 1983;9:4–13.

106. Lundberg, U. Influence of Paid and Unpaid Work on Psychophysiological Stress Responses of Men and Women. *Journal of Occupational Health Psychology* 1996;1(2):117–30.

107. Luecken, LJ, Suarez EC, Kuhn CM, Barefoot JC, Blumenthal JA, Siegler IC, et al. Stress in Employed Women: Impact of Marital Status and Children at Home on Neurohormone Output and Home Strain. *Psychosomatic Medicine* 1997;59(4):352–59.

108. Frankenhaeuser, M, Rauste von Wright M, Collins A, et al. Sex Differences in Psychoneuroendocrine Reactions to Examination Stress. *Psychosomatic Medicine* 1978;4:334–43.

109. Stoney, CM, Davis M, Matthews KA. Sex Differences in Physiological Responses to Stress and in Coronary Heart Disease. *Psychophysiology* 1987;4:127–31.

110. Goode, E. Women Found to React to Stress by Social Contact Rather Than "Fight or Flight." *New York Times* (May 19, 2000) A22.

111. Ezoe, S, Araki S, Ono Y, Kawakami N, Murata K. Work Stress in Japanese Computer Engineers: Effects of Computer Work on Bioeducational Factors. *Environmental Research* 1993;63(1):148–56.

112. Hinton, JW, Burton RF. A Psychophysiological Model of Psystress Causation and Response Applied to the Workplace. *Journal of Psychophysiology* 1997;11(3):200–17.

113. Marmot, MG, Theorell T. Social Class and Cardiovascular Disease: The Contribution of Work. *International Journal of Health Services* 1988;18:659–74.

114. Schnall, PL, Schwartz JE, Landsbergis PA, Warren K, Pickering TG. A Longitudinal Study of Job Strain and Ambulatory Blood Pressure: Results from a Three-Year Follow-Up. *Psychosomatic Medicine* 1998;60(6):697–706.

115. Cavanaugh, MA, Boswell WR, Roehling MV, Boudreau JW. An Empirical Examination of Self-Reported Work Stress among U.S. Managers. *Journal of Applied Psychology* 2000;85(1):65–75.

116. Karasek, RA. Job Demands, Job Decision Latitude, and Mental Strain: Implications for Job Redesign. *Administrative Science Quarterly* 1979;24(June):285–308.

117. Karasek, RA, Theorell T, Schwartz J, Schnall P, Pieper C, Michela J. Job Characteristics in Relation to the Prevalence of Myocardial Infarction in the U.S. *American Journal of Public Health* 1988;78:910–18.

118. Marmot, M, Siegrist J, Theorell T, Feeney A. Health and the Psychosocial Environment at Work. In: Marmot M, Wilkinson RG, editors. *Social Determinants of Health*. Oxford: Oxford University Press; 1999.

119. Frankenhaeuser, M, Gardell B. Underload and Overload in Working Life: Outline of a Multidisciplinary Approach. *Journal of Human Stress* 1976;2(3):35–46.

120. Bosma, H, Peter R, Siegrist J, Marmot M. Two Alternative Job Stress Models and the Risk of Coronary Heart Disease. *American Journal of Public Health* 1998;88(1):68–74.

121. Amick, BC, McDonough P, Chang H, Rogers WH, Pieper CF, Duncan G. Relationship between All-Cause Mortality and Cumulative Working Life Course Psychosocial and Physical Exposures in the United States Labor Market from 1968 to 1992. *Psychosomatic Medicine* 2002;64:370–81.

122. Marmot, MG, Rose G, Shipley M, Hamilton PJS. Employment Grade and Coronary Heart Disease in British Civil Servants. *Journal of Epidemiology and Community Health* 1978;32:244–49.

123. Marmot, MG, Smith GD, Stansfeld S, Patel C, North F, Head J, et al. Health Inequalities among British Civil Servants: The Whitehall II Study. *The Lancet* 1991;337:1387–93.

124. Karasek, R, Theorell TO, editors. *Healthy Work: Stress, Productivity and the Reconstruction of Working Life*. New York: Basic Books; 1990.

125. Pollard, TM, Ungpakorn G, Harrison GA, Parkes KR. Epinephrine and Cortisol Responses to Work: A Test of the Models of Frankenhaeuser and Karasek. *Annals of Behavioral Medicine* 1996;18(4):229–37.

126. Stokols, D, Pelletier KR, Fielding JE. Integration of Medical Care and Worksite Health Promotion. *Journal of the American Medical Association* 1995; 273(14):1136–41.

127. Brunner, E. The Social and Biological Basis of Cardiovascular Disease in Office Workers. In: Brunner E, Blane D, Wilkinson RG, editors. *Health and Social Organisation*. London: Routledge; 1996.

128. Navran, FJ. Organizational Systems and Employee Ethics. In: Korman AK, editor. *Human Dilemmas in Work Organizations: Strategies for Resolution*. New York: Guilford Press; 1994. p. 149–72.

129. Hymowitz, C. Can Workplace Stress Get Worse? *Wall Street Journal* (January 16, 2001) B1.

130. Brenner, MH. Political Economy and Health. In: Amick BC, Levine S, Tarlov AR, Walsh DC, editors. *Society and Health.* New York: Oxford University Press; 1995.

131. Jin, RL, Chandrakant PS, Svoboda TJ. The Impact of Unemployment on Health: A Review of the Evidence. *Canadian Medical Association Journal* 1995;153:538.

132. Hurrell, JJ. Editorial: Are You Certain?—Uncertainty, Health, and Safety in Contemporary Work. *American Journal of Public Health* 1998;88(7):1012–13.

133. Theodossiou, I. The Effects of Low-Pay and Unemployment on Psychological Well-Being: A Logistic Regression Approach. *Journal of Health Economics* 1998;17:85–104.

134. MacFadyen, AJ, MacFadyen HW, Prince NJ. Economic Stress and Psychological Well-Being: An Economic Psychology Framework. *Journal of Economic Psychology* 1996;17:291–311.

135. Klunk, SW. Conflict and Dynamic Organization. *Hospital Material Management Quarterly* 1997;19(2):37–44.

136. Oswald, AJ. Happiness and Economic Performance. *The Economic Journal* 1997;107:1815–31.

137. Marshall, GD. Stress and Immunology. Presentation to the Center for Society and Population Health, Houston Health Science Center, School of Public Health, April 13, 2001.

138. Molitch, M, Hou S. Neuroendocrine Alterations in Systemic Disease. *Clinics in Endocrinology & Metabolism* 1983;12(3):825–51.

139. Dabbs, JM, Dabbs MG. *Heroes, Rogues, and Lovers: Testosterone and Behavior.* New York: McGraw-Hill; 2000.

140. Blau, P. Co-operation and Competition in a Bureaucracy. *American Journal of Sociology* 1954;59(6):530–35.

141. Deutsch, MA. A Theory of Co-operation and Competition. *Human Relations* 1949; 2(April):129–51.

142. Haines, DB, McKeachie W. Cooperative versus Competitive Discussion Methods in Teaching Introductory Psychology. *Journal of Educational Psychology* 1967;58(6, Pt.1):386–90.

143. Naught, G, Newman W. The Effect of Anxiety on Motor Steadiness in Competition and Non-Competitive Conditions. *Psychonomic Science* 1966;6:519–20.

144. McCaul, KD, Gladue BA, Joppa M. Winning, Losing, Mood, and Testosterone. *Hormones & Behavior* 1992;26:486–504.

145. Mazur, A, Lamb TA. Testosterone, Status, and Mood in Human Males. *Hormones & Behavior* 1980;14:236–46.

146. Dabbs, JMJ. Salivary Testosterone Measurements in Behavioral Studies. In: Malamud, D, Tabak, LA, editors. *Saliva as a Diagnostic Fluid.* New York: New York Academy of Sciences; 1993. p. 177–83.

147. James, B, Collins D. Self-Presentational Sources of Competitive Stress during Performance. *Journal of Sport & Exercise Psychology* 1997;19(1):17–35.

148. Terry, P, Slade A. Discriminant Effectiveness of Psychological State Measures in Predicting Performance Outcome in Karate Competition. *Perceptual and Motor Skills* 1995;81(1):275–86.

149. Vaughn, J. An Experimental Study of Competition. *Journal of Applied Psychology* 1936;20:1–15.

150. Goetzel, RZ, Anderson DR, Whitmer RW, Ozminkowski RJ, Dunn RL, Wasserman J, et al. The Relationship between Modifiable Health Risks and Health Care Expenditures: An Analysis of the Multi-Employer HERO Health Risk and Cost Database. *Journal of Occupational and Environmental Medicine* 1998;40(10):843–54.

151. Matteson, MT, Ivancevich JM, editors. *Controlling Work Stress: Effective Human Resource and Management Strategies.* San Francisco: Jossey-Bass Publishers; 1987.

152. Burris, S. The Invisibility of Public Health: Population-Level Measures in a Politics of Market Individualism. *American Journal of Public Health* 1997;87(10):1607–10.

3

Competition's Mixed Results:
Individuals and Groups

It is not a logical, or even an economic, necessity that the market process generates a class of people with very low incomes, but it is a fact.[1, p. 20]

RESEARCH ON INDIVIDUAL AND GROUP competition from the fields of education, psychology, social psychology, anthropology, sociology, organizational theory, and sports offers some surprising results that conflict with the assumptions of the competition paradigm. These studies are reviewed in this chapter, and they suggest that, on balance, competition does not necessarily improve performance. We will see that where competition does increase productivity, it often diminishes quality. Only in one specific situation, when the task is entirely independent, is competition as efficient in promoting productivity as is cooperation. In general, however, intense competition is more often a minus than a plus for individuals and groups because so much of what we do in life is interdependent. This chapter shows that many factors directly or indirectly influence competition's impact on the quality or quantity of production. They include the nature of the task (what people are trying to do), how they are organized to get things done (as a group or as an individual unit of production), and individual characteristics, such as gender and personality. Studies also warn of largely unexpected externalities of competition. Psychopathologies, such as interpersonal hostility, aggression, generalized violence, deception, cheating, and fraud, are all associated in certain circumstances with too much competition, and these too are considered in this chapter. Again, a self-reinforcing spiral of destructive competition at the individual and group levels amplifies the disparity between winners and losers over time.

General Results: Competition Fails to Improve the Quantity and Quality of Production

The competition paradigm assumes that all forms of competition increase performance, productivity, and the quality of what is produced. But there is little evidence to support this view, and substantiation of the contrary is overwhelming. Performance is better in a cooperative environment than in a competitive equivalent on a wide array of interdependent tasks.[2-5] An exhaustive meta-analysis of studies that considers individual and group competition reported that cooperation is superior to competition in promoting achievement and productivity.[6, 50, 51, 57] Johnson and Johnson examined 521 studies of competition completed between 1899 and 1989 and concluded that, overall, cooperation produces higher productivity and achievement than competitive or individualistic efforts.[5, pp. 19, 41] Only about 10 percent of the studies assessed showed the opposite in this ninety-year period. Another review article summarized research carried out between 1939 and 1993 and suggested that interpersonal competition is less effective than cooperation for all subject areas and age-groups over a wide variety of tasks, including those involving motor skills, decoding, recall of factual information, and problem-solving categories that require a variety of different cognitive processes.[7]

Very few studies contradict these general trends. In these cases, competition was found to promote productivity more than does cooperation.[8-10] Two review articles indicated that evidence was conflicting.[11, 12] They are based on fewer studies than those that find cooperation to be superior. They have also been criticized for several reasons, including a possible bias concerning the selection of studies to be reviewed.[6, 13] In general, when competition is found to increase productivity, it is also reported to do so to a lesser extent than does cooperation. While productivity is generally found to be higher with cooperation than with competition, differences have been noted for various groups in different contexts. Still, a fair reading of the psychological literature gives the general impression that intense competition is far less effective than more moderate competition or cooperation at the level of the individual and the group.[14, 15]

There is little evidence that competition improves the quality of an individual's production. Many studies suggest that it even compromises quality.[16, 17] Quality reductions under conditions of rivalry or competition were noted in the 1920s.[18] Deutsch reports that the cooperative situation is superior to the competitive environment on both quality and quantity of work.[19] His research involved psychology students at the Massachusetts Institute of Technology who participated in human relations puzzle-solving problems with rewards that depended either on group performance or on an individual's personal functioning. Cooperative production is more efficient and produces better quality than competitive production, especially regarding interdependent tasks.[20] Only a few experiments report the opposite results, concluding that competition produces higher quantity and quality of performance.[21, 22]

When competition is intense, as with destructive competition, quality is especially likely to suffer. Sixteen percent of workers report that they are pressured to cut corners and reduce quality control.[23, p. 7] This is the case in the increasingly competitive health care sector, for example. Twenty-four percent of primary care physicians indicate that the scope of care they are expected to provide, now that the health system has become highly competitive, is greater than it should be.[24, p. 1980] Intense market competition means that doctors are being asked to perform in medical specialties different from those in which they were trained.[25] Patients do not receive optimal health care, and rehabilitation therapy may be denied them to save money because competition is so great.[26] A comparison of Arizona's Medicaid managed care program (organized around highly competitive bidding) with New Mexico's much less competitive, more traditional Medicaid program reveals substantially lower quality in the Arizona program.[27] The practice of "deskilling" in the hospital industry is adopted by many organizations in an effort to survive in the competitive marketplace. But it reduces the quality of care and hospital worker safety.[28] Deskilling means downgrading the responsibilities of a job or position. It also takes the form of hiring the employee with the lowest level of education and training possible to do a job. This is worrisome when patient lives depend on a narrow margin of error and good judgment is essential.

The reasons why the quality of individual and group production is better under conditions of cooperation than competition are known to some extent. Cooperative groups are better at communication than competitive groups. The laboratory experiments carried out at Princeton University by Alan Blinder and John Morgan surprisingly demonstrate the effectiveness of cooperative groups. They found that groups of people working together are just as quick at making decisions as individuals and that the quality of group decisions is superior to that made by individuals.[29] Individuals working in cooperative settings are more oriented toward the group than are those working in competitive settings. They have better team spirit and are more involved, more interested, and more motivated to achieve. They show greater acceptance of others' ideas. Cooperatively organized groups are better coordinated and are more likely to practice a division of labor that contributes to efficiency.[30–32] Finally, most people are happier working in a cooperative setting.[33–35]

Qualifying Competition's Impact

The purpose of competition is not to be fair in the sense of giving everyone, in all circumstances, an equal chance. Competition works differently, advantaging some and disadvantaging others, depending on the circumstances, the context, and the individual. Some people are simply better at competition than others. Population-level studies on this topic are almost nonexistent today. But data collected more than one hundred years ago suggest that while many people do perform effectively under competitive conditions, a substantial number do not. In 1897, Norman Triplett at the Psychological Laboratory of Indiana University studied the impact of competition in several competitive situations (bicycle races, ice-skating contests, and boat races) and in an experimental situation with a mechanical apparatus constructed for the purpose of his study. With meticulous attention to the effects of practice, the context of the competition, the order of the experimental conditions, and so on, he determined that competition did not affect his subjects in a uniform fashion. About half were positively stimulated and improved their performance. But a quarter were stimulated adversely and ended up doing worse on the task when required to compete compared to when they performed alone. The performance of the remaining 25 percent was little affected by competition one way or the other.[36, pp. 520–23]

It Depends on What You're Trying to Do and What Is Being Produced

It seems logical to expect that competition might improve performance of some tasks while other tasks could be better performed in a cooperative setting. In fact, this turns out to be the case. As noted previously, competition's effect on productivity is different for interdependent and independent tasks. Here is why. When a task is interdependent, cooperation, not competition, is the best way to get things done. In such situations, mutual assistance that comes about through cooperation and an agreed-on division of labor reached through communication improves performance. The workplace and educational settings are examples. This is true for general factory production[37] as well as for retail services and government organizations.[38] However, if a task is independent, then, in general, cooperating and interacting with others may be a distraction. Time spent coordinating with others can mean that it takes longer to get things done. This is also true if personality or cultural factors predispose one to try harder in competitive situations.

However, sometimes cooperative efforts have been found to give better results than competition even on tasks that have an independent component. These include lower-level tasks, such as those requiring motor skills,[39] decoding, memorization of facts,[6, 7, 40] and problem solving.[7, 16] The same results hold for school-related skills, such as "math and reading drill review, story problems, sequencing, triangle identification, and visual sorting."[41] Competition also lowers motivation for puzzle solving.[42, 43]

At school, children do better overall in a cooperative than a competitive setting. The learning of educational content has been found to be more effective under conditions of cooperation than of competition at most levels, including elementary[44] and junior high.[16, 45] Many different forms of class content show this pattern, including science material.[46] Some studies report no difference in competitive and cooperative senior high school biology classes[47] and junior high school physical science classes.[45] However, based on Clark's research at the University of Washington's Department of Psychology, graduate students seem to perform better under conditions of competition for grades, probably because the tasks they undertake require independent intellectual activity.[48]

One reason why competition works as well as cooperation for independent tasks can be understood as a function of human nature and the work environment. With interdependent tasks, one's competitive position can be improved either by blocking the productivity of others or by greater individual productivity.[8, p. 768] A number of studies report that the expected obstructive and aggressive behavior will develop under conditions of intense competition.[49] An example of this is when law students steal assigned readings that are available exclusively on library reserve. These students hope to improve their own class ranking by making it harder for other students in their class to do well on the exam. Laboratory studies suggest that competition between individuals in a group can reduce overall performance, especially in large groups with limited equipment or resources. In these instances, competition between members of a group may lead to a logjam in the production process.[50, p. 236] This illustrates that no matter how hard a highly competitive individual tries, the work environment can thwart their efforts if the task is interdependent.

The Unit of Production and Competition

Many studies suggest that internally cooperative groups are more productive than internally competitive groups.[19, 51–53] Cooperation within groups, combined with competition between these groups, works better than competition alone. Research supports the finding that in situations where groups compete with each other, achievement and productivity are greater for those groups that practice internal cooperation.[6, p. 57] But one study did find that group cooperation leads to higher productivity within groups and between groups.[8] Very rarely do any researchers report the opposite—that within-group competition leads to higher productivity than within-group cooperation.

There is evidence that the highest production levels are observed when cooperative groups function without reference to any other group. For example, Abaineh Workie of the Department of Psychology at Norfolk State University carried out research, based on carefully controlled experiments with 240 male high school students, involving structured card games. Conditions of play required either cooperation or competition between and within groups. Monetary rewards for points scored offered incentives under the various conditions of play and served as a measure of "productivity."[51] Still other researchers find little difference in achievement between cooperative and competitive groups.[54] Some studies completely contradict Workie's research and indicate that individuals do better if they are grouped into cooperative teams that compete with other teams than if they work alone.[55, 56] Competition between teams is thought to increase motivation and performance within each one of the teams involved.[50, p. 236] Emerging from these studies is the view that group interest can substitute for self-interest in motivating individuals to increase performance. However, some research calls into question any simple "one-to-one correspondence between people's objective interests and their group memberships."[57, p. 244]

Individual leadership style—cooperative or competitive—affects group performance. It seems to have an important effect on those supervised and on their productivity. For example, a study of medical laboratory technicians in ten hospitals found that supervisors with a cooperative orientation had, over-all, a more positive influence on employees than did supervisors with competitive orientations.[58] Again, cooperative leadership is difficult to maintain in an environment where supervisors and "leaders" are rewarded for "downsizing" and "multiskilling" their staff and where they must agree to job enlargement, taking on more tasks, if they aspire to advance.[28] This employment atmosphere undermines morale and worker loyalty to the employer while reducing internal group cooperation and increasing in-group competition for scarce resources.[59] This is discussed further in the next chapter.

People Are Different: Individual Characteristics and Competition

Some individuals are more likely than others to say they prefer competition or cooperation, and some are more predisposed than others to do well in competitive situations.[33, 34, 49, 60–62] About 50 percent of University of Zurich undergraduate students who participated in laboratory experiments involving cooperation and competition were conditional cooperators. This means that their behavior was motivated largely by feelings of equity, altruism, or fairness.[63] No one knows whether these findings can be generalized to the population as a whole or to individuals in other countries. But the question is, Why do people differ? Personality characteristics and gender, along with other variables including culture, unit of production, and task, are important in this respect. Just as with stress sensitivity (discussed in the previous chapter), certain known characteristics predispose people to be more or less responsive to cooperation and competition.[13]

Individual personality type influences performance under conditions of competition and cooperation. High achievement–motivated personalities do best when competing against equals.[64] Personality variables function as "mediators."[65] Competition's effects can be an especially negative force for those who already have severe personality disorders, such as narcissistic personality disturbances, where the person must win at all costs and cannot tolerate other people winning. However, at least one study reported that personality correlates are not strongly associated with performance under stressful competition.[66]

Cooperative learning environments promote interpersonal attraction more than do competitive experiences.[67] More than 180 studies going back to the 1940s support this finding. Interpersonal attraction increases under cooperative learning environments because cooperative interaction sets up a process of acceptance based on "frequent, accurate and open communication; accurate understanding of each other's perspective; inducibility; differentiated, dynamic, and realistic views of each other; high self-esteem; success and productivity; and expectations for positive and productive future interaction."[5, p. 126] Working in a cooperative environment increases social cohesiveness.[35] But of greatest importance is that people tend to expect that others will be like them. Individuals who perceive and define themselves as very competitive tend to anticipate competitive behavior from others. The opposite is also true for individuals who identify themselves as cooperative— they expect that others will also be cooperative.[68, p. 347] Those who favor cooperative environments have a more positive view of their peers—the people they are working with—than do those preferring a competitive style.[33, 34] In short, those who say that they prefer a competitive or a cooperative mode of functioning differ in important ways.

Research suggests that women, as a group, are less comfortable with competition than are men. They have more positive attitudes about cooperation than do men.[69] On the whole, women are found to perform better in cooperative settings than they do in a competitive setting.[16] As discussed in chapter 2, girls and women suffer more from the stress of competition,[70] and this is reported to have an effect on their self-image.[71] When women compete as a team, elements of both competition with the other team and social support among their own team members are engaged. This diminishes the overall stress effects of competition. Women, especially those with a strong sense of the nurturing role, associate competition with greed, envy, aggressiveness, and jealousy.[72] For some women, competition is to be feared, avoided, and even repressed.[73, p. 36, 74]

Gender effects regarding competition appear at an early age. Boys are more competitive than girls in general,[75, 76] and boys may not even experience cooperative winning as success.[77, p. 395] Overall, girls are more negative about competition than boys in both elementary school[78] and junior high.[3, 4, 79] Differences between boys' and girls' views of cooperation and competition narrow as they move into high school, but the differences do not ever disappear completely.[69, 80] A nationally representative study of high school seniors (from 1977 to 1991) found that females are less likely than males to accept competition.[81] Young women perform at lower levels when competing with men than they do when performing in all-women groups.[82] This has long been the rationale for all-girl schools and all-women colleges.

Adult men perform better than adult women in competitive performance situations.[83] Men behave more competitively in negotiations, though differences with women in a meta-analysis of sixty-two research projects were reported to be small.[84] Women, more than men, suffer decreased motivation when losing in competition,[42] and this was very apparent in school subjects in which boys have an advantage, such as science and math.[16] Finally, on the job, women respond better to cooperative leadership styles than to competitive leadership styles.[58] They are more responsive than men to cooperative communications.[85] Women's performance on competitive games of strategy depends a good deal on the structure and rules governing the game.[86] But in general, women are more cooperative than men here, too.[87] Nurses, a health provider category that in the United States is 94 percent female,[88, p. 28] have more cooperative and altruistic value systems, as measured on the Rokeach Survey of Values, than do male-dominated professional groups (such as business students, who are largely male).[89]

While, on balance, women are found to be less competitive than men, a caveat is in order concerning these gender differences. Much of this research was carried out in the 1970s or earlier.[90] It is possible that the previously observed gender differences no longer hold or are diminished in magnitude. A number of recent studies suggest as much.[91, 92] On the other hand, many of the differences between men and women and boys and girls were observed consistently throughout the period from the mid-1970s to the early 1990s. Some researchers argue that these differences show little sign of decreasing.[81, p. 436]

The Psychosocial and Behavioral Effects of Competition

Social interaction under conditions of competition has social, psychological, and behavioral consequences.[5, ch. 9] Overall, results indicate that the more cooperative an individual, the lower his or her psychopathology. This may be because of the self-reinforcing spiral of competition that exaggerates the effects of winning and losing at the individual levels.

In general, researchers attribute negative psychosocial effects to competition and positive effects to cooperation. Cooperation is said to restructure social situations along lines of agreement, affection, and affiliation.[14] It encourages friendship, reciprocity, and mutual sharing;[93] promotes empathy;[94] and "induces perceived similarity, trust, open communication, flexibility, concern for the other, emphasis on mutual interests, and attraction between the parties."[95, p. 99, 96] Confronting a perceived competitive situation, people become "suspicious, make unreasonable demands, pursue their own interests at the expense of others, and often fail to reach an agreement."[37, p. 237] Competition is reported to increase personal insecurity and lower trust.[19] As a result, it may do social harm.[97] It is said to encourage greed, envy, jealousy, deceit, betrayal, and exploitation.[73, 95, p. 100] Destructive competition has been associated with both selfishness and excessive individualism.[98, 99]

Competition brings out strong human emotions. It promotes interpersonal arguments. It increases the anger–aggression sequence. "People think about competitive situations in much more aggressive terms than cooperative situations."[100, p. 1024] Aggression is thought to result from competition for scarce resources, property, and territory as well as for self-esteem and self-respect.[101] Competition removes inhibition of hostility and aggression.[94]

Animal studies show much the same thing. When researchers hide food and forced members of a harmonious troop of chimpanzees to compete for food, within-group solidarity and affiliative behavior disappeared and was replaced with violence.[102]

Participants in internally competitive groups have more negative attitudes toward those they are competing against than is the case with internally cooperative groups.[103, 104] Under conditions of cooperative production, individuals give and receive more assistance and support from one another. Competitive groups pay more attention to task than to socioemotional relationships.[104] In cooperative groups, interaction is based more on persuasion and less on coercion.[38] Research in several countries confirms these findings about personal relationships and competition.[105]

A Negative Spiral of Individual Competition

Competition, in the absence of outside intervention, generates a self-reinforcing spiral of intensifying competition at the individual level just as was the case at the biological level.[96, p. 31] Success or failure under conditions of competition provides an individual with competence feedback and influences his or her perception of self-efficacy or the lack of it.[106] Those who have a sense of being competent are less likely to experience cognitive anxiety related to competition.[107] "Losers of competition experience a decrease in intrinsic motivation because they perceive themselves as less competent than winners."[108, p. 655, 109] Competition selects out and rewards winners at the same time that it creates losers. Being labeled a "winner" or a "loser" affects performance, probably because of the social evaluation related to each condition. This "informational feedback from the outcome of competition can have a potent effect on both task performance and intrinsic motivation."[106, p. 297] Losing is related to lower motivation in future tasks[108] and less overall enjoyment of the experience of competing.[77]

Labeling someone a winner or loser may generate a self-fulfilling prophecy. Individuals internalize labels and act in ways that are often consistent with the expectations of others. While labeling as such goes back centuries,[110] the first person to explain how this power-laden process works in sociological terms was Tannenbaum in 1938.[111, pp. 19–20] He suggested that labeling is a process of "tagging, defining, identifying, segregating, describing, emphasizing, making conscious and self-conscious; it becomes a way of stimulating, suggesting, emphasizing, and evoking the very traits that are complained of. . . . The person becomes the thing he is described as being." Interpretive sociologists in the fields of deviance, subcultures, and criminology, many of them phenomenologists, ethnomethodologists, symbolic interactionists, or social constructionists, further developed labeling theory in the 1950s, 1960s, and 1970s.[110, 112, 113]

This theory helps understand how the spiral of losing and winning works. It offers an explanation for losers who fail again and again. It helps understand how some repeat winners become unrealistically overvalued and compensated out of all proportion to their worth.[114–116] The label becomes a master code type that has an overriding impact on self-definition.[117] Others respond to an individual in terms of that internalized view, whether it be positive or negative.[118] People avoid losers and seek to express their affiliation with winners. For example, students were more likely to wear apparel that clearly identified them with their university on days after their school's football team won compared to days after their team lost. Even the size of the victory point margin predicted the magnitude of the association.[119]

Labeling is both a dependent and an independent variable,[120] which is why it contributes to the negative spiral of individual level competition. As an independent variable, it means that labeling someone a winner contributes to future gains. Labeling theorists examine how individuals are intellectually engaged in personal biographical reconstruction on an almost daily basis.[121] As a dependent variable, it points to the consequences of winning and losing. In both cases, there is an element of stereotyping and retrospective interpretation mixed in that influences societal rule making, interpersonal reactions, and organizational processing.[110, 122]

Cooperative learning experiences do not require labeling individuals as winners or losers to the same extent as does competitive learning environments. More participants in a cooperative activity end up with a positive attitude about themselves.[45, p. 351] Morale and psychological well-being are enhanced even in competition between small (cooperating) groups, even if one's group loses.

In general, individual losers in competition have much higher postcompetition state anxiety than do winners.[123, p. 271] The process of competition leads to defeatism on the part of losers.[124] Disposition improves for winners; they exhibit higher mood scores than do controls who are not involved in winning or losing.[125] Losers are more anxious, angry, and sullen than winners. Winners are more placid and relaxed after a game than are losers.[126] "Winning facilitated both actual competitive performance and intrinsic motivation relative to losing."[106, p. 291]

A spiral of self-reinforcing competition exists at the group level, too. Intense competition makes for limited communication with opposing groups. This, in turn, encourages even more and greater degrees of competition. Communication breaks down between competitors; in-group/out-group views of the world develop and are reinforced. This makes for even more limited communication and so forth.[5, p. 168]

Competition sets the context for future social relationships and therefore contributes to the negative self-reinforcing spiral of destructive competition. Subjects are found to respond to aid and to an offer of help on the basis of previous behavior and prior relationships between donor and recipient.[127, p. 213] People generally act more cooperatively with those they expect to interact with again in the future.[128, 129] Expectations of cooperation encourage feelings of empathy, and expectations of competition seem to promote the opposite emotions.[94, p. 543] At the same time, "an atmosphere of either cooperation or competition can be quickly altered in a situation of interdependence when one party clearly acts inconsistently with what is characteristic of that climate."[95, p. 99]

Competition may be quite impersonal in the context of the marketplace, but it is deeply personal at the individual level. This is because individuals who lose out in competitive life situations do not disappear, as do defunct enterprises. They remain part of society. If some competitors win repeatedly and pass those benefits that come with winning on to their children, generation after generation, the differences will be accentuated over time, whether by genetics, by learned proclivity, or by acquired social advantage. For individuals who are ill equipped to compete in the future, any number of outcomes are possible, each of which has societal repercussions: engagement in self-destructive activities, loss of employment, or social isolation.

Psychopathology and Competition

The effects of destructive competition can be severe and sometimes even pathological, with negative consequences for production and individual

performance. While the strongest statements about the pathological qualities of competition are generally theoretical, research in several different
contexts supports the possibility of serious psychopathological aspects of
competition. Extreme, intense competitiveness can generate a social dynamic that makes status, power, and dominance an obsession.[130] Televised
sports competition has been found to link metaphors of recklessness, aggressiveness, masculinity, violence, and war in a positive fashion.[131] Competition over jobs and status was linked to sexual harassment in a 1994 study
of university employees who filled out questionnaires[132, p. 73] and even to
"classic 'trivial altercation' homicide" in another study.[133, pp. 59–73]

The pathological consequences of competition seem to be associated with
a wide range of life situations. Competition can become a matter of "life and
death."[73] Psychological testing of incarcerated prisoners showed that "competitive attitudes were somewhat related . . . with psychological pathology,
alienation, and criminal attitudes."[134, p. 131] Extreme competition also seems to
be linked with aggressiveness.[135] "A competitive process leads to a suspicious,
hostile attitude, and it increases the readiness to exploit the other's requests."[96, p. 30] One author suggests that competition increases "affectless aggression" and perhaps violence.[100, p. 1029] Another indicates that most suicides
are the consequence of failure in competition.[136, p. 165] Laboratory research
confirms that high levels of pathological forms of hostility result from competitive situations. The "competition-primed subjects unnecessarily killed
more video game characters . . . than cooperation-primed subjects. The
increase in kill ratio occurred in the absence of changes in hostility, friendli-
ness, or liking for one's game partner."[100, p. 1020] Finally, violence and combativeness in the premarital relationship have been studied and found to be a
function of unpleasant competitiveness as measured by need to control, expressed in the use of sarcasm and being excessively boastful.[137, 138]

In the extreme, a whole range of problems has been associated with
competition. Though it is unlikely that competition is the only cause in any
of these cases, competition is said to trigger international conflict.[139]
Competition-driven aggression may lead to extreme antisocial behavior.[140]
Chester Insko reports that competitive group relations evolve into a tit-for-tat
or an eye-for-an-eye type of negative reciprocity far more quickly than is the
case for individual-to-individual relations. He and his colleagues at the University of North Carolina suggest that "competitiveness rationally leads to
non-cooperativeness or defensive withdrawal."[141, pp. 68–69] Morton Deutsch said
that it encourages one side to assume the worst about the other group, and
this may encourage paranoia. "There are pathogenic processes inherent in
competitive conflict—such as perceptual distortion, self-deception, unwitting
involvement—that tend to magnify and perpetuate conflict."[96, p. 47]

With the rise of the competition paradigm, there has been a dramatic increase of cheating in schools. Simultaneity, however, does not indicate exactly how or why the two might be associated. In the 1950s, only 20 percent of students admitted to cheating. Half a century later, it was between 75 and 98 percent.[142] The Internet complicates the situation and may even encourage plagiarism. At the same time, there is competition to invent and market Internet systems to catch those who copy off the Internet.[143] Teachers cheat on state and national exams to make it appear that their class and their school has higher achievement levels than other classes or schools. They are driven to do so not by concern for prestige but more by competition for salary rewards, according to the National Education Association. This is called the "battle for performance dollars."[144, p. A18]

Competition may be a source of prejudice and bias. It expresses the failure to cooperate, as an asocial form of behavior that "increases sensitivity to differences and threats while minimizing awareness of similarities. It permits behavior that would be considered outrageous if directed toward someone like oneself."[145, p. 40] Competition has even been advanced as a "precipitant and underlying conditions of race riots."[146, p. 171] Competition can be a powerful antisocial force if it makes for a view of the world as divided between an in-group and an out-group, which can lead to stereotyping. Even the anticipation of competition intensifies in-group/out-group hostility in the absence of actual competition.

The famous Robbers' Cave experiments of Sherif and Sherif found that aggression, hostility, and collective fighting increased after twelve-year-old boys were encouraged to play competitive games at summer camp.[147] In-group solidarity translated, in the presence of competition, into out-group discrimination, hostility, and aggression.[148] One experimenter reported, "Sometimes intergroup antagonism grew so intense that the experiments had to be discontinued."[148, 149, p. 72] The impact of competition-generated hostility and aggression was found to be long lasting and difficult to reverse.[150] Only imposed superordinate goals that required groups to work together toward a common objective improved the relationship between the groups.[147, 151, p. 100]

College-level sports athletes, both men and women, are more competitive than the general population,[152] sometimes to the point of pathology. Those who experience prolonged exposure to competitive sports have reduced altruistic behavior patterns and are more rivalrous.[153] The higher testosterone levels that result from winning in competition make for more rambunctious and rowdy behavior.[154] Scores on competitiveness among college men are "significantly correlated with reported sexual aggression and athletic participation."[155, p. 1379] The National Association for Sports and Physical Education now counsels its members that it is inappropriate to focus activities on competition with other students.[100, p. 1029, 156]

Accounting for the Unexpected

The research reviewed here surprisingly suggests that in most cases a competitive approach does not lead to increased productivity. Various explanations are possible with regard to the discrepancy between what basic research reveals about competition and the competition paradigm's assumptions about the virtues of competition.

First, the basic research may simply be wrong. This explanation, while plausible, is unlikely because the body of research is so substantial and consistent across such a long period of time. There are disagreements and some conflicting findings, as has been mentioned. But these are the exceptions in what is a relatively consistent set of research findings.

Second, the basic research may be valid, but the results may not apply outside the laboratory to anyone other than the kind of subjects with whom these experiments were performed, in any contexts other than those that served as a basis for the studies reviewed. This explanation is quite possible because laboratory research is artificial, and it constitutes a naive version of society.[157] Empirical research is often undertaken in highly simplified circumstances, which means that conclusions may or may not be applicable to real-world conditions. Applications of basic research findings on competition from one context to another always risk inappropriate generalization.

At the same time, completely ignoring this body of research would be unwise. Not all the research discussed took place in the laboratory. The results reviewed come from a number of different situations including various educational sites, informal settings such as summer camps, professional and amateur sports competitions, and industrial organizations. They involve different types of subjects, ranging from workers to students and from children to adults. In addition, some of the findings, including those concerning reduced production under competitive conditions, were consistent across settings and subjects, thus lending weight to their probable accuracy.

Third, the results discussed in this chapter may be limited in that they do not apply to all forms of competition. Many studies of individual and group competition have, in the past, failed to distinguish between destructive and constructive competition, between appropriate and inappropriate competition, and between goal-oriented and interpersonal competition.[158] In this body of research, competition is frequently defined as zero sum. As explained in chapter 1, it is among the most destructive forms of competition, and this means that the results apply with certainty only to the most extreme forms of competition. The findings in this chapter remain relevant to the extent that the competition paradigm similarly fails to distinguish between unfettered and more benign forms of this phenomenon.

Fourth, this research on competition may be accurate, and competition may not be superior to cooperation in some areas. If this is true, it is important to determine those sectors where competition is superior and where it is not exceptional. The competition paradigm makes no room for this type of qualification. Much evidence suggests that it should be revised.

Fifth, competition may not be as productive as cooperation for many individuals and groups, but the short-term variance between the two is not great and may be evident only in the long run. If this is the case, then the competition paradigm, with its commitment to unrelenting competition, may not constitute a major handicap immediately, but it could have serious negative consequences in the long run.

Notes

1. Solow, RM. Welfare: The Cheapest Country. *New York Review of Books* (March 23, 2000) 20–23.

2. Johnson, DW, Johnson RT. Instructional Goal Structure: Cooperative, Competitive or Individualistic. *Review of Educational Research* 1974;4(2):213–40.

3. Johnson, DW, Ahlgren A. Relationship between Students' Attitudes about Cooperative Learning and Competition and Attitudes toward Schooling. *Journal of Educational Psychology* 1976;68:29–102.

4. Johnson, DW, Johnson R, Anderson D. Relationship between Student Cooperative, Competitive, and Individualistic Attitudes toward Schooling. *Journal of Psychology* 1978;100:183–99.

5. Johnson, DW, Johnson RT. *Cooperation and Competition: Theory and Research.* Edina, MN: Interaction Book Company; 1989.

6. Johnson, DW, Maruyama G, Johnson R, Nelson D, Skon L. Effects of Cooperative, Competitive, and Individualistic Goals Structures on Achievement: A Meta-Analysis. *Psychological Bulletin* 1981;89(1):47–62.

7. Qin, Z, Johnson DW, Johnson RT. Cooperative versus Competitive Efforts and Problem Solving. *Review of Educational Research* 1995;65(2):129–43.

8. Miller, LK, Hamblin RL. Interdependence, Differential Rewarding and Productivity. *American Sociological Review* 1963;28:768–78.

9. Tjosvold, D, Fraser S. Cooperation Theory and Organizations. *Human Relations* 1984;37(9):743–67.

10. May, M. A Research Note on Co-operative and Competitive Behavior. *American Journal of Sociology* 1937;42:887–91.

11. Michaels, JW. Classroom Reward Structures and Academic Performance. *Review of Educational Research* 1977;47:87–98.

12. Schmitt, D. Competition: Some Behavioral Issues. *Behavior Analyst* 1986;9(1):27–34.

13. Deutsch, M. Education and Distributive Justice: Some Reflections on Grading Systems. *American Psychologist* 1979;34(5):391–401.

14. Rocha, RF, Rogers RW. Ares and Babbitt in the Classroom: Effects of Competition and Reward on Children's Aggression. *Journal of Personality and Social Psychology* 1976;33(5):588–93.

15. Lambert, R. Cooperation et Competition Dans Des Petits Groupes (Cooperation and Competition in Small Groups). *Revue Française de Sociologie* 1960;1(1):61–72.

16. Johnson, RT, Johnson DW, Stanne MB. Effects of Cooperative, Competitive, and Individualistic Goal Structures on Computer-Assisted Instruction. *Journal of Educational Psychology* 1985;77(6):668–77.

17. Whittemore, IC. The Influence of Competition on Performance: An Experimental Study. *Journal of Abnormal and Social Psychology* 1924;19:236–53.

18. Allport, FH. *Social Psychology*. Boston: Houghton Mifflin Company; 1924.

19. Deutsch, M. An Experimental Study of the Effects of Co-operation and Competition upon Group Process. *Human Relations* 1949;2(July):199–232.

20. Rosenbaum, ME, Moore DL, Cotton JL, Cook MS, Hieser RA, Shovar MN, et al. Group Productivity and Process: Pure and Mixed Reward Structures and Task Interdependence. *Journal of Personality and Social Psychology* 1980;39(4):626–42.

21. Julian, JW, Perry FA. Cooperation Contrasted with Intra-Group and Inter-Group Competition. *Sociometry* 1967;30(1):79–90.

22. Williams, D. Effects of Competition between Groups in a Training Situation. *Occupational Psychology* 1956;30:85–93.

23. American Society of Chartered Life Underwriters and Chartered Financial Consultants, and Ethics Officer Association. Sources and Consequences of Workplace Pressure: Increasing the Risk of Unethical and Illegal Business Practices. Belmont, MA: Ethics Officer Association; 1997.

24. St. Peter, RF, Reed MC, Kemper P, Blumenthal D. Changes in the Scope of Care Provided by Primary Care Physicians. *New England Journal of Medicine* 1999;341(26):1980–85.

25. Grumbach, K. Primary Care in the United States—The Best of Times, the Worst of Times. *New England Journal of Medicine* 1999;341(26):2008–10.

26. Retchin, SM, Brown RS, Yeh SH, Chu D, Moreno L. Outcomes of Stroke Patients in Medicare Fee for Service and Managed Care. *Journal of the American Medical Association* 1997;278:119–24.

27. McCall, N. Lessons from Arizona's Medicaid Managed Care Program. *Health Affairs* 1997;16(5):194–99.

28. Pindus, N, Greiner A. The Effects of Health Care Industry Changes on Health Care Worker and Quality of Patient Care: Summary of Literature and Research. Washington, DC: Urban Institute; 1997.

29. Blinder, AS, Morgan J. Are Two Heads Better Than One?: An Experimental Analysis of Group vs. Individual Decisionmaking. Cambridge, MA: National Bureau of Economic Research; 2000. p. 47.

30. Crawford, T, Sidowski JB. Monetary Incentive and Cooperative/Competitive Instructions in Minimal Social Situation. *Psychological Reports* 1964;150:233–34.

31. Raven, BH, Eachus TM. Cooperation and Competition in Means-Interdependent Triads. *Journal of Abnormal and Social Psychology* 1963;67:307–16.

32. Smith, AJ, Madden HE, Sobol R. Productivity and Recall in Cooperative and Competitive Discussion Groups. *Journal of Psychology* 1957;43:193–204.

33. Cohen, J. Cooperative and Competitive Styles—The Construct and Its Relevance. *Human Relations* 1982;35(8):621–33.

34. Cohen, J. Theoretical Considerations of Peer Tutoring. *Psychology in the Schools* 1986;23(2):175–86.

35. Phillips, B, D'Amico L. Effects of Cooperation and Competition on the Cohesiveness of Small Face-to-Face Groups. *Journal of Educational Psychology* 1956;47:65–70.

36. Triplett, N. The Dynamogenic Factors in Pacemaking and Competition. *American Journal of Psychology* 1898;9:507–33.

37. Tjosvold, D, Chia LC. Conflict between Managers and Workers: The Role of Cooperation and Competition. *Journal of Social Psychology* 1989;129(2):235–47.

38. Tjosvold, D. Power in Cooperative and Competitive Organizational Contexts. *Journal of Social Psychology* 1990;130(2):249–58.

39. Stanne, MB, Johnson DW, Johnson RT. Does Competition Enhance or Inhibit Motor Performance: A Meta-Analysis. *Psychological Bulletin* 1999;125(1):133–54.

40. Slavin, R. *Cooperative Learning.* New York: Longman; 1983.

41. Johnson, DW, Johnson RT, Skon L. Student Achievement on Different Types of Tasks under Cooperative, Competitive, and Individualistic Conditions. *Contemporary Educational Psychology* 1979;4(2):99–106.

42. Deci, EL, Betley G, Kahle J, Abrams L, Porac J. When Trying to Win: Competition and Intrinsic Motivation. *Personality and Social Psychology Bulletin* 1981;7:79–83.

43. Haines, DB, McKeachie W. Cooperative versus Competitive Discussion Methods in Teaching Introductory Psychology. *Journal of Educational Psychology* 1967;58(6, Pt.1):386–90.

44. French, DC, Brownell CA, Graziano WG, Hartup WW. Effects of Cooperative, Competitive, and Individualistic Sets on Performance in Children's Groups. *Journal of Experimental Child Psychology* 1977;24(1):1–10.

45. Humphreys, B, Johnson RT, Johnson DW. Effects of Cooperative, Competitive, and Individualistic Learning on Students' Achievement in Science Class. *Journal of Research in Science Teaching* 1982;19(5):351–56.

46. Okebukola, PA, Ogunniyi MB. Cooperative, Competitive, and Individualistic Science Laboratory Interaction Patterns—Effects on Students' Achievement and Acquisition of Practical Skills. *Journal of Research in Science Teaching* 1984;21(9):875–84.

47. Sherman, LW. A Comparative Study of Cooperative and Competitive Achievement in Two Secondary Biology Classrooms: The Group Investigation Model versus an Individually Competitive Goal Structure. *Journal of Research in Science Teaching* 1988;26(1):55–64.

48. Clark, DC. Competition for Grades and Graduate-Student Performance. *Journal of Educational Research* 1969;62(8):351–54.

49. Pepitone, EA. *Children in Cooperation and Competition: Toward a Developmental Social Psychology.* Lexington, MA: Lexington Books; 1980.

50. Hare, AP, Blumberg HH, Davies MF, Kent MV. *Small Group Research: A Handbook.* Norwood, NJ: Ablex Publishing Corporation; 1994.

51. Workie, A. The Relative Productivity of Cooperation and Competition. *Journal of Social Psychology* 1974;92:225–30.

52. Goldman, M, Stockbauer JW, McAjliffe TG. Intergroup and Intragroup Competition and Cooperation. *Journal of Experimental Social Psychology* 1977;13(1):81–88.

53. Gump, PV. The School as a Social Situation. In: Rosenweig MR, Porter LW, editors. *Annual Review of Psychology.* Palo Alto, CA: Annual Reviews Inc.; 1980. p. 553–82.

54. Ryan, FL, Wheeler R. Effects of Cooperative and Competitive Classroom Environments on the Attitudes and Achievement of Elementary School Students Engaged in Social Studies Inquiry Activities. *Journal of Educational Psychology* 1973;65(3):402–7.

55. Okun, MA, di Vesta FJ. Cooperation and Competition in Coacting Groups. *Journal of Personality and Social Psychology* 1975;31:615–20.

56. Hulten, B, DeVries DL. Team Competition and Group Practice: Effects on Student Achievement and Attitudes. Baltimore: Psychological Abstracts of Center for Social Organization of Schools Report, Johns Hopkins University; 1976. p. 4766.

57. Turner, JC. Anthropological and Cross-Cultural Perspectives. In: Colman AM, editor. *Cooperation and Competition in Human and Animals.* Wokingham, England: Van Nostrand Reinhold; 1982. p. 219–49.

58. Tjosvold, D, Andrews R. Cooperative and Competitive Relationships between Leaders and Subordinates. *Human Relations* 1983;36(12):1111–24.

59. Shepherd, G, Muijen M, Hadley TR, Goldman H. Effects of Mental Health Services Reform on Clinical Practice in the United Kingdom. *Psychiatric Services* 1996;47(12):1351–55.

60. Cosier, RA, Dalton DR. Competition and Cooperation: Effects of Value Dissensus and Predisposition to Help. *Human Relations* 1988;41(11):823–39.

61. Zander, A. The Psychology of Group Processes. In: Rosenzweig MR, Proter LW, editors. *Annual Review of Psychology.* Palo Alto, CA: Annual Reviews Inc.; 1979.

62. McClintock, CG. Preferences among Alternative Test Outcomes: A Classroom Measure of Social Motives. *Journal of Personality and Social Psychology* 1978;26(2):21–27.

63. Fischbacher, U, Gatchter S, Fehr E. Are People Conditionally Cooperative? Evidence from a Public Goods Experiment. *Economics Letter* 2001;71:397–404.

64. Gasser, OF. The Differential Effect of Competition on Physical Performance of Individuals with High and Low Levels of Achievement Motivation and Anxiety. *Dissertation Abstracts International* 1973;33(7-A):3380-A.

65. Prapavessis, H, Grove JR. Personality Variables as Antecedents of Precompetitive Mood States. *International Journal of Sports Psychology* 1994;25:81–99.

66. Mogar, R. Competition, Achievement, and Personality. *Journal of Counseling Psychology* 1962;9(2):168–72.

67. Johnson, RT, Johnson DW. Effects of Cooperative, Competitive, and Individualistic Learning Experiences on Social Development. *Exceptional Children* 1983;49(4):323–29.

68. Grossack, M. Some Effects of Cooperation and Competition upon Small Group Behavior. *Journal of Abnormal and Social Psychology* 1954;49:341–48.

69. Ahlgren, A, Johnson DW. Sex Differences in Cooperative and Competitive Attitudes from the 2nd through the 12th Grades. *Developmental Psychology* 1979;15(1):45–49.

70. Ratner, C. Concretizing the Concept of Social Stress. *Journal of Social Distress and the Homeless* 1992;1(1):7–22.

71. Kishton, J, Dixon A. Self-Perception Changes among Sports Camp Participants. *Journal of Social Psychology* 1995;135(2):135–41.

72. Horner, M. The Motive to Avoid Success and Changing Aspirations in College Women. In: Bardwick J, editor. *Readings in the Psychology of Women*. New York: Harper & Row; 1972.

73. Wallach, T. Competition and Gender in Group Psychotherapy. *Group* 1994;18(1):29–36.

74. Taylor, SE, Klein LC, Lewis BP, Gruenewald TL, Gurung RAR, Updegraff JA. Biobehavioral Responses to Stress in Females: Tend-and-Befriend, Not Fight-or-Flight. *Psychological Review* 2000;107(3):411–29.

75. McClintock, CG, Moskowitz JM. Children's Preferences for Individualistic Cooperative and Competitive Outcomes. *Journal of Personality and Social Psychology* 1976;34:543–55.

76. Moely, BE, Skarin K, Weil S. Sex Differences in Competition-Cooperation Behavior of Children at Two Age Levels. *Sex Roles* 1979;5(3):329–42.

77. Crockenberg, SB, Bryant BK, Wilce LS. The Effects of Cooperatively and Competitively Structured Learning Environments on Inter- and Intrapersonal Behavior. *Child Development* 1976;47:386–96.

78. Stockdale, DF, Galejs I, Wolins L. Cooperative-Competitive Preferences and Behavioral Correlates as a Function of Sex and Age of School-Age Children. *Psychological Reports* 1983;53:739–50.

79. Johnson, DW, Johnson RT. *Learning Together and Alone: Cooperation, Competition, and Individualization*. Englewood Cliffs, NJ: Prentice Hall; 1975.

80. Ahlgren, A. Sex Differences in the Correlates of Cooperative and Competitive School Attitudes. *Developmental Psychology* 1983;19(6):881–88.

81. Beutel, AM, Marini MM. Gender and Values. *American Sociological Review* 1995;60(June):436–48.

82. Weisfeld, CC, Weisfeld GE, Warren RA, Freedman DG. The Spelling Bee: A Naturalistic Study of Female Inhibition in Mixed-Sex Competition. *Adolescence* 1983;18(71):695–708.

83. White, SA. Effects of Gender and Competitive Coaction on Motor Performance. *Perceptual and Motor Skills* 1991;73:581–82.

84. Walters, AE, Stuhlmacher AF, Meyer LL. Gender and Negotiator Competitiveness: A Meta-Analysis. *Organizational Behavior and Human Decision Processes* 1998;76(1):1–29.

85. Bonoma, TV, Tedeschi JT, Helm B. Some Effects of Target Cooperation and Reciprocated Promises on Conflict Resolution. *Sociometry* 1974;37(2):251–61.

86. Sherif, CW. Females in the Competitive Process. In: Harris DV, editor. *Women and Sport: A National Research Conference*. University Park: Pennsylvania State University Press; 1972. p. 115–39.

87. Hartup, WW, Yonas A. Developmental Psychology. In: Mussen PH, Rosenzweig MR, editors. *Annual Review of Psychology.* Palo Alto, CA: Annual Reviews Inc.; 1971. p. 337–92.

88. United States Health Resources and Services Administration. *Minorities and Women in the Health Field.* Rockville, MD: U.S. Department of Health and Human Services; 1994.

89. Killeen, J, McCarrey M. Relations of Altruistic versus Competitive Values, Course of Study, and Behavioral Intentions to Help or Compete. *Psychological Reports* 1986;59:895–98.

90. Blumberg, HH. Cooperation, Competition, and Conflict Resolution. In: Hare AP, Blumberg HH, Davies MF, Kent MV, editors. *Small Group Research: A Handbook.* Norwood, NJ: Ablex Publishing Corporation; 1994. p. 213–36.

91. Eckel, CC, Grossman PJ. Are Women Less Selfish Than Men?: Evidence from Dictator Experiments. *The Economic Journal* 1998;108(May):726–35.

92. Cashdan, E. Are Men More Competitive Than Women? *British Journal of Social Psychology* 1998;37:213–29.

93. Wilkinson, R. Commentary: Liberty, Fraternity, Equality. *International Journal of Epidemiology* 2002;31(3):538–43.

94. Lanzetta, JT, Englis BG. Expectations of Cooperation and Competition and Their Effects on Observers' Vicarious Emotional Responses. *Journal of Personality and Social Psychology* 1989;56(4):543–54.

95. Lindskold, S, Betz B, Walters PS. Transforming Competitive or Cooperative Climates. *Journal of Conflict Resolution* 1986;30(1):99–114.

96. Deutsch, M. *The Resolution of Conflict: Constructive and Destructive Processes.* New Haven, CT: Yale University Press; 1973.

97. Dunn, RE, Goldman M. Competition and Noncompetition in Relationship to Satisfaction and Feelings toward Own-Group and Nongroup Members. *Journal of Social Psychology* 1966;68:299–311.

98. Coleman, JW. Toward an Integrated Theory of White-Collar Crime. *American Journal of Sociology* 1987;93(2):406–39.

99. Hertzman, C, Marmot M. The Leading Hypothesis and Its Discontents: A Synthesis of Evidence and Outstanding Issues regarding the East-West Life Expectancy Gap. In: Hertzman C, editor. *East-West Life Expectancy Gap in Europe.* Dordrecht, Netherlands: Kluwer Academic Publishers; 1996.

100. Anderson, CA, Morrow M. Competitive Aggression without Interaction: Effects of Competitive versus Cooperative Instructions on Aggressive Behavior in Video Games. *Personality and Social Psychology Bulletin* 1995;21(10):1020–30.

101. Megargee, EI. *The Psychology of Violence and Aggression.* Morristown, NJ: General Learning Press; 1972.

102. de Waal, FBM. The Reconciled Hierarchy. In: Chance MRA, editor. *Social Fabrics of the Mind.* London: Lawrence Erlbaum Associates; 1989. p. 105–35.

103. Rabbie, JM, Wilkens G. Intergroup Competition and Its Effect on Intragroup and Intergroup Relations. *Journal of European Social Psychology* 1971;1(2):215–34.

104. Rabbie, JM, Benoist F, Oosterbaan H, Visser L. Differential Power and Effects of Expected Competitive and Cooperative Intergroup Interaction on Intragroup and Outgroup Attitudes. *Journal of Personality and Social Psychology* 1974;30(1):46–56.

105. Yu, F-Y. Competition or Noncompetition: Its Impact on Interpersonal Relationships in a Computer-Assisted Learning Environment. *Journal of Educational Technology Systems* 1997;25(1):13–24.

106. Reeve, J, Olson BC, Cole SG. Motivation and Performance: Two Consequences of Winning and Losing in Competition. *Motivation and Emotion* 1985;9(3):291–98.

107. Ommundsen, Y, Pedersen BH. The Role of Achievement Goal Orientations and Perceived Ability upon Somatic and Cognitive Indices of Sport Competition Trait Anxiety. *Medicine & Science in Sports* 1999;9(6):333–43.

108. Vallerand, RJ, Gauvin LI, Halliwell WR. Negative Effects of Competition on Children's Intrinsic Motivation. *Journal of Social Psychology* 1986;126(5):649–57.

109. Deci, EL, Ryan RM. *Intrinsic Motivation and Self-Determination in Human Behavior.* New York: Plenum Press; 1985.

110. Ericson, RV. *Criminal Reactions: The Labelling Perspective.* Lexington, MA: Saxon House Lexington Books; 1975.

111. Tannenbaum, F. *Crime and the Community.* Boston: Ginn; 1938.

112. Becker, HS. Labelling Theory Reconsidered. In: Becker HS, editor. *Outsiders.* New York: Free Press; 1973. p. 177–208.

113. Garfinkel, H. Conditions of Successful Degradation Ceremonies. *American Journal of Sociology* 1956;61:420–24.

114. Himmelberg, CP, Hubbard RG, Palia D. Understanding the Determinants of Managerial Ownership and the Link between Ownership and Performance. *Journal of Financial Economics* 1999;53(3):353–84.

115. Frank, RH, Cook PJ. *The Winner-Take-All Society: Why the Few at the Top Get So Much More Than the Rest of Us.* New York: Free Press; 1995.

116. Korn/Ferry International. Global Demand for Top Executives Soars in Second Quarter, according to Korn/Ferry International's Index. New York: Korn/Ferry International; 1999.

117. Becker, HS. *Outsiders: Studies in the Sociology of Deviance.* New York: Free Press; 1963.

118. Matza, D. *Becoming Deviant.* Englewood Cliffs, NJ: Prentice Hall; 1969.

119. Cialdini, RB, Borden RJ, Thorne A, Walker MR, Freeman S, Sloan LR. Basking in Reflected Glory: Three (Football) Field Studies. In: Baumeister RF, editor. *The Self in Social Psychology.* Cleveland: Psychology Press, Taylor & Francis Group; 1999. p. 436–45.

120. Gove, WR. The Labelling Perspective: An Overview. In: Gove WR, editor. *The Labelling of Deviance: Evaluating a Perspective.* New York: John Wiley & Sons; 1975. p. 3–20.

121. Lofland, J. *Deviance and Identity.* Englewood Cliffs, NJ: Prentice Hall; 1969.

122. Schur, EM. *Labelling Deviant Behavior: Its Sociological Implications.* New York: Harper & Row; 1971.

123. Corbin, CB, Barnett MA, Matthews KA. The Effects of Direct and Indirect Competition on Children's State Anxiety. *Journal of Leisure Research* 1979;11(4):271–77.

124. Shaw, ME. Some Motivational Factors in Cooperation and Competition. *Journal of Personality* 1958;26:155–69.

125. McCaul, KD, Gladue BA, Joppa M. Winning, Losing, Mood, and Testosterone. *Hormones & Behavior* 1992;26:486–504.

126. Wilson, GV, Kerr JH. Affective Responses to Success and Failure: A Study of Winning and Losing in Competitive Rugby. *Personality and Individual Differences* 1999;27(1):85–99.

127. Worchel, SW, Wong FY, Scheltema KE. Improving Intergroup Relations: Comparative Effects of Anticipated Cooperation and Helping on Attraction for an Aid-Giver. *Social Psychology Quarterly* 1989;52(3):213–19.

128. Gerald, HB, Miller N. Group Dynamics. In: Fransworth PR, NcNemar O, McNemar Q, editors. *Annual Review of Psychology.* Palo Alto, CA: Annual Reviews Inc.; 1967. p. 287–329.

129. Marlowe, D, Gergen KJ, Doob AN. Opponent's Personality, Expectations of Social Interaction, and Interpersonal Bargaining. *Journal of Personality and Social Psychology* 1966;3:206–13.

130. Gilbert, P. *Human Nature and Suffering.* Hillsdale, NJ: Lawrence Erlbaum Associates; 1989.

131. Messner, MA, Dunbar M, Hunt D. The Televised Sport Manhood Formula. *Journal of Sport & Social Issues* 2000;24(4):380–94.

132. Bjorkqvist, K, Osterman K, Hjeltback M. Aggression among University Employees. *Aggressive Behavior* 1994;20(3):173–84.

133. Wilson, M, Daly M. Competitiveness, Risk Taking, and Violence: The Young Male Syndrome. *Ethnology and Sociobiology* 1985;6:59–73.

134. James, NL, Johnson DW. The Relationship between Attitudes toward Social Interdependence and Psychological Health within Three Criminal Populations. *Journal of Social Psychology* 1983;121(1):131–43.

135. Wiggins, JA. Interaction Structure, Frustration, and the Extensiveness and Intensity of Aggression. *Sociometry* 1965;28:197–209.

136. Davidson, HA. Competition, The Cradle of Anxiety. *Education* 1955;76:162–66.

137. Laner, MR. Competition and Combativeness in Courtship: Reports from Women. *Journal of Family Violence* 1989;4(2):181–95.

138. Laner, MR. Competitive vs. Noncompetitive Styles: Which Is Most Valued in Courtship? *Sex Roles* 1989;20(3-4):165–72.

139. Rabbie, JM. Group Processes as Stimulants of Aggression. In: Groebel J, Hinde RA, editors. *Aggression and War: Their Biological and Social Bases.* New York: Cambridge University Press; 1989. p. 141–55.

140. Bay-Hinitz, AK, Peterson RF, Quilitch R. Cooperative Games: A Way to Modify Aggressive and Cooperative Behaviors in Young Children. *Journal of Applied Behavior Analysis* 1994;27(3):435–46.

141. Insko, CA, Schopler J, Hoyle RH, Dardis GJ, Graetz KA. Individual-Group Discontinuity as a Function of Fear and Greed. *Journal of Personality and Social Psychology* 1990;58(1):68–79.

142. Kleiner, C, Lord M. The Cheating Game. *U.S. News & World Report* (November 22, 1999) 55–57, 61–64, 66.

143. Hafner, K. Lessons in Internet Plagiarism. *New York Times* (June 28, 2001) G1.

144. Clines, FX. Cheating Report Renews Debate over Use of Tests to Evaluate Schools. *New York Times* (June 12, 2000) A18.

145. Deutsch, MA. Subjective Features of Conflict Resolution: Psychological, Social and Cultural Influences. In: Vayrynen R, editor. *New Directions in Conflict Theory: Conflict Resolution and Conflict Transformation.* Newbury Park, CA: Sage Publications; 1991. p. 26–56.

146. Lieberson, S, Silverman AR. The Precipitants and Underlying Conditions of Race Riots. In: Megargee EI, Hokanson JE, editors. *The Dynamics of Aggression: Individual, Group, and International Analyses.* New York: Harper & Row; 1970.

147. Sherif, M, Harvey OJ, White BJ, Hood WR, Sherif CW. *Intergroup Conflict and Cooperation: The Robbers' Cave Experiment.* Norman: Institute of Group Relations, University of Oklahoma; 1961.

148. Sherif, M, Sherif CW. *Groups in Harmony and Tension: An Integration of Studies on Intergroup Relations.* New York: Harper; 1953.

149. Blake, RR, Mouton JS. From Theory to Practice in Intergroup Problem Solving. In: Worchel S, Austin WG, editors. *Psychology of Intergroup Relations.* Chicago: Nelson-Hall; 1986.

150. Sherif, M, Sherif CW. Groups in Harmony and Tension. In: Megargee EI, Hokanson JE, editors. *The Dynamics of Aggression: Individual, Group, and International Analyses.* New York: Harper & Row; 1970. p. 190–210.

151. Goldstein, AP. *The Ecology of Aggression.* New York: Plenum Press; 1994.

152. Finkenberg, ME, Moode FM, DiNucci JM. Analysis of Sport Orientation of Female Collegiate Athletes. *Perceptual and Motor Skills* 1998;86(2):647–50.

153. Kagan, S, Madsen M. Experimental Analyses of Cooperation and Competition of Anglo-American and Mexican Children. *Developmental Psychology* 1972;6(1):49–59.

154. Dabbs, JMJ. Salivary Testosterone Measurements in Behavioral Studies. In: Malamud D, Tabak LA, editors. *Saliva as a Diagnostic Fluid.* New York: New York Academy of Sciences; 1993. p. 177–83.

155. Caron, SL, Halteman WA, Stacy C. Athletes and Rape: Is There a Connection? *Perceptual and Motor Skills* 1997;85(3):1379–93.

156. National Association for Sport and Physical Education. Appropriate Practices for High School Physical Education. Reston, VA: National Association for Sport and Physical Education; 1998. p. 23.

157. Helmreich, R, Bakeman R, Scherwitz L. The Study of Small Groups. In: Mussen PH, Rosenzweig MR, editors. *Annual Review of Psychology.* Palo Alto, CA: Annual Reviews Inc.; 1973. p. 337+.

158. Gordon, FM, Welch KR, Offringa G, Katz N. The Complexity of Social Outcomes from Cooperative, Competitive, and Individualistic Reward Systems. *Social Justice Research* 2000;13(3):237–69.

4

Competition Can Be Counterproductive for Organizations

It is hard for many economists to accept the proposition that competition may be excessive because the received theory regards competition as always good, and the more there is, the better.[1, pp. 6-7]

THERE SEEMS TO BE A national consensus in the United States about how competition benefits organizations. Representatives of the business community, the media, and political leaders all assume that intense competition shapes organizational structure and behavior in the best way. Articles in *The Economist, Forbes,* and *BusinessWeek* say the same thing. The competition paradigm supports the view that competition increases productivity, efficiency, and innovation at the level of the organization, be it a department, a firm, or a corporation. It is assumed to be as good for schools and hospitals as it is for business.

There is little doubt that constructive competition has some important advantages and yields certain benefits for organizations. It can both increase and diminish choices. It sometimes reduces costs. In these cases, it may make goods and services cheaper so that more people can afford a product or a service. It forges the link between those who have money to invest and those with the entrepreneurial skills at the organizational level who can do something with that money. In the best of cases, it rewards efficiency and weeds out economic failure. It allocates goods and services without excessive administrative input. It is said to reduce bureaucratic rigidity. It does all this without requiring unrealistic or optimistic philosophical assumptions about human nature.

Studies reviewed in this chapter indicate that all the benefits derived from competition are not without costs, even though the competition paradigm does not speak to these issues. In sum, we will see that destructive forms of competition may bring stress to an organization or commercially oriented enterprise in the same way they do to individuals and groups.[2,3] It leads managers to act in ways that make no sense at all. For example, they may increase competition internal to the organization, a practice found to reduce performance. Intense competition means that profits are lower because management is focused on the short term, and decisions are sometimes self-defeating. Measures likely to increase earnings in the long term are ignored. Finally, intense competition means customary business ethics are set aside at the long-term expense of the business community as a whole. A self-reinforcing spiral of competition reduces the possibility of constructive competition altogether.

Competition Shapes Organizational Structure and Behavior, but the Effects on Productivity Are Mixed

Intense competition changes the context within which organizations function. It rearranges power relationships and transforms corporate cultures.[4] It precipitates structural adaptation in very specific ways. Whether this is good or bad, functional or dysfunctional, is not necessarily clear. Sometimes it depends on one's point of view and personal situation in the organization. Ironically, there is little evidence that such changes actually improve organizational productivity or overall performance. They come about simply because they seem to be the right thing to do.

Centralized Power—Decentralized Accountability

Historically, it was thought that the greater the degree of competition, the closer the control and coordination of every aspect of the production process.[2, p. 278, 5] This makes sense—in a highly competitive environment, mistakes cannot be afforded, and top efficiency is required. To achieve these goals, organizations limit discretionary behavior.[6] At the same time, the number of managers and middle-level supervisors is reduced in periods of high competition.[7] Some studies find that a "taller" organizational structure evolves under these conditions.[8] However, there are reasons to question all these trends, and the opposite is often observed. For example, U.S.-based firms made greater use in recent years of outsourcing and semiautonomous work teams despite increased competition. There may be a point at which competition becomes so intense that normal rules do not apply and experimentation becomes the main imperative.

Leadership is said to be more critical during periods of high competition than under normal conditions.[9] The power of those at the top and of those with more competitively oriented personalities is increased.[10] Data suggest that chief executive officers (CEOs) are better compensated relative to other workers during periods of intense competition. Elmer Johnson, writing in the *Harvard Business Review,* compares CEO salaries in 1960 (a less competitive period) and 1988 (a more competitive period) and confirms this trend.[11] But it is also possible that CEO salaries continue to rise in economic sectors where intense competition leads to extreme market concentration or oligopoly.[12] This is discussed here.

An environment of destructive competition and high organizational stress changes the way organizations function. Increased review is typical, and strict accountability is taken more seriously. Reduced worker discretion at lower levels has been observed.[13] Competition also means that the actual number of job classifications in large organizations is reduced as workers at each level are expected to be available for more and different tasks. As a result, mobility between the ranks is harder to attain.[14, pp. 589, 592]

While power is centralized, accountability may be more dispersed during periods of high competition. This increased accountability sometimes means greater responsibility for performance and productivity.[14] Companies transfer more managerial discretion, relegating hiring and firing to lower-level managers. Frequency of reporting is increased, and monitoring up and down the hierarchy, rather than horizontally, is characteristic. Communication is more likely to be oral than written under conditions of high competition.[2, p. 278]

Ironically, none of these modified centralization/decentralization relationships resulting from intense competition are known to increase organizational performance. No one has systematically studied whether they do any good. They may, in fact, be so complicated that definitive research about their effects is almost impossible to carry out.

Change for the Sake of Change Alone? Layoffs, Downsizing, Outsourcing, and the Erosion of Job Benefits

Destructive competition precipitates broad structural and functional organizational changes. Again, it is not always clear whether the resulting organizational modifications and adjustments amount to much more than activity for its own sake. However, in the face of crisis, action, even for its own sake, may feel better than inaction. Sometimes action is taken simply because it seems to be what other organizations are doing. One result is clear: America's work force is unhappy. Sixty percent of workers report substantial job-related pressure; about a third report job insecurity.[15]

The makeup of the workforce changes under conditions of high competition. Organizational downsizing (or "right sizing") is often part of the restructuring that many experts attribute to higher levels of competition.[16, p. 866, 17]

Organizations reduce their workforces. This is as true of the newspaper sectors[18] as it is of the health insurance sector[19] and the automobile industry.[20] Reduced job security is a related effect of high competition.[17, 21] Some research suggests that the probability of employees finding another, even better paying job, actually increases in periods of high competition,[22] but this is true only in periods of economic expansion.[23] And even during expansion, there are exceptions. Older, highly educated workers with lots of seniority are more likely to be laid off than was the case in the past, and few of them find new positions at the same level and rate of pay.

Overall, increased competition appears to make for a decline in job stability.[24, 25] At least half of American firms reduced the number of people they employed in the first half of the 1990s.[7] Data from the Department of Labor indicate that forty-three million jobs were lost between 1979 and 1995.[26] A representative sample of some of America's major large and midsize firms and industries found that 50 percent downsized in 1995. Layoffs function in the same manner. Forty-nine percent of these companies eliminated jobs in 1996, and 51 percent did so in 1997.[27] In 2000, a time of high competition and full employment, some companies laid off workers at the same time that they were hiring others.[28]

According to Ted Baker, director of the Weinert Applied Ventures in Entrepreneurship (WAVE) Program and assistant professor at the University of Wisconsin, empirical evidence suggests that the practice of downsizing "has no positive effect on financial outcomes and may even have a negative effect."[29, p. 53] Higher retention rates actually improve profits and increase growth.[30–32] Certainly some downsizing practices work better than others. After downsizing, some companies report greater productivity from remaining workers and higher levels of overall productivity.[33] In a few cases, especially in the short term, downsizing does increase profits.[7, 17] But for most, employment downsizing does not increase returns or improve profits.[27, pp. 12–13, 34] Nevertheless, downsizing seems to please stockholders, especially when it accompanies restructuring in the form of acquisitions or mergers.[35]

The effects of downsizing and layoffs on the behavior and attitudes of those not laid off have consequences for an organization beyond undermining trust and morale (discussed later in this chapter). These workers who are not let go are profoundly distressed, and they experience guilt, and anxiety, and so on.[36, 37] Stress, anger, and denial are common.[3, 38, 39] The potential health effects on the individual worker were reviewed in preceding chapters. Restructuring increases depression, despair, and detachment among those who remain.[40, 41] Much, however, depends on the context and conditions of the layoffs, whether they are viewed as fair and equitable, and how the departing workers are treated.[36, 42, 43] Enron set an example of how not to lay off workers. The day after it sought and obtained the protection of the court under U.S. bankruptcy legislation, Enron informed half its employees that they were nonessential and that they should go home. The same afternoon these employees received phone messages indicating that they were fired.[44] If downsizing and layoffs have a negative effect on remaining employee attitudes and health, this translates into reduced company revenues.[45–47] Greater accountability rests with the workers who are retained, some of whom do not welcome added responsibilities.[48]

A long-term perspective suggests that personnel downsizing generates indirect costs that may not be offset by benefits to a company in terms of increased productivity. These include the loss of experience and knowledge as well as the expense of filling vacant positions when needed in the future.[49, 50] Good companies avoid downsizing even in periods of economic contraction. For example, Southwest Airlines, one of the most financially successful in the United States, did not lay off workers in the aftermath of the September 11, 2001, events. No surprise here. Its retention rate is 92 percent, and its employees agreed to give back some of their pay, temporarily, in this crisis.[51] Ironically, laying off an employee is not good for the health of those who do the firing. It appears to increase a manager's chance of a heart attack more than twofold in the following week.[52]

The higher pay and promotions associated with the seniority system are disappearing under conditions of increased competition. Where seniority still exists, there is a significant decline in rewards deriving from it for workers.[53, 54] Starting in the mid-1980s, seniority benefits in many companies simply collapsed.[14, p. 583, 25] The age discrimination that penalizes older workers is also thought to result from high levels of competition.[55]

Under conditions of high competition, companies look outside their organization for personnel rather than to existing staff for promotions, retraining, and so on.[14] Outsourcing, contracting out, and temporary employment are common.[56–58] Numerous studies suggest that by the mid-1980s, about a quarter of the workforce in America was "externalized" in the form of temporary help provided by an outside contractor or consultant.[59, 60] Even highly skilled professionals are now part of America's temporary workforce.[61] Hiring services from companies outside an organization rather than using in-house services is common in highly competitive conditions to reduce costs.[62] This is the case not only for private companies but for public sector organizations as well.[63, pp. A6, A1]

Employers believe that there are substantial benefits to hiring temporary workers. Temporary employees are thought to increase organizational flexibility.[64] They cost less because many do not have employer-provided health insurance and other benefits;[65, 66] this reduces the immediately evident fixed costs of employment. They have been found, in some studies, to be more productive than regular employees.[67] Turning to external subcontractors is especially helpful if the product market is new and unfamiliar.[68]

Research results on the cost of subcontracting under conditions of intense competition are mixed. Subcontracting and outsourcing make for employee uncertainty.[69] "Contractors work on site using the owner's equipment alongside the owner's employees. The contractors hire and manage their own workteams, negotiating pay and employment terms sometimes independently for each worker."[14, p. 563] An environment of uncertainty discourages internal organizational cooperation and lowers productivity.[70, 71] In some cases, it reduces profits.[72]

Employee relations have less importance during periods of high competition. Total quality management (TQM) programs are phased out even though they have been shown to improve employee moral, product quality, accounting, stock performance, and overall organizational productivity.[73] Under the pressure generated by high competition, features such as TQM become a luxury that is suddenly redefined as "distracting" from the drive for market leadership, market share, and higher profits. In addition, TQM is criticized because in a highly competitive environment it might turn over too much authority to employees.[8]

Intense competition forces organizations to change their behavior with respect to employees on everything from compensation and job security to benefits and retirement. Employees' commitment to their employer is diminished. In an effort to minimize costs, organizations in more competitive markets reduce employer-provided health insurance benefits.[74] Employees face higher copays and deductibles.

Destructive competition has implications for the way an organization functions when workers are terminated. Outplacement assistance, that is, help in finding another position for laid-off workers, is reduced during periods of high competition, even though such counseling has been found to be cost effective.[75] One survey indicated that in 1995, about 44 percent of employers offered such assistance. In 1996, only 39 percent did so. In 1997, the figure was 38 percent. Early retirement and voluntary separation agreements have also diminished over the same time. Severance pay is less likely to be offered.[27] Where it is still offered, it is a fraction of what it was in the past.[76]

During periods of intense market competition, employees bear a greater part of the risk involved in pensions and retirement.[77] The number of workers with a "defined-benefits" pension plan, in which they will receive a predetermined pension benefit, is diminishing. In a highly competitive environment, this type of commitment for the entire life span of the employee is difficult to justify to an organization. Employers are increasingly likely to contribute to a health plan that disappears when the worker retires. On the other hand, some companies, such as Campbell Soup, Procter and Gamble, and Walt Disney, through "resourceful accounting" methods, figured out a way to use retiree medical benefits to boost the bottom line.[78] The actual pension benefit today is often a function of the employee's, not the employer's, investment choices.[79] The wisdom of this approach is open to debate. Defined-benefits retirement programs are being transformed into worker-at-risk pension plans. These changes are having a substantial negative effect on older workers. Loss of pension benefits altogether is increasingly a problem. Even where postretirement health insurance benefits were promised for life, the employers' right to reduce benefits or cancel such promises has been upheld in court.[80–82]

To survive in periods of intense competition, companies attempt to pay their workers less so as to reduce costs. Unions seek to protect the wages of the lowest-paid workers,[83] and overall, unionized workers are paid more and have better benefits than nonunionized workers. One means for employers to circumvent union protections of workers has been to employ temporary workers who are, in many cases, exempt from federal regulations[14] and are very difficult for unions to organize. Another mechanism is to move production to geographic regions (the South) or to countries where unions are less in evidence.[84, pp. 184–98] The overall result is that unionization is reduced during periods of intense competition.

And Government Organizations Change, Too

The business sector is not the only organizational arena to experience structural and behavioral change for its own sake during periods of intense competition. Government organizations also have looked to competition for solutions. They employ it with the goal of restoring confidence and improving performance. The transformation in public services is aptly described in the publicity description of the "global public management revolution":

> This reform movement has shared a common set of six core characteristics: productivity—finding ways to squeeze more services from the same—or smaller—revenue base; marketization—replacing traditional bureaucratic mechanisms with market strategies; service orientation-putting citizens-as-service-recipients first; decentralization—transferring more service-delivery responsibilities to local governments and to front-line managers; policy—explicitly separating government's role as purchaser of services from its role in providing them; and accountability for results—focusing more on outputs and outcomes instead of processes and structures.[85]

Governments have been little concerned with evaluating the results of providing public management through the policy experiments. But report cards for government agencies, adopted by the George W. Bush administration, are one attempt to include a program evaluation component into the budget allocation process.[86] However, as implemented, it defines performance very narrowly, as agency compliance with the competition model. Other more objective criteria of evaluation might be desirable.

The education sector is one example of governments turning to competition as a means to solve problems. The school choice movement, voucher programs, charter schools, and the privatization of public schools all fit with the discourse of the competition paradigm. Their intent is to increase competition between public and private-sector schools. Some case studies of specific schools suggest success in terms of reduced cost and improved student performance. But broader, better-designed research calls any unequivocal conclusion regarding increased productivity and cost savings into question.[87-90]

Albert Hirschman's book *Exit, Voice, and Loyalty*[91] anticipated some of the consequences of depending exclusively on competition to improve performance of government organizations, including schools. "Exit" is defined as when "some customers stop buying the firm's products or some members leave the organization."[91, p. 4] But when there is a monopoly situation—the case with government in the past—members or customers cannot leave but must rather resort to what he calls "voice." The voice option leads to expressing one's dissatisfaction to authorities, management, and the press and to protesting when things go wrong. Introducing competition into government (a monopoly) means offering the exit option to governments' customers. This results in the most aggressive, skilled, and alert "consumers" leaving first. Hirschman argues that it weakens the institutions of government and leaves the burden of providing services to those whose "business" is undesirable to the provider of last resort—the U.S. taxpayers.

Private-sector competition with government services is a trade-off. To deny exit and require that the critical consumers remain in the monopoly pool—this is what defines government provision of services—and use their voices to change things when it is necessary is to impinge on individual rights. To offer the option of exit to them is to weaken societal-level institutions.[91]

School privatization programs do appeal to voters. They give the impression that something is being done in terms of an evident problem. As with private-sector companies in trouble, taking action—any action—may be a comfort to policymakers, legislators, and citizens. It makes people feel effective, at least in the short term.

Does It Really Make Sense for Organizations to Encourage Internal Competition?

The competition paradigm assumes that competition internal to the organization will improve performance. The underlying logic is that if competition between companies is a good thing, then competition within the organization will also have positive effects. The business community has an almost unqualified commitment to this view.[92] The evidence, however, is that an internal environment of cooperation increases performance much more than does internal competition.[93, 94] Still, management often holds to the view that reducing internal competition means that the organization will fail.[95, p. 163]

Anecdotal evidence suggests that internal competition makes each member of a production unit an "individual entrepreneur" who puts his or her own interest above that of the company.[96] When and where competition internal to an organization is reduced, results are very different from those anticipated by the competition paradigm. Productivity, profits, and product quality do not suffer. Employing group rewards in industry yield better results because cooperative groups are better able to deal with complex problems than are individual competitors working alone.[97]

Mechanisms designed to increase internal competition are widespread in conditions of destructive competition. Some are so taken for granted that we are hardly aware of their function—to increase competition among employees within an organization. Such devices include preferred parking space assignments, employee-of-the-month awards, individual recognition through titles, honorary pins, public recognition rewards, performance reviews with ranking, and prizes for perfect attendance. "Report cards" and competitive zero-sum grading schemes are more obvious tactics designed to set worker against worker within an organization.[98, 99] Enron consciously sought to encourage competition between its employees with its famous "rank and yank" philosophy. It was an example of how to create an atmosphere where everyone "shoots for number one. And you don't get there by being a nice guy."[100, p. B1] But Enron was far from unique. John F. Welch Jr., former chairman and CEO of General Electric, put it this way: "A company that bets its future on its people must remove that lower 10 percent, and keep removing it every year—always raising the bar of performance and increasing the quality of its leadership."[98, p. A1] Similarly, zero-sum pay for performance and merit pay increase internal competition, set up barriers to communication inside the organization, and may end up lowering overall organizational effectiveness.[101, 102] Ford Motor Company experimented with report cards but dispensed with them because management concluded that they had a bad effect on morale and proved to be ineffective and discriminatory.[103, 104]

Evidence that internal noncompetitive workplace structures and incentives improve performance comes from case studies in a range of different economic sectors, in several different countries, for large and small companies, going back fifty years.[105, 106] Self-management and industrial democracy experiments increased productivity between 10 and 40 percent. The Gaines Pet Food plant in Kansas implemented such innovations and found that they increased output and reduced accidents. The Volvo plant in Kalmar, Sweden, carried out numerous workplace experiments that increased internal cooperation and gave workers more freedom and autonomy at the same time. These arrangements increased efficiency and reduced absenteeism dramatically.[107–111] Workers organized into autonomous cooperative teams exhibited higher product quality, lower absenteeism, and reduced turnover.[112, 113, 114, pp. viii–x] The combination of such high-performance work practices gives better results than could be expected if the benefits of each, alone, were simply added together.[115] Results are the same across many studies in different circumstances.[29] Even the most conservative estimates suggest that workplace innovations that increase internal cooperation and that empower employees do not harm employers.[116, 117] On the macrolevel, national economic growth is correlated with higher levels of organizational internal cooperation, not competition.[118]

Cooperation internal to an organization leads to increased corporate profits. It can be achieved by creating a "sense of ownership" among employees. Profits increase when employees are briefed on how they fit in with the organization's corporate strategy and how their behavior affects the success or failure of the company. Sharing information with employees as to company strategy in terms of its competitors improves employee cooperation and commitment.[119, 120] Company-level "town hall meetings" make for an increased sense of employee participation at the local level, where suggestions can best be implemented. They increase corporate profits, too, even in periods of economic slowdown and layoffs.[121] Financial incentives may also increase productivity, but they are most effective when everyone working for the organization benefits if the company does well. Profit sharing and pay increases tied to customer satisfaction ratings are examples.[45] They increase internal cooperation rather than internal competition.

If cooperative internal organizational cultures are so successful, why do more companies not take measures to create them? External levels of competition experienced by an organization are not within the control of management; little can be done about them. But the level of competition and cooperation internal to the organization is subject to direct determination by management. This is an area where corporations that depart from the competition paradigm would be at an important advantage, but few move in this direction. Why is it that employers ignore the wealth of experimental evidence and numerous field studies that promise increased profits from cooperative internal organizational structures? The reasons are not clear, but some hypotheses are suggestive.

Personal beliefs, prior intellectual orientations, and ideological considerations, reinforced by the competition paradigm, seem to override evidence. Business leaders act on their beliefs that competition is more effective and cooperation less so. The competition paradigm suggests as much. Many leaders of business and corporate organizations believe that individual accountability is essential. Ron Zarella, chief of General Motors' North American operations, says that internal competition is a good thing. "When the ball gets dropped," he says he wants people "to scramble to pick it up." He argues this is how "you know who your good people are."[20, p. A1] Cooperation and teamwork do not fit with this intellectual perspective. As explained in the pages of the *Harvard Business Review*, "Most executives distrust the entire notion . . . of mutual accountability." Noncompetitive work organization, it is commonly assumed, "is seldom the most efficient way of getting something accomplished."[10, pp. 86, 87]

Some organizational leaders resist setting aside internal competition because they believe that a cooperative internal environment will jeopardize their influence and diminish their power.[122] Managers fear "losing the powers and prerogatives that they currently enjoy."[110, p. 18] They worry that they will be threatened by challenges to their expertise and knowledge.[112, p. 389] In one case, managers saw "their own positions threatened because the workers performed almost too well."[123, p. 78] Some executives view the potential increase in profits from cooperative production as not worth the risk if it undermines traditional authority patterns.

The well-researched sociological phenomenon of the self-fulfilling prophecy plays a role. It proposes that strongly held beliefs influence one's expectations and behavior. Unsystematic personal experience confirms philosophical preference.[122, p. 230] These individual expectations take precedence over more systematic information. Even when upper-level executives participate in workplace innovations involving less competitive internal organizational structures, they are quick to declare failure and abandon them even when evidence contradicts their view.[112]

Faith in supervision and the self-enhancement effect are related reasons for refusing to moderate competition and the associated hierarchically organized forms of workplace production. The self-enhancement effect means that managers tend to judge a product more favorably if they were personally involved in its production. Faith in supervision means that managers will tend to find work done under the control of a supervisor to be of better quality than identical work done without a supervisor.[124]

Inertia is another explanation for failure to curtail competition internal to an organization and replace it with a more cooperative environment. If a company is making a profit using internal competition, management sees no reason to change even if greater profits are likely. Is this because change increases uncertainty?

Resistance to employing internal cooperation to improve organizational performance is overwhelming. Upper-level management argues that employees in affiliated production facilities that do not use cooperative production techniques will experience decreased morale.[112] Middle-level managers resist such changes for the reasons outlined previously. Union leaders see cooperative production as a "management trick: a way of getting workers to accept gimmicks instead of real gains in wages and benefits."[95, pp. 163–64] In addition, because it requires close collaboration between workers and management, the trade union's power might be reduced.

The Downside of Intense Competition for Organizations

In this section, how excessive competition directly or indirectly affects organizations is examined. It appears to discourage new entrants to the marketplace, and this reduces innovation. Internal to the organization, too much competition inhibits job redesign, job enhancement, employee participation, and other programs that increase creativity, inventiveness, product quality, and the profit margin. Intense competition leads to lower quality and safety, organizational demise, loss of trust, and lower employee morale. All these reduce productivity.[125] An environment of destructive competition can also increase dishonest and illegal organizational behavior.

Reduced Innovation

In his summary of the literature, Will Mitchell, professor of international management at Duke University, suggests that a highly competitive market environment discourages start-up entrants to an economic sector.[126, p. 577] And he is not alone. Carroll and Hannan indicate that the "start-up rate is inversely proportional to the intensity of competition."[127, p. 116] "Intensified competition lowers founding rates." [128, p. 49] Newly established organizations suffer a disproportionate number of failures and bankruptcies. "The number of organizations operating in an industry at the time of start-up has a persisting positive effect on the organization's probability of death."[127, p. 119] This is because "environmental conditions set a finite carrying capacity, more competitors means that the potential gains from starting an organization will be smaller."[127, p. 116] It makes no sense to begin a new enterprise where there are already so many others competing.

Since intense competition leads to fewer start-up organizations, a decline in innovation results. It is more difficult to innovate and develop a new product in a highly competitive environment.[9] The market system may be a "device for conducting and evaluating experiments in economic organization,"[126, p. 576, 129, p. 277] but much of the expected benefit will not be available when competition is very intense. Under conditions of such destructive competition, these experiments never materialize to begin with or are prematurely ended.[130, 131] Without them, existing competitors may not be doing the best job possible. Novel ideas that might emerge from new entrants never have a chance to be tested in the market.

In many circumstances, intense competition discourages novel, inventive, and often-profitable workplace redesign internal to organizations.[111] Many of these innovations reduce competition internal to organizations and were discussed previously. They include innovations that involve job enrichment or give workers more control over their lives. They frequently lead to increased productivity[112, 113] and almost always improve quality.[132] Johnson & Johnson experienced a 50 percent reduction in absenteeism after innovating with flexible time schedules. Xerox indicates that its experiment with flexible scheduling led to a 10 percent increase in productivity. Switching from traditional assembly-line scheduling to flexible work production scheduling reduces stress and lowers turnover as well.[133] Such innovations cost corporations little in terms of increases in salary and benefits.[134] Women are especially likely to benefit.

Ironically, many corporations faced with a highly competitive market environment move away from innovations that could increase profits. Pioneering programs that involve workers in management have been found to increase productivity and product quality.[122] Worker participation in an organization can extend the firm's longevity and make it more profitable.[135] Flatter, less hierarchical organizational structures with greater worker participation are more responsive to environmental change.[93] Workplace innovation often leads to lower stress and higher profits.[132]

Sometimes when low unemployment accompanies excessive competition, workplace innovation survives. In these conditions, employers may feel the need to compete not just in terms of what they produce but also for primary, scarce resources (that is, quality employees). Demand for labor increases, especially where labor pools are confined geographically and where demand is high for trained technical professionals.[27] Employers may adopt internal innovation to attract and maintain personnel. Those who offer flexible work arrangements are at an advantage.[134] Without these innovations, employees might leave for positions in other companies.

Diminished Quality

Competition about quality is related to certain specific market stages. Market environments evolve over time, ranging from immature to mature. In the immature market, many sellers fiercely compete under conditions of high uncertainty. As competition increases, profits decline and, according to economic theory, should "go to zero." This is an environment where "every individual firm considered in isolation is barely getting by, so that a single false step will be its undoing."[91, p. 9] With close-to-zero profits, quality considerations are less important than offering lower prices and merely surviving. Expert opinion indicates that the effect of this type of destructive competition is largely about prices. The problem is that "lowering quality, through cheaper materials, shoddy workmanship, and misrepresentation, is the major resource of small competitive industries."[136, p. 26]

In the mature market, a few sellers compete under conditions of relative certainty where market share is well established. Constructive competition is more common in the mature market, and quality compromises may not be so evident. In these markets, it is reasonable for consumers to assume that price and quality are related.[16, p. 435]

Price and profitability are extremely important for long-term viability. But during the immature-market period, profitability may be sacrificed in the short term to acquire market share. The "profit-maximizing firm may be at a disadvantage if a rival 'blindly' pursues a sales-maximizing strategy, even if the former is more efficient."[137, p. 516] The health care economic sector, where intense market competition developed after 1993, is an example.[138] Patient mortality rates at hospitals in highly competitive markets are greater than in less competitive markets.[139] This indicates lower quality. In the highly competitive health sector of the 1990s, about 28 percent of employers and more than 60 percent of physician group representatives say that "cost pressures are hurting quality."[140, p. 2, 141] Quality may be hard to maintain because in such highly competitive markets, price and market share are, necessarily, the most important consideration.[84] Only when the immature-market shakeout period is over and the mature marketplace emerges may providers give more attention to quality considerations.

The trend toward lower quality under conditions of intense competition can be explained in several ways. Producers have a short-term perspective. Price is the first thing most customers think about. It is easy to determine the costs of a product prior to purchase. But product quality is often determined after the purchase and over the life of the product. This is true for services as well. For example, the lowest-cost provider may not be providing high-quality wireless telephone services.[142] Whether purchasing lower-cost health insurance results in inferior health care is almost impossible to know in advance of being sick and making use of the insurance. If quality is not good, if the product fails, or if service is poor, consumers are likely to be unhappy. But the consequences usually come later rather than earlier. The organization's focus in the highly competitive market is necessarily on immediate survival.

The short-term focus imposed by destructive competition means that producers must make choices that have negative long-term consequences. Advertising budgets win out in the short term over research expenditures. But without research, quality improvements lag. If price is the principal concern for purchasers, then the result is "to minimize efforts to produce significant improvements . . . in products if they are likely to increase minimum required selling price without increasing sales."[84, p. 195] In some markets, quality may not be important to consumers, so price reductions are the primary selling point, even in the long term. In other sectors (for example, health services), as the trade-off between cost and quality becomes evident, employers begin to include it in their purchasing decisions.[143]

Decreased Safety

Increased competition may make for lower attention to safety considerations in the workplace. The reasons are not always evident. It may be due to a decline in regulation or an increased drive for profit. If competition increases individual stress, this would augment organizational accident rates due to inattention, carelessness, and distraction. Mindy Fried, project director for the National Work/Life Measurement Project at Boston College, Center for Work and Family, says, "The research is pretty clear that as people work over a certain number of hours, productivity goes down, stress goes up, and work isn't as good." An organizational culture that "encourages individualism, survival of the fittest, macho heroics, and can-do reactions" may seem desirable because it is more competitive.[144, p. C8] But it can also lead to disaster. On the other hand, workers trained to cooperate have better safety records.[145] Cooperation is said to be an essential skill in commercial sectors where dangerous activities are common, such as the airline industry.[146, p. 378]

Intense competition between rival companies can offer an incentive to actually create safety hazards. This happened in the utility sector in the United States. In filings with the Federal Energy Regulatory Commission, several utility companies charged that their rivals suspended routine power deliveries over shared lines. The consequences for the customers of these rival companies were enormous. This happened in the summer of 1998, when the Midwest suffered repeated brownouts due to disruptions in transmission. While the official reason for suspending deliveries was said to be a risk of an overload on the lines, others interpreted it as an explicit attempt to damage the competitors. In either case, the indirect result of this intense competition was harm to the competitor's customers.[147]

The impact of competition on safety is less important for products that are without great social or economic consequences. Here, lower prices may be worth reduced quality for many people if safety considerations play no role. If an inexpensive, throwaway toaster burns the morning toast, it is simple enough to watch it more closely or purchase another toaster. It is a different story when a lapse in safety results in the loss of human life or when the toaster is so defective that it burns the house down. Similarly, the cost cutting that was achieved by increasing competition through privatization of the airline security and baggage inspection is a case study of the worst sort.[148] Airline executives and the General Accounting Office pointed to the problem long before September 11, 2001, but U.S. commitment to competition was unwavering.[149] From Maine to Boston to New York, the assumption has been that "faster, leaner, meaner" and cheaper carry-on baggage inspection has no downside. And even if this is largely true, the exceptions have probably eaten all the "savings." Only after the terrorist attack did government assume responsibility for airport security.[150]

The Federal Aviation Administration (FAA) has had a difficult time adjusting to the deregulation of the airline industry and the frenzy of competitive activity unleashed by the competitive market.[151] The number of passenger miles traveled has increased. Prices on competitive routes have gone down. Service to less traveled geographic locations has been reduced. But more important, has there been a reduction in safety in the airline industry?[152]

Experts worry about whether the intensely competitive market might have contributed to some recent airline crashes.[153, ch. 5] Such speculation has become common, supported by data from FAA audits of major airlines.[154] In the case of the 1998 Swissair tragedy, journalists pointed out that an American Airlines executive had taken over Swissair's daily operations with an eye to bringing experience from the U.S. competitive market to make Swissair more competitive. "Like other European carriers, Swissair has faced an increasingly competitive business environment as governments increasingly allow deregulation and airlines struggle for passengers."[155, p. B6] A USAir accident on July 2, 1994, was attributed to poor pilot-safety and training programs and trying to save money by neglecting required repairs to aircraft.[152] Deaths were reported to have been higher because USAir "resisted retrofitting cabins" with new flame-retardant material because it cost too much.[152, p. A19]

Low-priced airlines feel that they have to take extreme measures to survive in the exceptionally competitive airline industry. Strong, large players are willing to accept short-term losses to discourage new competitors from entering the market or to eliminate them if they do enter. The large carriers in the airline industry report that newer, smaller competitors modify aircraft maintenance schedules to reduce costs. They imply that this is dangerous for passengers. Whatever the case, it constitutes a form of destructive competition.[156]

ValuJet was under severe competitive pressure just prior to the tragic May 11, 1996, Florida crash.[157] To save money, it skimped on personnel training with regard to carrying hazardous materials. Poor maintenance record keeping probably jeopardizes safety as well.[158] Schwartz points out that ValuJet "offered very low fares yet had the highest profit margin in the airline industry."[159, p. 45] The hearings held later concerning the crash of ValuJet flight 592 revealed that maintenance workers had been rushing and functioned under intense pressure to meet deadlines and impress potential customers.[160] A court case found the company guilty and levied large fines, but the employees involved were not found guilty. Following the January 31, 2000, crash of an Alaska Air plane off the coast of California, mechanics at the Seattle maintenance facility said that they had been "pressured, threatened and intimidated" to cut corners.[161, p. A25]

Destructive competition may lead to compromises regarding safety, but the problem is that checks internal to the dynamics of market competition itself are very weak. For example, if accidents increase, worker compensation benefits rise, and employers cease to view workplace accidents as inevitable and instead they develop programs to improve safety.[162] To do otherwise would mean that they had to pay more than their competitors for workers' compensation costs. In addition, customers will avoid purchasing unsafe products. But when the stakes are high, such as is the case with the airline industry, these market dynamics are too little, and they come too late.

Bankruptcy: Organizational Mortality Is on the Rise

While economists see bankruptcies as a natural and perhaps even desirable consequence of competition, the costs are far from trivial. The total annual bankruptcy filings increased from around 331,264 to 1,492,129 between 1980 and 2001.[163] Those who experience the consequences include shareholders, creditors, managers, and employees.[16, 164] For example, small investors in Enron stock lost a great deal at the same time that the company's leaders sold shares, before the company declared bankruptcy on the morning of December 4, 2001.[165, 166] Even a "winning" competitor may bear the cost of a rival company's going bankrupt. In the health service industry in some states, the remaining viable organizations must take over responsibility for services to the patients of defunct health maintenance organizations.[167, 168]

Destructive competition increases failure rates.[127, 169] Historically, it was thought that bankruptcies or "failure rates" declined during periods of economic prosperity.[170] And indeed, ten of the largest bankruptcies since 1980, including that of WorldCom, occurred in 2001 and 2002.[171] But even economic prosperity does not always protect against bankruptcy.[172] The Congressional Budget Office suggests that seeking protection of the court under U.S. bankruptcy legislation increases during periods of economic expansion.[173] Part of the problem has to do with the business climate that accompanies destructive competition. Hiring prestigious managers is assumed to protect against bankruptcy. But because such hiring costs so much, the practice may actually increase the probability of bankruptcy.[174, p. 135]

Where competition is extremely intense, the "resources needed to build and maintain organizations have already been claimed by other organizations. Intense competition exhausts supplies of potential organizers, members, patrons, and resources. . . . Markets are packed tightly."[175, p. 116] Competition increases with higher rates of organizational density,[128, 176, 177] and organizational demise is greater where there are a large number of organizations already operating. Many studies show that this trend, "the density-delay" effect, lasts through the life of the organization.[175, 119, 120] Young start-up organizations have higher rates of failure in general, no matter what the level of competition.[178–180] But this too may depend on timing, the strength of the organization in specific markets (declining sales or increasing sales), and so on.[181]

Certainly not all organizations facing financial default need fail in the classic sense of bankruptcy, even in the most competitive markets. Some simply disappear through acquisition, mergers, or reorganization. In many instances, these devices reduce the costs of bankruptcy to society. More often than not, this "downward spiral" of bankruptcy experienced by corporations headed toward demise is viewed as manageable in the right hands, even in conditions of intense competition.[182] Many organizations at risk of financial failure seek economic support to restructure. Some are successful at avoiding bankruptcy with this strategy.[183, 184]

Loss of Trust and Lower Morale in the Workplace

Trust and cooperation are essential to many elements of market competition, including information diffusion, coordination, and entrepreneurship. Exchange theories of the firm posit a "nexus of contracts" between employees, creditors, shareholders, and management.[185] These unwritten contracts constitute an organizational and institutional prerequisite to commerce. They are grounded on the assumption that though they rest on trust and cooperation, they will be respected.[186] In addition, they are contingent on trust being established and maintained within the organization.

Trust is, however, a fragile commodity.[187, 188] It is not an inherent human trait, nor is it a genetic characteristic. Rather, it is something that is built up on the basis of experience, slowly over time, the result of many repeated confidence-building interactions.[189–191] One betrayal can destroy it, and once done, the damage is very difficult to repair.[192–195] When trust breaks down, people become self-protective and supervigilant. To reestablish trust requires taking a big risk—giving the benefit of the doubt to the very person or organization that initially offended.[196]

Many of the structural and functional changes described here that accompany high levels of competition reduce employee trust and morale.[197] These, in turn, translate into lower productivity and profits.[60] Among these trust breakers is the use of temporary workers and free agency.[198, 199] Organizations that emphasize temporary employment have greater salary differentials that translate into higher turnover among their lower-paid employees.[200] As Brian McQuaid, executive director of human resources at MCI Communications (at the time of the interview), points out, turnover is costly. "A new hire can accomplish only 60% as much in the first three months as an experienced worker, and serves customers less well."[46, p. B1] Reduced stability and duration of employment leads to poorer morale among employees.[14, pp. 585–86] In the end, the organization suffers.

Distrust of management increases substantially after downsizing and layoffs. This too was discussed previously. Both increase pressure and stress on employees substantially.[15] The evidence is overwhelming. Downsizing makes for lower worker morale.[7, 17, 201] Layoffs have the same effects.[194] Worker insecurity is high because of "the threat of layoff and the comparison with other jobless workers. It is also increased by the fact that companies in the same economic sector were undergoing the same type of restructuring."[14, p. 593] In addition, both employees and unions in many cases realize that employers in some industries have the option of moving production to Third World countries. Outsourcing also appears to reduce trust and morale.[202, 203] Typically, the survivors of the most recent wave of layoffs, those with the most ability and talent, exit in large numbers.[204]

Distrust arises as well from the surveillance procedures common in the highly competitive industrial workplace today.[205–207] "Because of psychological reactance, even honest employees may try to cheat or sabotage monitoring systems."[192, p. 591, 208]

In an environment of destructive competition, organizations underinvest in their employees' training and career development, which in turn means that employees are less loyal and committed to the organization and are less trusting of coworkers as well. Underinvestment in an employee and the failure to commit to a relatively long-term relationship with workers lead to lower performance and poorer attitudes.[209, p. 1117] Investment in employees is a paying proposition—increasing profits, lowering turnover, minimizing costly retraining, improving morale, and enhancing worker productivity.[46, 210] It increases shareholder returns as well.[211] However, it is more and more common to require training take place on the employees' own time.[212]

Where employers make a commitment to employees in terms of a long-term relationship, employees perform better and are happier.[34, 213, 214] They respond favorably to this type of employer allegiance and are more productive.[209] Uncertainties about future employment status and job loss are related to poor physical and psychological health of employees.[215, 216] Surveys in Britain and the United States indicated that unemployment takes a toll on an individual's feelings of well-being and happiness.[217, 218] Even the fear of unemployment has such effects.[219] There is a direct link between employee satisfaction and profits. One study found that each time worker contentment increased 5 percent, customer satisfaction increased 1.3 percent and revenues 5 percent.[45]

Fraud, Mistakes, and Cover-Ups

The competition paradigm assumes that free markets reduce fraud and crime and protect against them while they increase efficiency. This argument is based on the expectation that consumers have full knowledge and would prefer to do business with firms that are accountable.[220, p. 6, 221] In theory, an honest business concern has a competitive advantage over those that are dishonest. But it does not always work out this way in the real world, where full transparency and voluntary, complete disclosure are rare.[222, 223]

Virtuous business practices are likely to lead to financial success in the long term. But when destructive competition takes hold, the rules change. Competition may be so intense, as was the case of America's gas and oil sector in the 1990s, as to actually push some organizations to the point of actions that, while of dubious legality, seemed necessary for survival. Responsible companies fear that they may not be around long enough to reap the potential long-term benefits of integrity.

Even some of America's greatest corporate citizens, with formidable reputations, have been involved in dubious activities, such as billing after service is terminated, charging for services never ordered by the customer, and airing television commercials whose attractive claims are undercut by small type that appears briefly on the television screen. On December 18, 2001, this type of activity was documented by the television program *60 Minutes*. AT&T, MCI, and Sprint were "competing by cheating; . . . these are scams." This is a very strong statement. And these practices were said to be "typical of companies that have had impeccable reputations and broad public respect."[224]

Too much demand and a market so competitive that a seller cannot raise prices may mean that "customers become supplicants and there is no economic disincentive to incivility, surliness and arrogance"[221, p. 244] or even fraud. Deregulation can do the same thing. Outsourcing makes it difficult for the customer to identify the responsible party when a problem develops with a product. The normal mechanisms by which exemplary business practices may be financially beneficial and enhance product appeal break down.[221, p. 243]

Excess fear, loss of control, and greater uncertainty under conditions of intense competition may create negative incentives for organizations. Destructive competition increases incentives for organizations to cover up defects as long as the cover-up is not illegal, or, if the cover-up is illegal, then the chances are that one will not be caught.[225] "Aggressive accounting" practices, or "creative accounting," for example, did not require listing stock options as an expense. The practice did, however, disguise the true earnings figures of a company. To fail to practice creative accounting might put a company at a competitive disadvantage.[226–228] The situation was so bad in the mid-1990s that 47 percent of corporate executives questioned indicated a willingness to ignore personal ethics and commit some types of accounting fraud.[229]

The same logic has pushed large U.S. companies doing business in foreign countries to violate U.S. laws prohibiting them from bribing foreign officials. To fail to do so put their shareholders at a disadvantage.[230, p. 71] Too often good companies were less than honest regarding the reports they submitted to the Securities and Exchange Commission. Those hired to do the audits also acted as consultants and found themselves in conflict-of-interest situations.[231, 232] They attempted to bend over backward to help their clients. They were therefore reluctant to take action or speak out in ways that might discourage return business.[233, p. 66, 234, 235]

When companies increase profits through dishonest behavior, they are competing at the wrong thing.[236] This type of corporate "competition" was common beginning in the late 1990s. Companies "competed" at exploiting loopholes in the law. Energy companies artificially created congestion on power lines so as to receive special compensation for removing said congestion.[237] They "competed" at inventing techniques to make it appear that their trade volume was higher than it really was and thus give the impression that they were a really "big player." They did this by "selling" large quantities of electricity back and forth with a partner company. Such bogus trades were common and were probably quite legal at the time. Enron staged fake trading rooms and used clerical employees to pose as traders to give the impression to visiting investors that Enron Energy Services was a dynamic and profitable company.[238] While this activity enhanced the company's reputation—perhaps artificially elevating its stock price—it is not about fair business competition that increases value and accurately reflects productivity.[239]

The health sector is another example of competing at the wrong things.[240] Between 1992 and 1999, prosecutions against health care providers increased from 83 to 506.[241] Fraud and the act of covering it up are illegal. Columbia HCA's paid kickbacks, falsified Medicare claims, upcoding the severity of patient illness when requesting government reimbursement, and other criminal activities coincided with the full development of market competition in the health sector.[242–246] The question becomes this: Did other companies in the same sector feel that they had to match Columbia HCA's illegal corporate behavior in order to be competitive? If this is the case, then the winners turn out to be the organizations that are not caught. Columbia HCA lost out; it ended up paying more than $800 million in settlement payments.[247, 248] Vencor, a corporate provider of nursing home care, was also caught—in this case, for illegally discharging patients who ran out of money and had to move to Medicaid coverage.[249] Medicaid did not pay as much as private insurance, and therefore Medicaid patients were avoided. Tenet (when it was called National Medical Enterprises) held patients "hostage" at its inpatient psychiatric hospitals, drugging them and restraining them against their will, until the patients' health insurance benefits had been exhausted. The goal was to maximize revenue to the hospital even if this amounted to what courts called kidnapping.[250] The incentives for health providers to be manipulative and secretive are overwhelming because the stakes are so high during the shakeout period of competition.

Of course, fraud, mistakes, and cover-ups are not only the result of destructive competition. The world is much too complicated to assume any such singular and oversimplified explanation. Even in environments entirely free of competition, fraud is still evident. In countries where, on occasion, there is substantial cooperation between firms (for example, Japan), fraud is a problem. In this case, little competition, together with pro-business regulation, created an environment where corruption was common. In the United States, some companies developed a culture of carelessness that resulted in scandal after scandal regardless of the level of competition. Arthur Andersen's record of accounting problems with Sunbeam, Waste Management, and the Baptist Foundation of Arizona are examples.[251–253] It culminated in Andersen's felony conviction for obstruction of justice in the Securities and Exchange Commission's Enron inquiry.[254, 255] Corporate crime, corruption, and fraud may indeed be the result of individual greed or personal self-protection. Arthur Andersen's shredding of incriminating Enron-related documents and deleting associated email messages in the face of a federal inquiry is an example of illegal behavior designed to conceal incriminating evidence.[256, 257] Experts in corporate organizational behavior agree that companies are more likely to resort to fraud under certain identifiable conditions, as when competition becomes too intense, when pressure from rivals increases substantially, and when prices are expected to fall.[258] Problems range from simple omissions to criminal violations. Activities include rackets, dishonest insurance claims, fire-loss claims, and tax claims for capital losses. During World War II, compliance with price controls was much more likely for an organization if profits were rising than if they were declining, and compliance was lower for depressed industrial sectors than for those that were not depressed.[259, 260] Antitrust violators were found to have experienced lower profits just before their antitrust problems.[261] Poorly performing firms had higher levels of antitrust law violations.[262, p. 142] Many studies suggest that low profitability resulting from increased competition leads to corporate crime, including price-fixing.[263, p. 431] Cartels engage in price-fixing as profits are squeezed.[264]

Does intense competition always lead to more mistakes and greater effort at cover-ups? Most of the evidence is anecdotal, but it does suggest that this is the case.[265] High pressure to produce may make for impossible goals resulting from stiff competition. Medical care, again, is a good example. Hospitals that are not doing well from a financial point of view have higher rates of adverse patient outcomes: patient injuries that result from mistakes in medical management. During periods of intense financial competition, such hospitals may not be able to spend enough on patient care to avoid negligence.[266] Errors are found to increase when nurse caseloads are unusually high. Stress and fatigue, high workloads, and time pressures contribute to increased mistakes and higher error rates.[267] Intense competition exacerbates these conditions. Under intense competition, many teaching hospitals affiliated with medical schools violate legal limitations on the number of hours a resident can work. Tired residents make more mistakes.[268, 269] Lower profits for pharmacies in a managed care environment, together with longer shifts, fewer breaks, and more pressure on pharmacists, are hypothesized to increase errors in filling prescriptions.[270] There is another incentive to overlook medical errors, according to Lucian Leape. Errors "generate revenues in a fee-for-service system."[271, p. 3] But the cost of errors to hospitals can also be high.[272, 273] Although the causes of mistakes and errors in medicine have been known for years, little has changed, and cover-ups continue.[274, 275]

Mistakes and marginally unfair business practices can sometimes be profitable to a corporation in a competitive environment, and when this is the case, they may become routine practice.[276, 277] For example, some managed care companies have routine policies of "deny, delay and down-code" regarding approval of physician requests for patient procedures and reimbursement.[278] They reimburse doctors later rather than promptly, on receipt of a bill, deriving a fiscal advantage over competitors. A study of hospital billing revealed that 99 percent of bills contained errors, and most of these favored the hospital.[279–281] Mistakes increase where staff cutbacks result in inadequate supervision of residents.[269] Pressure to meet deadlines and increase productivity, higher under conditions of excess competition, results in more mistakes.[282]

What Happened to Business Ethics?

Another downside of destructive competition is that it destabilizes the ethical norms of the business community. When Ed Schultz, the former executive of gun manufacturer Smith and Wesson introduced the "smart gun" that allows only the owner to operate the weapon, it was the "right" thing to do. It would save lives and prevent accidents. But opposition from customers, retailers, and the National Rifle Association was instantaneous. Competitors profited by setting aside ethics and focusing on the bottom line. They quite correctly saw the situation as an opportunity to increase their market share, whether it was the "right" thing to do or not.[283]

A convincing case can be made that there is a fundamental incompatibility between laissez-faire competition and social ethics. The argument is this: The efficiency assumption requires "giving the best player the best hand, the fastest runner the benefit of the handicap, and thus flagrantly violates the . . . conditions of fairness in the game."[284, p. 62] Intense competition certainly segments lifestyles and sets up conflicting demands. It leads to a situation where there is a sharp differentiation between behaviors expected in public and those expected in private. It does nothing to discourage the view that any business practice not expressly prohibited by legal authorities is by definition acceptable. It makes for a harsher workplace environment. All these trends undermine business ethics.[285, 286]

Destructive competition does not have to be pervasive in a particular economic sector to have these effects. Even if only a few companies in a sector engage in dubious ethical behavior, it has an impact on the entire profession or sector.[287] The gas and oil industry is an example of how ethically dubious behavior leads to a race to the bottom. Enron pushed corporate behavior beyond ethical limits in a sector that was typified by its formal commitment to unrestricted competition. Its practice of "shedding debt" to subsidiaries and affiliates was a loophole in the law that afforded the company a device to improve the bottom and increase their stock share price in the short term.[288, 289] Enron's "creative accounting" was only the tip of the iceberg. Twenty-nine executives sold over $1 billion in stock (17.3 million shares) in the two years before Enron declared bankruptcy—at the same time these executives advised others to buy Enron stock, emphasizing that the company was a sound financial investment.[290] Telecommunications executives in more than 100 companies did much the same.[291] Company after company in this sector adopted these often legal but ethically worrisome practices.[292, 293]

Business ethics and professional competence are assumed to ensure proper organizational conduct through a combination of informal self-regulating mechanisms and formal public professional norms. This should, in theory, alleviate the problems associated with ethical failure including fraud and other dishonest business practices. But these devices seem insufficient. The view that business ethics may mean, at most, responsibility to stockholders is worrisome to many in the business community.[294, 295]

In the highly competitive environment, "there is little factual or logical basis for the conviction that honesty is the best policy. . . . The evidence that treachery can pay seems compelling."[296, p. 121] Research confirms that when unethical practices result in rewards, including higher profits, this type of behavior will increase.[297] The new business code of conduct, supposedly more in line with the competition paradigm, is dependent on cunning, speed, and surprise.[298, p. 245]

Research on business ethics dating back decades points to increasing competition as, at least in part, responsible for declining ethical business practice. In surveys, business executives "admit to and point out the presence of numerous generally accepted practices in their industry which they consider unethical."[299, p. 7] Laboratory experiments with graduate business students suggest that unethical behavior is much higher under conditions of intense destructive competition.[297] Most of thirty recent Harvard Business School graduates interviewed said that they had been pressured to do things that were "sleazy, unethical or illegal."[300, p. B1] Managers underline that the absence of predictability both inside and outside their organization means that they have to do whatever they can to survive.[301] By 1977, a survey of more than 1,000 *Harvard Business Review* readers indicated a decline in ethical commitments. The reason offered was that "competition today is stiffer than ever. As a result, many businesses find themselves forced to resort to practices which are considered shady, but which appear necessary for survival."[302, p. 62] Chief executive officers and supervisors push workers, in this environment, to "get results no matter how." Sometimes this means violating ethical standards. A representative survey of 1,324 workers revealed that 56 percent felt pressured to act unethically or illegally. Forty-eight percent actually engaged in illegal or unethical behavior.[15]

Recent observations in the health sector confirm these trends. Twenty-four percent of the sample in this sector reports intense pressure to act unethically or even illegally.[15, p. 13] "Stakeholders in the increasingly market-driven U.S. health care system have few incentives to explore the harms of the technologies from which they stand to profit."[303, 304, p. 452] Many doctors admit that they have to lie to insurance companies to get needed treatment for patients, and they have few qualms about doing so because it has become routine.[305, 306] Is this the indirect result of the extremely competitive character of the health sector?

Several reasons are given for violating business ethics at times of intense competition. Some say that they did not know the activity in question was illegal or immoral. Others do so because they are complying with orders from senior management.[229] Still others argue that the "activity is in the corporation's best interest and therefore will be condoned." Many say that they engage in such behavior because they do not think that they will be caught. Most believe that if they are caught, the company will protect its unethical employee.[307, p. 85] "Damage control" is very effective. In any case, they say, the penalties for white-collar crime have been minimal.[308] Finally, the now famous excuse may be an adequate defense: "It was an 'administrative error.'"

No matter how successful the damage control, or what rationale is offered for violating business ethics, "once the rules are successfully broken, there is no going back; the games take on a new and dirtier form."[309, p. x] Whether or not the corporate reform, oversight, and honesty in accounting legislation adopted by Congress in 2002 will result in a higher ethics in the business world remains to be seen.[310]

A Self-Reinforcing Spiral of Competition at the Organizational Level

A spiral of self-reinforcing competition at the organizational level resembles that observed at the individual and group levels. Winners get bigger, and losers have less and less of a chance to succeed.[311] In the business world, some companies grow larger through consolidations, acquisitions, and mergers.[312, p. 125, 313] Others go bankrupt and cease to exist. In the absence of any outside intervention, market concentration takes place, and the possibility of fair constructive competition is reduced. Oligopolistic and monopolistic competition among a small number of large firms results.[314, pp. 568–70] Some economists argue that this type of market structure is inevitable; the forces generating it are irresistible because at sufficiently large volumes production yields economies of scale that small companies cannot match.[315, p. 245, 316, ch. 4] Historically, regulation discouraged these trends, but the competition paradigm counsels against government playing such a role in the evolution of the marketplace.

Internal to this spiral of competition is a process that undermines the integrity of the market. Unrestricted destructive competition interferes with the mechanisms that ensure equilibrium. The self-reinforcing spiral of competition means that when there are only a few large competitors left, these enterprises, collectively, have considerable influence over the degree and timing of competition.[317] This is discussed in detail in the next chapter because, ironically, it is an arrangement that is openly sought out and carefully cultivated by organizations as a means to avoid competing.

Eventually, changes in market structure related to the spiral of competition create an environment in which survival of the organization is less seriously in question on a day-to-day basis. Highly concentrated oligopolies make for higher certainty as to the terms of doing business. Destructive competition disappears, but all too often so does the opportunity for constructive competition.

The competition paradigm assumes that there is a natural dynamic at work that restores balance. As large corporations get lazy, inflate prices, and reduce quality, customers become discontented. The window of opportunity develops for the entry of new, young, dynamic organizations. But the spiral of competition means that the power of these few large competitors may become so great over time that they can take action to discourage the entry of new producers.

The vicious spiral of self-reinforcing intense, destructive competition is transformed into a not-so-benign process of sustained preservation. The discussion of how this works continues in the next chapter. Possible solutions to the dilemma of not-too-much and not-too-little competition, however, await the conclusion.

Notes

1. Telser, LG. *A Theory of Efficient Cooperation and Competition.* Cambridge, U.K.: Cambridge University Press; 1987.

2. Pfeffer, J, Leblebici H. The Effect of Competition on Some Dimensions of Organizational Structure. *Social Forces* 1973;52:268–79.

3. Gordon, JR. *A Diagnostic Approach to Organizational Behavior.* 3rd ed. Boston: Allyn & Bacon; 1991.

4. Ilinitch, AY, Lewin AY, D'Aveni RD, editors. *Managing in Times of Disorder: Hypercompetitive Organizational Responses.* Thousand Oaks, CA: Sage Publications; 1998.

5. Woodward, J. *Industrial Organization: Theory and Practice.* London: Oxford University Press; 1965.

6. Chamberlain, NW. *Enterprise and Environment.* New York: McGraw-Hill; 1968.

7. American Management Association. 1994 AMA Survey on Downsizing: Summary of Key Findings. New York: American Management Association; 1994.

8. Niven, D. When Times Get Tough, What Happens to TQM? *Harvard Business Review* 1993;71(May/June):20–34.

9. Bowen, HK, Clark KB, Holloway CA, Wheelwright SC. Make Projects the School for Leaders. *Harvard Business Review* 1994;72(September–October 1994):131–40.

10. Katzenbach, JR. The Myth of the Top Management Team. *Harvard Business Review* 1997;75(6):83–91.

11. Johnson, EW. An Insider's Call for Outside Direction. *Harvard Business Review* 1990;68(March–April 1990):46–55.

12. Dunham, KJ. The Jungle/Focus on Retirement, Pay and Getting Ahead. *Wall Street Journal* (April 2, 2002) B10.

13. Marmot, MG, Bosma H, Hemingway H, Brunner E, Stansfeld S. Contribution of Job Control and Other Risk Factors to Social Variations in Coronary Heart Disease Incidence. *The Lancet* 1997;350:235–39.

14. Cappelli, P. Rethinking Employment. *British Journal of Industrial Relations* 1995;33(December):563–602.

15. American Society of Chartered Life Underwriters and Chartered Financial Consultants, and Ethics Officer Association. Sources and Consequences of Workplace Pressure: Increasing the Risk of Unethical and Illegal Business Practices. Belmont, MA: Ethics Officer Association; 1997.

16. Stiglitz, JE. *Economics.* 2nd ed. New York: W. W. Norton & Company; 1997.

17. Wyatt Company. *Wyatt's 1993 Survey of Corporate Restructuring—Best Practices in Corporate Restructuring.* New York: Wyatt Company; 1993.

18. Gleick, E. Read All about It. *Time* 1996;148(19):66–69.

19. Freudenheim, M. Aetna to Cut 4,400 More Jobs as It Shifts to Managed Care. *New York Times* (October 11, 1996) A1, A19.

20. White, GL. Hitting the Brakes: In Order to Grow, GM Finds that the Order of the Day Is Cutbacks. *Wall Street Journal* (December 18, 2000) A1.

21. Anonymous. Do Workplace Woes Signal End of the American Dream? *USA Today* 1995;124 (2603) A1, A2.

22. Levinson, M. Capitalism with a Safety Net? *Harvard Business Review* 1996;74:173–80.

23. Uchitelle, L. Data Show Growing Trend toward Permanent Layoffs. *New York Times* (August 22, 2002) C9, col. 5.

24. Swinnerton, K, Wail H. Is Job Stability Declining in the US Economy? *Industrial Relations Review* 1995;48:293–304.

25. Marcotte, DE. Has Job Stability Declined? Evidence from the Panel Study of Income Dynamics. *American Journal of Economics and Sociology* 1999;58(2):197–217.

26. Uchitelle, L, Kleinfield N. On the Battlefields of Business, Millions of Casualties. *New York Times* (March 3, 1996) A1.

27. American Management Association. 1997 AMA Survey on Downsizing: Summary of Key Findings. New York: American Management Association; 1997.

28. Barta, P. Zero Sum Gain: In Current Expansion, as Business Booms, So, Too, Do Layoffs. *Wall Street Journal* (March 13, 2000) A1, A16.

29. Baker, T. *Doing Well by Doing Good: The Bottom Line on Workplace Practices.* Washington, DC: Economic Policy Institute; 1999.

30. Reichheld, FF. *Loyalty Rules! How Leaders Build Lasting Relationships in the Digital Age.* Boston: Harvard Business School Publishing; 2001.

31. Reichheld, FF, editor. *The Quest for Loyalty: Creating Value through Partnerships.* Boston: Harvard Business School Publishing; 1996.

32. Reichheld, FF. *The Loyalty Effect: The Hidden Force behind Growth, Profits, and Lasting Value.* Boston: Harvard Business School Publishing; 2001.

33. American Management Association. 1996 AMA Survey on Downsizing: Summary of Key Findings. New York: American Management Association; 1996.

34. Cascio, WF, Young CE, Morris JR. Financial Consequences of Employment-Change Decisions in Major US Corporations. *Academy of Management Journal* 1997;40:1175–89.

35. Spindle, B. Sony's Planned Cutbacks Intensify Trend in Japan toward Major Restructurings. *Wall Street Journal* (March 10, 1999) A14, A19.

36. Brockner, J. The Effects of Work Layoffs on Survivors: Research, Theory, and Practice. *Research in Organizational Behavior* 1988;10:213–55.

37. Sutton, RI. Organizational Decline Processes: A Social Psychological Perspective. *Research in Organizational Behavior* 1990;12:205–53.

38. Short, JD. Psychological Effects of Stress from Restructuring and Reorganization: Assessment, Intervention, and Prevention Strategies. *AAOHN Journal (American Association of Occupational Health Nurses)* 1997;45(11):597–606.

39. Murray, M. Stress Mounts as More Firms Announce Large Layoffs, but Don't Say Who or When. *Wall Street Journal* (March 13, 2001) B1.

40. Greenberg, PE, Finkelstein SN, Berndt ER. Economic Consequences of Illness in the Workplace. *Sloan Management Review* 1995;36:26–38.

41. Wilkinson, R, Marmot M, editors. *The Solid Facts: Social Determinants of Health.* Copenhagen: World Health Organization Regional Office for Europe and London International Centre for Health and Society, University of London; 1998.

42. Dunham, KJ. The Kinder, Gentler Way to Lay Off Employees. *Wall Street Journal* (March 13, 2001) B1, B10.

43. Stybel, LJ, Peabody M. The Right Way to Be Fired. *Harvard Business Review* 2001;79(7):87–95.

44. Oppel RA, Jr., Atlas RD. Hobbled Enron Tries to Stay on Its Feet. *New York Times* (December 4, 2001) C1, C8.

45. Rucci, AJ, Kirn SP, Quinn RT. The Employee-Customer-Profit Chain at Sears. *Harvard Business Review* 1998;76(1):83–97.

46. Shellenbarger, S. Companies Are Finding It Really Pays to Be Nice to Employees. *Wall Street Journal* (July 22, 1998) B1.

47. Elovainio, M, Kivimaki M, Vahtera J. Organizational Justice: Evidence of a New Psychosocial Predictor of Health. *American Journal of Public Health* 2002;92(1):105–8.

48. Aeppel, T. Missing the Boss: Not All Workers Find Idea of Empowerment as Neat as It Sounds. *Wall Street Journal* (September 8, 1997) A1, A13.

49. Jaffe, A. Firing: There's (Almost) Always a Better Way. *Psychology Today* (August, 1989) 68–69.

50. Ansberry, C. In the New Workplace, Jobs Morph to Suit Rapid Pace of Change. *Wall Street Journal* (March 22, 2002) A1, A7.

51. Beardon, T. High Flyer. *Jim Lehrer News Hour.* PBS; 2001.

52. Mittleman, MA, Malone MA, Maclure M, Sherwood JB, Muller JE. Workplace Stress as a Trigger of Acute Myocardial Infarction. *Circulation* 1998;97(8):821.

53. Marcotte, DE. The Wage Premium for Job Seniority during the 1980s and Early 1990s. *Industrial Relations* 1998;37(4):419–39.

54. Chauvin, KW. Firm-Specific Wage Growth and Changes in the Labor Market for Managers. *Management and Decision Economics* 1994;15:21–37.

55. Patel, B, Kleiner BH. New Developments in Age Discrimination. *Equal Opportunities International* 1995;14(6,7):69–79.

56. Belous, RS. *The Contingent Economy: The Growth of the Temporary, Part-Time, and Subcontracted Workforce.* Washington, DC: National Planning Association; 1989.

57. Mishel, L, Bernstein J. *The State of Working America, 1994–1995.* Washington, DC: Economic Policy Institute; 1995.

58. Mishel, L, Bernstein J, Schmitt J. *The State of Working America, 2000–2001.* Ithaca, NY: Cornell University Press; 2001.

59. Pfeffer, J. *New Directions for Organization Theory: Problems and Prospects.* New York: Oxford University Press; 1997.

60. Pink, DH. *Free Agent Nation: How America's New Independent Workers Are Transforming the Way We Live.* New York: Warner Books; 2001.

61. Zipkin, A. Temporary Work is Sidestepping a Slowdown. *New York Times* (July 22, 2001) 4, Business.

62. Levine, HZ. The View from the Board: The State of Compensation and Benefits Today. *Compensation & Benefits Review* 1992;24(2):24–29.

63. Zachary, GP. For France's Gemplus, the Secret of Success Is Made in the U.S.A. *Wall Street Journal* (June 8, 1998) A1, A10.

64. Davis-Blake, A, Uzzi B. Determinants of Employment Externalization: A Study of Temporary Workers and Independent Contractors. *Administrative Science Quarterly* 1993;38:195–223.

65. Casey, B. *Temporary Employment: Practices and Policy in Britain.* London: Policy Studies Institute and Anglo-German Foundation; 1989.

66. Christopherson, S. Flexibility in the U.S. Service Economy and the Emerging Spatial Division of Labour. *Transactions of the Institute of British Geography* 1989;14:131–43.

67. Caudron, S. Contingent Work Force Spurs HR Planning. *Personnel Journal* 1994;July:52–60.

68. Rosenau, MD. From Experience: Faster New Product Development. *Journal of Production Innovation and Management* 1988;5:150–53.

69. Yergin, D, Stanislaw J. *The Commanding Heights: The Battle between Government and the Marketplace That Is Remaking the Modern World.* New York: Simon & Schuster; 1998.

70. Berwick, D, Smith R. Cooperating, Not Competing, to Improve Health Care. *British Medical Journal* 1995;310(6991):1349–50.

71. Clemmer, TP, Spuhler VJ, Berwick DM, Nolan TW. Cooperation: The Foundation of Improvement. *Annals of Internal Medicine* 1998;128(12, Pt. 1, June 15):1004–9.

72. Bernhardt, I, Mackenzie KD. Measuring Seller Unconcentration, Segmentation and Product Differentiation. *Western Economic Journal* 1968;6:395–403.

73. Easton, GS, Jarrell SL. The Effects of Total Quality Management on Corporate Performance: An Empirical Investigation. *Journal of Business* 1998;71(2):253–305.

74. Ho, R. Fewer Small Businesses Are Offering Health Care and Retirement Benefits. *Wall Street Journal* (June 24, 1998) B2.

75. Feldman, R, Wholey D, Christianson J. Economic and Organizational Determinants of HMO Mergers and Failures. *Inquiry* 1996;33:118–32.

76. Hymowitz, C. Firms That Get Stingy with Layoff Packages May Pay a High Price. *Wall Street Journal* (October 30, 2001) B1.

77. Wyatt, E. Pension Change Puts the Burden on the Worker. *New York Times* (April 5, 2002) A1, C2.

78. Schultz, EE. Health Advisory: Investors Should Do a Checkup on Firms That Use Medical Plans to Lift Profits. *Wall Street Journal* (October 25, 2000) C1.

79. Ippolito, RA. Toward Explaining the Growth of Defined Contribution Plans. *Industrial Relations* 1995;34:1–20.

80. Swoboda, F, Crenshaw A. Court Says GM Can Cut Benefits. *Washington Post* (January 9, 1998) G1, G4.

81. Scanlon, WJ. Retiree Health Insurance: Erosion in Retiree Health Benefits Offered by Larger Employers. Washington, DC: Subcommittee on Oversight: House Committee on Ways and Means; 1998. p. 12.

82. Freudenheim, M. Companies Trim Health Benefits for Many Retirees as Costs Surge. *New York Times* (May 10, 2002) A1.

83. Blackburn, ML, Bloom DE, Freeman RB. The Declining Economic Position of Less-Skilled American Men. In: Burtless G, editor. *A Future of Lousy Jobs? The Changing Structure of US Wages.* Washington, DC: Brookings Institution Press; 1990.

84. Meehan, EJ. *Social Inquiry: Needs, Possibilities, Limits.* Chatham, NJ: Chatham House Publishers; 1994.

85. Kettl, DF. *The Global Public Management Revolution.* Washington, DC: Brookings Institution Press; 2000.

86. Stevenson, RW. Budget Links Dollars to Deeds in Rating Agencies. *New York Times* (February 3, 2002) A1, A23.

87. Egan, T. Failures Raise Questions for Charter Schools. *New York Times* (April 5, 2002) A14.

88. Schemo, DJ. Voucher Study Indicates No Steady Gains in Learning. *New York Times* (December 9, 2001) A33.

89. Steinberg, J. For-Profit School Venture Has Yet to Turn a Profit. *New York Times* (April 8, 2002) A17.

90. Gill, BP, Timpane PM, Ross KE, Brewer DJ. *Rhetoric versus Reality: What We Know and What We Need to Know about Vouchers and Charter Schools.* Santa Monica, CA: Rand Corporation; 2001.

91. Hirschman, AO. *Exit, Voice, and Loyalty.* Cambridge, MA: Harvard University Press; 1970.

92. Hymowitz, C. Ranking Systems Gain Popularity but Have Many Staffers Riled. *Wall Street Journal* (May 15, 2001) B1.

93. Beer, M, Walton E. Developing the Competitive Organization: Interventions and Strategies. *American Psychologist* 1990;45(2):154–61.

94. Prusak, L, Cohen D. *In Good Company: How Social Capital Makes Organizations Work.* Cambridge, MA: Harvard Business School Press; 2000.

95. Bolman, LG, Deal TE. *Reframing Organizations: Artistry, Choice, and Leadership.* San Francisco: Jossey-Bass Publishers; 1991.

96. Aeppel, T. Tricks of the Trade: On Factory Floors, Top Workers Hide Secrets to Success. *Wall Street Journal* (July 1, 2002) A1, A10.

97. Qin, Z, Johnson DW, Johnson RT. Cooperative versus Competitive Efforts and Problem Solving. *Review of Educational Research* 1995;65(2):129–43.

98. Abelson, R. Companies Turn to Grades, and Employees Go to Court. *New York Times* (March 19, 2001) A1.

99. Coens, T, Jenkins M, Block P. *Abolishing Performance Appraisals: Why They Backfire and What to Do Instead.* San Francisco: Berret-Koehler Publisher; 2000.

100. Barrionuevo, A. Jobless in a Flash, Enron's Ex-Employees Are Stunned, Bitter, Ashamed. *Wall Street Journal* (December 11, 2001) B1.

101. Berwick, DM. The Toxicity of Pay for Performance. *Quality Management in Health Care* 1995;4(1):27–33.

102. Berwick, D. Appraising Appraisal. *Quality Connection* 1991;1(1):1–4.

103. Shirouzu, N. Ford Stops Using Letter Rankings to Rate Workers. *Wall Street Journal* (July 11, 2001) B1, B4.

104. Hymowitz, C. Using Layoffs to Battle Downturns Often Costs More Than It Saves. *Wall Street Journal* (July 24, 2001) A1.

105. Walton, RE. How to Counter Alienation in the Plant. *Harvard Business Review* 1972(November–December):70–81.

106. Simmons, J, Mares W. *Working Together.* New York: Alfred A. Knopf; 1983.

107. Gibson, CH. Volvo Increases Productivity through Job Enrichment. *California Management Review* 1973;15(4):64–66.

108. Gyllenhammar, PG. *People at Work.* Reading, MA: Addison-Wesley Publishing Company; 1977.

109. Gyllenhammar, PG. How Volvo Adapts Work to People. *Harvard Business Review* 1977(July–August):102–13.

110. Karasek, R, Theorell TO, editors. *Healthy Work: Stress, Productivity and the Reconstruction of Working Life.* New York: Basic Books; 1990.

111. FitzRoy, FR, Acs ZJ, Gerlowski DA. *Management and Economics of Organization.* London: Prentice Hall Europe; 1998.

112. Thierauf, RJ. *Decision Support Systems for Effective Planning and Control: A Case Study Approach.* Englewood Cliffs, N. J.: Prentice Hall; 1982.

113. Management Review. The Plant That Runs on Individual Initiative. *Management Review* 1972(July):20–25.

114. Berggren, C. *The Volvo Experience: Alternatives to Lean Production in the Swedish Auto Industry.* Paperback with special introduction ed. Ithaca, NY: Cornell University Press; 1992.

115. Kruse, D, Blasi J. The New Employee-Employer Relationship. In: Ellwood DT, Blank RM, Blasi J, Kruse D, Niskanen WA, Lynn-Dyson K, editors. *A Working Nation: Workers, Work, and Government in the New Economy.* New York: Russell Sage Foundation; 2000. p. 42–91.

116. Neumark, D, Cappelli P. Do "High Performance" Work Practices Improve Establishment-Level Outcomes? NBER Report No. W7374. October 1999. Cambridge, MA: National Bureau of Economic Research.

117. Cappelli, P, Neumark D. External Job Churning and Internal Job Flexibility. *Industrial Relations: A Journal of Economy and Society* (forthcoming).

118. Hicks, A, Kenworthy L. Cooperation and Political Economic Performance in Affluent Democratic Capitalism. *American Journal of Sociology* 1998;103(6):1631–72.

119. Jaworski, BJ, Kohli AK. Market Orientation: Antecedents and Consequences. *Journal of Marketing* 1993;57(3):53–70.

120. Appelbaum, E, Bailey T, Berg P, Kalleberg AL. *Manufacturing Advantage: Why High-Performance Work Systems Pay Off.* Ithaca, NY: Cornell University Press; 2000.

121. Royal, W. A Factory's Crash Course in Economics Pays Off. *New York Times* (April 25, 2001) C9.

122. Lawler, EE. *High-Involvement Management: Participative Strategies for Improving Organizational Performance.* San Francisco: Jossey-Bass Publishers; 1986.

123. *BusinessWeek.* Stonewalling Plant Democracy. *BusinessWeek* (March 28, 1977) 78–83.

124. Pfeffer, J, Cialdini RB, Hanna B, Knopoff K. Faith in Supervision and the Self-Enhancement Bias: Two Psychological Reasons Why Managers Don't Empower Workers. *Basic & Applied Social Psychology* 1998;20(4):313–21.

125. Amick, BC, Lavis JN. Labor Markets and Health: A Framework and Set of Applications. In: Tarlov AR, St. Peter RF, editors. *The Society and Population Health Reader.* New York: New Press; 2000. p. 178–209.

126. Mitchell, W. The Dynamics of Evolving Markets: The Effects of Business Sales and Age on Dissolutions and Divestitures. *Administrative Science Quarterly* 1994;39:575–602.

127. Carroll, GR, Hannan MT. An Introduction to Density-Dependent Evolution. In: Carroll GR, Hannan MT, editors. *Organizations in Industry.* New York: Oxford University Press; 1995. p. 115–20.

128. Hannan, MT, Carroll GR. *Dynamics of Organizational Populations: Density, Legitimation, and Competition.* New York: Oxford University Press; 1992.

129. Nelson, RR, Winter SG. *An Evolutionary Theory of Economic Change.* Cambridge, MA: Harvard University Press; 1982.

130. Romer, PM, Griliches Z. Implementing a National Technology Strategy with Self-Organizing Industry Investment Boards. *Brookings Papers on Economic Activity* 1993;2:345–99.

131. Wysocki, B. Wealth of Nations: For This Economist, Long-Term Prosperity Hangs on Good Ideas. *Wall Street Journal* (January 21, 1997) A1, A8.

132. Kopelman, RE. Job Redesign and Productivity: A Review of the Evidence. *National Productivity Review* 1985;4(3):237–55.

133. Melin, B, Lundberg U, Soderlund J, Granqvist M. Psychological and Physiological Stress Reactions of Male and Female Assembly Workers: A Comparison between Two Different Forms of Work Organization. *Journal of Organizational Behavior* 1999;20:47–61.

134. Rose, K. Work/Life Flexibility: A Key to Maximizing Productivity. Insights & Solutions: Management Issues ed. Price Waterhouse Coopers; at www.pricewaterhousecoopers.com/extweb/manissue.nsf/DocID/6850ED3F9BAB2B888525662E004AABA2 (accessed December 8, 1999).

135. Wholey, DR, Christianson JB. Organization Size and Failure among Health Maintenance Organizations. *American Sociological Review* 1992;57:829–42.

136. Frank, LK. *Society as the Patient: Essays on Culture and Personality.* New Brunswick, NJ: Rutgers University Press; 1950.

137. Van Witteloostuijn, A. Bridging Behavioral and Economic Theories of Decline: Organizational Inertia, Strategic Competition, and Chronic Failure. *Management Science* 1998;44(4):501–19.

138. Rosenau, PV. Market Structure and Performance: Evaluating the U.S. Health System Reform. *Journal of Health and Social Policy* 2001;13(1):41–72.

139. Shortell, SM, Hughes EFX. The Effects of Regulation, Competition, and Ownership on Mortality Rates among Hospital Inpatients. *New England Journal of Medicine* 1988;318(17):1100–7.

140. Watson Wyatt Worldwide. Delivering Value in Health Care. Westchester, NY: Watson Wyatt Worldwide; 1998.

141. Angell, M, Kassirer JP. Quality and the Medical Marketplace—Following Elephants. *New England Journal of Medicine* 1996;335(12):883–85.

142. Jensen, E. Yakking It Up: For Wireless Services, Talk Gets Far Cheaper as Competition Rages. *Wall Street Journal* (April 27, 1998) A1, A8.

143. Martinez, B. Business Consortium to Launch Effort Seeking Higher Standards at Hospitals. *Wall Street Journal* (November 15, 2000) A12.

144. Kaufman, L. Some Companies Derail the "Burnout" Track. *New York Times* (May 4, 1999) A1, C8.

145. Orlady, HW, Foushee HC. Cockpit Resource Management Training. Springfield, VA: National Technical Information Service; 1987.

146. Weick, KE, Roberts KH. Collective Mind in Organizations: Heedful Interrelating on Flight Decks. *Administrative Science Quarterly* 1993;38:357–81.

147. Kranhold, K, Emshwiller JR. New Rules Blamed for Power Shortages. *Wall Street Journal* (July 24, 1998) A2.

148. Power, S. Federal Takeover of Airline Security Draws New Support. *Wall Street Journal* (September 24, 2001) A26.

149. Krugman, P. Paying the Price. *New York Times* (September 16, 2001) sec. 4, p. 11.

150. Wald, ML. U.S. Begins Taking Over Screening at Airports. *New York Times* (May 1, 2002) A16.

151. Shapiro, M. FAA under Pressure to Reform Airline Inspections. *Conde Nast Traveler* (November, 1997) 43, 47–48, 50, 164–67, 213, 17–20.

152. Frantz, D, Blumenthal R. USAir's Troubles: Cruel Coincidence or the Reflections of Airline Lapses? *New York Times* (November 13, 1994) A1, A18, A19.

153. Nance, JJ. *Blind Trust*. New York: William Morrow and Company; 1986.

154. Wald, ML. Audits of Big U.S. Airlines by F.A.A. Find Problems. *New York Times* (February 24, 2002) sec. 1, p. 26, col. 5.

155. Cushman, JH. A Mostly Reliable Plane, but with Flaws in Its Past. *New York Times* (September 5, 1998) B6.

156. Pasztor, A. Airlines Call for More Oversight of Maintenance. *Wall Street Journal* (June 6, 2000) B1, B4.

157. Brannigan, M, Abramson J. ValuJet Crash Ended the Success Story of Its Founders and Major Investors. *Wall Street Journal* (May 17, 1996) C8.

158. Wald, ML. Cargo in Hold of Jet in Crash Was Improper. *New York Times* (May 16, 1996) A1, A14.

159. Schwartz, H. Startling Similarities between ValuJet, HMOs. *Houston Chronicle* (June 13, 1996) 45, Outlook.

160. Davis, R. ValuJet Probe: Workers Were Rushed. *USA Today* (November 19, 1996) A3.

161. Verhovek, SH. Alaska Airlines Center in Turmoil after Complaint by Mechanics. *New York Times* (March 19, 2000) A25.

162. Krueger, AB. Fewer Workplace Injuries and Illnesses Are Adding to Economic Strength. *New York Times* (September 14, 2000) C2.

163. American Bankruptcy Institute. ABI World: U.S. Bankruptcy Filings 1980–2001 (Business, Non-Business, Total). Alexandria, VA: American Bankruptcy Institute; 2002.

164. D'Aveni, RD. Dependability and Organizational Bankruptcy: An Application of Agency and Prospect Theory. *Management Science* 1989;35(9):1120–38.

165. Gilpin, KN. Plenty of Pain to Go Around for Small Investors, Funds, Workers and Creditors. *New York Times* (December 4, 2001) C8.

166. Pacelle, M. Called to Account: Enron Awards to Officials Outrage Laid-Off Workers. *Wall Street Journal* (June 18, 2002) C18.

167. Anonymous. Health Maintenance Organizations Held to Be Domestic Insurance Companies Subject to State Rehabilitation and Liquidation Laws. *Journal of Insurance Regulation* 1997;16(2):232–35.

168. Bell, A. Georgia Department Takes Over Augusta HMO, Says Service Will Continue. *National Underwriter (Life/Health/Financial Services)* 1997;101(29):41.

169. Dewing, AS. *The Financial Policy of Corporations.* New York: The Ronald Press Company; 1953.

170. Platt, HD. *Why Companies Fail: Strategies for Detecting, Avoiding, and Profiting from Bankruptcy.* Lexington, MA: Lexington Books; 1985.

171. Romero, S, Atlas RD. WorldCom Files for Bankruptcy; Largest U.S. Case. *New York Times* (July 22, 2002) A1, A12.

172. Dun & Bradstreet Corporation. Business Failure Record; 1995.

173. Clark, K. Why So Many Americans Are Going Bankrupt. *Fortune* (August 4, 1997) 24.

174. D'Aveni, RA. Top Managerial Prestige and Organizational Bankruptcy. *Organizational Science* 1990;1(2):121–42.

175. Carroll, GR, Hannan MT, editors. *Organizations in Industry: Strategy, Structure, and Selection.* New York: Oxford University Press; 1995.

176. Baum, JAC, Mezias S. Localized Competition and Organizational Failure in the Manhattan Hotel Industry, 1898–1990. *Administrative Science Quarterly* 1992;37:580–604.

177. Hannan, MT, Carroll GR, Dundon EA, Torres JC. Organizational Evolution in a Multinational Context: Entries of Automobile Manufacturers in Belgium, Britain, France, Germany, and Italy. *American Sociological Review* 1995;60(August):509–28.

178. Stinchcombe, AL. Organizations and Social Structure. In: March JG, editor. *Handbook of Organizations.* Chicago: Rand-McNally; 1965. p. 142–93.

179. Freeman, J. Organizational Life Cycles and Natural Selection Processes. In: Staw BM, Cummings LL, editors. *Research in Organizational Behavior.* Greenwich, CT: JAI Press; 1982. p. 1–32.

180. Freeman, J, Carroll GR, Hannan MT. The Liability of Newness: Age Dependence in Organizational Death Rates. *American Sociological Review* 1983;48:692–710.

181. Romanelli, E. Environments and Strategies of Organization Start-Up: Effects on Early Survival. *Administrative Science Quarterly* 1989;34:369–87.

182. Hambrick, DC, D'Aveni RA. Large Corporate Failures as Downward Spirals. *Administrative Science Quarterly* 1988;33(March):1–23.

183. Rundle, RL. How FPA Landed in Bankruptcy Court. *Wall Street Journal* (July 21, 1998) B5.

184. Whitman, J. No Deal: M&A Activity among Small Firms Plunged Last Year. Is It Poised for a Turnaround? *Wall Street Journal* (March 27, 2002) R16–R17, Small Business.

185. Chadwick-Jones, JK. *Social Exchange Theory: Its Structure and Influence in Social Psychology*. New York: Academic Press; 1976.

186. Coase, RH. The Nature of the Firm. *Economica* 1937;4(16):386–405.

187. Levi, M, Stoker L. Political Trust and Trustworthiness. *Annual Review of Political Science* 2000;3:475–507.

188. Bok, S. *Lying: Moral Choice in Public and Private Life*. Updated ed. New York: Alfred A. Knopf; 1999.

189. Clark, K, Sefton M. The Sequential Prisoner's Dilemma: Evidence on Reciprocation. *The Economic Journal* 2001;111(468):51–68.

190. Glaeser, EL, Liaibson DI, Scheinkman JA, Soutter CL. Measuring Trust. *The Quarterly Journal of Economics* 2000;115(3):811–46.

191. Alesina, A, La Ferrara E. Who Trusts Others? *Journal of Public Economics* 2002;85(2):207–34.

192. Kramer, RM. Trust and Distrust in Organizations: Emerging Perspectives, Enduring Questions. *Annual Review of Psychology* 1999;50:569–98.

193. Messick, DM, Kramer RM. Trust as a Form of Shallow Morality. In: Cook KS, editor. *Trust in Society*. New York: Russell Sage Foundation; 2001. p. 89–118.

194. Lester, RK. *The Productive Edge: How U.S. Industries Are Pointing the Way to a New Era of Economic Growth*. New York: W. W. Norton & Company; 1998.

195. Goldberg, RK. Regaining Public Trust. *Health Affairs* 1998;17(6):138–41.

196. Holmes, JS. The Effects of Ownership and Ownership Change on Nursing Home Industry Costs. *Health Services Research* 1996;31(3):327–46.

197. Uchitelle, L. These Days, Layoffs Compete with Loyalty. *New York Times* (August 19, 2001) sec. 3, p. 4, col. 5.

198. Pfeffer, J, Baron JN. Taking the Workers Back Out: Recent Trends in the Structuring of Employment. *Research in Organizational Behavior*. Greenwich, CT: JAI Press; 1988. p. 257–303.

199. Pfeffer, J. What's Wrong with Management Practices in Silicon Valley? A Lot. *MIT Sloan Management Review* 2001;42(3).

200. Pfeffer, J, Davis-Blake A. Salary Dispersion, Location in the Salary Distribution, and Turnover among College Administrators. *Industrial and Labor Relations Review* 1992;45:753–63.

201. Yankelovich, D. Got to Give to Get. *Mother Jones* (July 1997) 60–63.

202. Bradsher, K. Labor's Peace with G.M. Unraveling at Saturn Plant. *New York Times* (July 22, 1998) A1, C2.

203. Blumenstein, R, Warner F. Saturn's Workers Move toward a Strike, Pointing to Flaws in Partnership Model. *Wall Street Journal* (July 20, 1998) A4.

204. Hymowitz, C. In the Lead: Managers Who Fought to Lure Talent in 2000 Must Now Ponder Cuts. *Wall Street Journal* (December 26, 2000) B1.

205. Cialdini, R. The Triple Tumor Structure of Organizational Behavior. In: Messick DM, Tenbrunsel AE, editors. *Codes of Conduct.* New York: Russell Sage Foundation; 1996. p. 44–58.

206. Kruglanski, AW. Attributing Trustworthiness in Supervisor-Worker Relations. *Journal of Experimental Social Psychology* 1970;6:214–32.

207. Strickland, LH. Surveillance and Trust. *Journal of Personality* 1958;26:200–15.

208. Prusak, L, Cohen D. How to Invest in Social Capital. *Harvard Business Review* 2001;79(6):86–93.

209. Tsui, AS, Pearce JL, Porter LW, Tripoli AM. Alternative Approaches to the Employee-Organization Relationship: Does Investment in Employees Pay Off? *Academy of Management Journal* 1997;40(5):1089–121.

210. Kanter, RM. *The Change Masters: Innovations for Productivity in the American Corporation.* New York: Simon & Schuster; 1983.

211. Watson Wyatt Worldwide. Human Capital Index: Linking Human Capital and Shareholder Value. Westchester, NY: Watson Wyatt Worldwide; 2000.

212. Shellenbarger, S. New Training Methods Allow Jobs to Intrude Further into Off Hours. *Wall Street Journal* (July 11, 2001) B1.

213. Hurrell, JJ. Editorial: Are You Certain?—Uncertainty, Health, and Safety in Contemporary Work. *American Journal of Public Health* 1998;88(7):1012–13.

214. Drucker, PF. They're Not Employees, They're People. *Harvard Business Review* 2002;80(2):70–77.

215. Ferrie, JE, Shipley MJ, Marmot MJ, Stansfeld S, Smith GD. Health Effects of Anticipation of Job Change and Non-Employment: Longitudinal Data from the Whitehall II Study. *British Medical Journal* 1995;311:1264–69.

216. Ferrie, JE, Shipley MJ, Marmot MJ, Stansfeld S, Smith GD. An Uncertain Future: The Health Effects of Threats to Employment Security in White-Collar Men and Women. *American Journal of Public Health* 1998;88:1030–36.

217. Blanchflower, DG, Oswald AJ. Well-Being Over Time in Britain and the USA. Warwick: University of Warwick; 2001. p. 44.

218. Argyle, M. *The Psychology of Happiness.* 2nd ed. New York: Routledge; 2001.

219. Di Tella, R, MacCulloch RJ, Oswald AJ. The Macroeconomics of Happiness. Warwick: University of Warwick; 2001. p. 40.

220. Handler, JF. *Down from Bureaucracy: The Ambiguity of Privatization and Empowerment.* Princeton, NJ: Princeton University Press; 1996.

221. Mueller, J. *Capitalism, Democracy, and Ralph's Pretty Good Grocery.* Princeton, NJ: Princeton University Press; 1999.

222. Maremont, M. Tyco Made $8 Billion of Acquisitions over 3 Years but Didn't Disclose Them. *Wall Street Journal* (February 4, 2002) A3.

223. Henriques, DB, Eichenwald K. A Fog over Enron, and the Legal Landscape. *New York Times* (January 27, 2002) BU1, BU13.

224. CBS. Connecticut AG Slams Telecom Companies. *60 Minutes.* CBS; 2001.

225. Kramer, RC. Corporate Crime: An Organizational Perspective. In: Wickman P, Dailey T, editors. *White-Collar and Economic Crime.* Lexington, MA: Lexington Books; 1982. p. 75–94.

226. Hitt, G, Schlesinger JM. Stock Options Come Under Fire in Wake of Enron's Collapse. *Wall Street Journal* (March 26, 2002) A1, A8.

227. Sherman, HD, Young SD. Tread Lightly through These Accounting Minefields. *Harvard Business Review* 2001;79(7):129–35.

228. Brown, K. Creative Accounting: How to Buff a Company. *Wall Street Journal* (February 21, 2002) C1, C18.

229. Brief, AP, Dukerich JM, Brown PR, Brett JF. What's Wrong with the Treadway Commission Report? Experimental Analysis of the Effects of Personal Values and Codes of Conduct on Fraudulent Financial Reporting. *Journal of Business Ethics* 1996;15:183–98.

230. Martin, RL. The Virtue Matrix: Calculating the Return on Corporate Responsibility. *Harvard Business Review* 2002;80(3):69–75.

231. Weil, J. Double Enron Role Played by Andersen Raises Questions. *Wall Street Journal* (December 14, 2001) A4.

232. Herrick, T, Barrionuevo A. Were Auditor and Client Too Close-Knit? *Wall Street Journal* (January 21, 2002) C1, C14.

233. Kleiner, C, Lord M. The Cheating Game. *U.S. News & World Report* (November 22, 1999) 55–57, 61–64, 66.

234. Norris, F. Top Accounting Firm Settles S.E.C. Fraud Charges. *New York Times* (June 20, 2001) A1.

235. Norris, F. A Top Five Accounting Firm to Pay $7 Million over Fraud. *New York Times* (June 19, 2001) A1, C7.

236. Culbertson, JM. *Competition, Constructive and Destructive.* Madison, WI: Twenty-First Century Press; 1985.

237. Banerjee, N, Barboza D, Oppel RA Jr., Kahn J. Will It Be California Redux? *New York Times* (May 12, 2002) 1, 10.

238. Leopold, J. Enron Executives Helped to Create Fake Trading Room. *Wall Street Journal* (February 20, 2002) A4.

239. Benson, M, Cummins C, Sapsford J. Trade Disclosures Shake Faith in Damaged Electricity Market. *Wall Street Journal* (May 13, 2002) A1, A8.

240. Labaton, S. The World Gets Tough on Price Fixers: With Consumers Pinched at Every Turn, U.S. Leads a Crackdown. *New York Times* (June 3, 2001) sec. 3, p. 1, 7, Money and Business.

241. Steinhauer, J. Chasing Health Care Fraud Quietly Becomes Profitable. *New York Times* (January 23, 2001) A1, A17.

242. Rodriguez, EM, Lagnado L. Columbia Inquiry Yields First Indictments— Three Midlevel Executives Plotted to Defraud U.S., Federal Prosecutors Say. *Wall Street Journal* (July 31, 1997) A3, A6.

243. Eichenwald, K. Columbia/HCA Discussions on Cost Shifting Were Secretly Taped by U.S. Informants. *New York Times* (September 2, 1997) D2.

244. Eichenwald, K. 2 Leaders Are Out at Health Giant as Inquiry Goes On. *New York Times* (July 26, 1997) 1, 22.

245. Lagnado, L. Columbia/HCA to Pay the U.S. $745 Million. *Wall Street Journal* (May 19, 2000) A3.

246. Gottlieb, M, Eichenwald K. A Hospital Chain's Brass Knuckles, and the Backlash—Opponents Rally to Stop the March of Columbia/HCA. *New York Times* (May 11, 1997) F1, F10–F11.

247. Eichenwald, K. HCA to Pay $95 Million in Fraud Case. New York Times (December 15, 2000) C1.

248. Lagnado, L. HCA Faces New U.S. Filings on Medicare. Wall Street Journal (March 19, 2001) B13.

249. Adams, C, Moss M. Bed News: The Business Potential of Nursing Homes Is Elusive, Vencor Finds. Wall Street Journal (December 24, 1998) A1, A10.

250. Sharp, K. Hospital Chain's Critics Call Recovery Incomplete. New York Times (August 6, 2000) 4, Business.

251. Weil, J. Andersen, in Reversal, Agrees to Pay to Settle Suit by Baptist Group. Wall Street Journal (May 7, 2002) C1, C15.

252. Eichenwald, K. Andersen's Past Stumbles Haunt It in Court. New York Times (May 8, 2002) C6.

253. Eichenwald, K, Henriques DB. Enron Buffed Image to a Shine Even as It Rotted from Within. New York Times (February 10, 2002) A1, A26.

254. Brown, K. Andersen Might Face More Legal Problems beyond Guilty Verdict. Wall Street Journal (June 17, 2002) C1.

255. Bryan-Low, C. Some Offices to Close; Others Are Acquired by Rival Companies. Wall Street Journal (June 17, 2002) C1.

256. Brown, K, Pacelle M, Bryan-Low C, Weil J, Frank R, Craig S. Called to Account: Indictment of Andersen in Shredding Case Puts Its Future in Question. Wall Street Journal (March 15, 2002) A1, A4.

257. Wilke, JR, Raghavan A, Barrionuevo A. U.S. Will Argue Andersen Knew of Missteps. Wall Street Journal (May 7, 2002) C1, C18.

258. Barboza, D. Tearing Down the Facade of "Vitamins Inc." New York Times (October 10, 1999) B1, B11.

259. Katona, G. Price Control and Business. Bloomington: Indiana University Press; 1946.

260. Lane, RE. The Regulation of Businessmen: Social Conditions of Government Control. New Haven, CT: Yale University Press; 1954.

261. Staw, BM, Szwajkowski E. The Scarcity-Munificence Component of Organizational Environments and the Commission of Illegal Acts. Administrative Science Quarterly 1975;20:345–54.

262. Clinard, MB, Yeager PC. Corporate Crime. New York: Free Press; 1980.

263. Coleman, JW. Toward an Integrated Theory of White-Collar Crime. American Journal of Sociology 1987;93(2):406–39.

264. Schlesinger, JM. Possible Paths: The Embrace of Capitalism Could Be Just Beginning—Or Disappear in the Next Recession. A Case Can Be Made for Both. Wall Street Journal (September 27, 1999) R23.

265. Vaughan, D. The Dark Side of Organizations: Mistake, Misconduct, and Disaster. Annual Review of Sociology 1999;25:271–305.

266. Burstin, HR, Lipsitz SR, Udvarhelyi IS, Brennan TA. The Effect of Hospital Financial Characteristics on Quality of Care. Journal of the American Medical Association 1993;270(7):845–49.

267. Leape, LL. Error in Medicine. Journal of the American Medical Association 1994;272(23):1851–57.

268. Pear, R. Interns' Long Workdays Prompt First Crackdown: Medical Training Group Is Enforcing Rules. New York Times (June 11, 2000) sec. 1, p. 18, col. 5.

269. McKee, M, Black N. Does the Current Use of Junior Doctors in the United Kingdom Affect the Quality of Medical Care? *Social Science and Medicine* 1992;34:549–58.

270. Sowers, L. Rx for Trouble: Are Pharmacists Failing to Detect Possible Adverse Drug Interactions? *Houston Chronicle* (October 1, 1996) 1D, 4D.

271. Leape, LL. Out of the Darkness: Hospitals Begin to Take Mistakes Seriously. *Health Systems Review* 1996;29(6):21–24.

272. Bates, DW, Spell N, Cullen DJ, Burdick E, Laird N, Petersen LA, et al. The Costs of Adverse Drug Events in Hospitalized Patients. *Journal of the American Medical Association* 1997;277(4):307–11.

273. Classen, DC, Pestotnik SL, Evans RS, Lloyd JF, Burke JP. Adverse Drug Events in Hospitalized Patients: Excess Length of Stay, Extra Costs, and Attributable Mortality. *Journal of the American Medical Association* 1997;277(4):301–6.

274. Kilborn, PT. Ambitious Effort to Cut Mistakes in U.S. Hospitals. *New York Times* (December 26, 1999) 1, 14.

275. Pear, R. Report Outlines Medical Errors in V.A. Hospitals. *New York Times* (December 19, 1999) A1, A36.

276. Landau, M, Chisholm D. The Arrogance of Optimism: Notes on Failure-Avoidance Management. *Journal of Contingencies and Crisis Management* 1995;3(2):67–78.

277. Singer, BD. Assessing Social Errors. *Social Policy* 1978;9:27–34.

278. Jackson, C. Downcoding, Denial of Claims by Insurers Are Facts of Life for Many Doctors. *American Medical News* (December 25, 2000); at www.ama-assn.org/sci-pubs/amnews/pick_00/bisa1225.htm#rbar_add.

279. Rosenthal, E. Confusion and Error Are Rife in Hospital Billing Practices. *New York Times* (January 27, 1993) C16.

280. Kerr, P. Glossing over Health Care Fraud. *New York Times* (April 5, 1992) F17.

281. U.S. General Accounting Office. Health Insurance: Remedies Needed to Reduce Losses from Fraud and Abuse—Testimony. Washington, DC: United States General Accounting Office; 1993.

282. Riemer, JW. "Mistakes at Work": The Social Organization of Error in Building Construction Work. *Social Problems* 1976;23(3):255–67.

283. Seglin, JL. The Right Thing; When Good Ethics Aren't Good Business. *New York Times* (March 18, 2001) sec. 3, p. 4, col. 2.

284. Knight, F. The Ethics of Competition. *The Quarterly Journal of Economics* 1923;37:579–624.

285. Sullivan, WM. *Work and Integrity.* New York: HarperBusiness; 1995.

286. Reich, RB. *The Work of Nations: Preparing Ourselves for 21st-Century Capitalism.* New York: Alfred A. Knopf; 1991.

287. McDowell, B. *Ethical Conduct and the Professional's Dilemma: Choosing between Service and Success.* New York: Quorum Books; 1991.

288. Norris, F, Kahn J. Rule Makers Take on Loopholes That Enron Used in Hiding Debt. *New York Times* (February 14, 2002) A1, C8.

289. Emshwiller, JR, Smith R. Murky Waters: A Primer on Enron Partnerships. *Wall Street Journal* (January 21, 2002) C1, C14.

290. Wayne, L. Before Debacle, Enron Insiders Cashed in $1.1 Billion in Shares. *New York Times* (January 13, 2002) A1, A27.

291. Leonhardt, D. Bubble Beneficiaries. *New York Times* (August 25, 2002) sec. 3, p. 10, col. 4.

292. Sapsford, J, Beckett P. Number Crunching: Enron Rival Used Complex Accounting to Burnish Its Profile. *Wall Street Journal* (April 3, 2002) A1, A9.

293. Wessel, D. Venal Sins: Why the Bad Guys of the Boardroom Emerged en Masse. *Wall Street Journal* (June 20, 2002) A1, A6.

294. Harwood, J. Public's Esteem for Business Falls in Wake of Enron Scandal. *Wall Street Journal* (April 11, 2002) D5.

295. *The Economist.* Economics Focus: Curse of the Ethical Executive. *The Economist* (November 17, 2001) 70.

296. Bhide, A, Stevenson HH. Why Be Honest if Honesty Doesn't Pay. *Harvard Business Review* 1990;68(5):121–29.

297. Hegarty, WH, Sims HP. Some Determinants of Unethical Decision Behavior: An Experiment. *Journal of Applied Psychology* 1978;63(4):451–57.

298. D'Aveni, RA, Gunther R. *Hypercompetitive Rivalries: Competing in Highly Dynamic Environments.* New York: Free Press; 1995.

299. Baumhart, RC. How Ethical Are Businessmen? *Harvard Business Review* 1961;39(July–August):156–76.

300. Hymowitz, C. In the Lead: CEOs Set the Tone for How to Handle Questions of Ethics. *Wall Street Journal* (December 22, 1998) B1.

301. Stevenson, HH, Moldoveanu MC. The Power of Predictability. *Harvard Business Review* 1995;73(4):140–43.

302. Brenner, SN, Molander EA. Is the Ethics of Business Changing? *Harvard Business Review* 1977;55(January–February):57–71.

303. Deyo, RA, Psaty BM, Simon G, Wagner EH, Omenn GS. The Messenger under Attack: Intimidation of Researchers by Special-Interest Groups. *New England Journal of Medicine* 1997;336:1176–80.

304. Fisher, ES, Welch HG. Avoiding the Unintended Consequences of Growth in Medical Care: How Might More Be Worse? *Journal of the American Medical Association* 1999;281(5):446–53.

305. Freeman, VG, Rathore SS, Weinfurt KP, Schulman KA, Sulmasy DP. Lying for Patients: Physician Deception of Third-Party Payers. *Archives of Internal Medicine* 1999;159(October 25):2263–70.

306. Kinghorn, W. Should Doctors Ever Lie on Behalf of Clients? *MSJAMA* (November 3, 1999) 1674–75.

307. Gellerman, SW. Why 'Good' Managers Make Bad Ethical Choices. *Harvard Business Review* 1986;64(4):85–90.

308. Eichenwald, K. White-Collar Defense Stance: The Criminal-less Crime. *New York Times* (March 3, 2002) 3, Week in Review.

309. Burke, T, Genn-Bash A, Haines B. *Competition in Theory and Practice.* London: Routledge; 1991.

310. Lublin, JS, Bryan-Low C, Schmitt RB, Dunham KJ, Gavin R. Oversight Bill Will Mean Change; Boardrooms to Be More Nervous. *Wall Street Journal* (July 29, 2002) B1, B4.

311. Thomas, LG. The Two Faces of Competition: Dynamic Resourcefulness and the Hypercompetitive Shift. *Management Science* 1996;7(3):221.

312. Greer, DF. *Industrial Organization and Public Policy.* 2nd ed. New York: Macmillan; 1984.

313. Lipin, S. Corporations' Dreams Converge in One Idea: It's Time to Do a Deal—Merger Wave Gathers Force as Strategies Demand Buying or Being Bought—"You Need to Be a Gorilla." *Wall Street Journal* (February 26, 1997) A1, A12.

314. Samuelson, PA, Nordhaus WD. *Economics.* 13th ed. New York: McGraw-Hill Book Company; 1989.

315. Byrns, RT, Stone GW. *Microeconomics.* 6th ed. New York: HarperCollins College Publishers; 1995.

316. Scherer, FM, Ross D. *Industrial Market Structure and Economic Performance.* 3rd ed. Boston: Houghton Mifflin Company; 1990.

317. Scherer, FM. *Industrial Market Structure and Economic Performance.* 2nd ed. Boston: Houghton Mifflin Company; 1980.

5

How and When Organizations Avoid Competition

The primary goal of business strategy is to negate the necessity to engage in the competitive process.[1, p. 224]

IN THE REAL WORLD, MOST individuals, groups, businesses, and nations compete not because they like to compete but rather to eliminate "the competition." This chapter is about the race to avoid destructive competition altogether among those who laud it most. At the same time that on the intellectual level the merit of competition goes unquestioned, the discrepancy between words and actions grows. Discourse and behavior do not match, basically because competition is not the unqualified good it is claimed to be.

Corporate and business leaders overwhelmingly express confidence in the competition paradigm, though this endorsement is not always directly to the point. Support may be expressed as enthusiasm for "individual accountability," a belief in "every man for himself,"[2] a call for freedom from regulation, or an expression of confidence in "the market." But organizational strategies formulated by leadership aim to avoid, not to embrace, intense competition much of the time. No surprise here—the goal of a corporate organization, any business, is not to compete for the sake of competition. The intent is to make a profit, to reward stockholders, and to stay in business. Competition is the process, not the end. There are innumerable ways in which organizations may and do avoid competition because this so often enhances profits. If competition were as good for you as cod liver oil, as the Advanced Micro Devices advertisement quoted in the introductory chapter of this book suggests, one might expect that people would want more of it even if the taste were not so great. But they do not.[3, 4]

Individuals and societies often seek to avoid destructive competition too. It is easy to find examples. Tenure for professors and union membership for workers are two mechanisms individuals use to avoid competition (these are discussed in this chapter). But there are few systematic studies of competition-averse human behavior.[5, 6] What research is available comes from the fields of psychology, economics, and management.[7] Research results on the topic of conflict aversion are pertinent if, as Karl Deutsch suggests, competition is merely a subcategory of conflict. People are often uncomfortable when information and the sources of that information are incongruent. Agreeing messages, even ambiguous information, are preferred.[8] Some societies (for example, Japan) seem to be so competition averse that they strive to avoid any appearance of success in situations of interpersonal competition.[9, 10]

The principal focus of this chapter is on commerce and corporate enterprises rather than on the individual. This choice is partly because of the surprising transparency evident in business practices. For example, when Microsoft sought to quash the competition, it was relatively open about it. In the business community, the obvious efforts to avoid competition are on the surface rather than buried deeply in the inner psyche, as in the case of individuals.

Many corporate executives say that they believe in competition, but they clearly act as if avoiding intense competition will increase productivity and profits.[11] The business community seems to be telling us that competition is not always the most efficient way to get things done. Still, a corporation is subject to criticism if it is viewed as "less competitive" or if its leadership is somewhat risk averse, appears indecisive, and is too relaxed about becoming leaner and meaner.[12] In fact, almost all businesses seek to create just such a loose environment—to be in a situation of less challenge and more certainty. Ron Baron, owner–manager of the Baron Mutual Fund Company, puts it right up front: He seeks to invest in companies that successfully avoid competition. "We want to be sure the businesses in which we invest will continue to prosper over the several year time horizon in which we intend to be shareholders. Barriers to competitors will help them do so."[13, p. 3] There is even an economic theory with a long historical tradition that argues that cooperation is more efficient than competition.[14–18] Such views are at odds with the competition paradigm for the simple reason that they represent the opposite problem, namely, the absence of competition altogether.

There are several very good reasons for organizations to avoid competition, and all of them call the competition paradigm into question. Self-interest is an important element. In many cases, cooperation is simply more efficient and more profitable than intense competition for most enterprises.[19–21] Output quotas set by either a complete vertically integrated network or a coalition of producers are apparently highly efficient, noncompetitive examples of cooperation in the corporate world.[22, p. 8] It should be no surprise if intense, destructive competition reduces profits and brings on bankruptcy. It is designed to do exactly that.[23]

If the evidence about the superiority of competition is in doubt, the discrepancy between deeds and words is an additional caution. Intense competition is likely to be observed in areas where results are not very important to society and where failure is tolerable from society's point of view. At the end of this chapter, we will see that when things are critically important, the focus is on cooperating, organizing, and planning. The inefficiency of bureaucracy receives less attention and almost no complaints. This is why in cases of national emergency, war, and national disaster, competition is set aside.

Muddling Through—Organizations Respond to Intense Competition

The range and variety of mechanisms for routinely avoiding competition, especially intense, destructive forms of competition, are many. Several such techniques employed in the corporate world to avoid destructive competition are considered here. Not all these strategies are pursued equally by every member of the business community.

Merging, Consolidating, Acquiring "the Competition," and Organizing for Oligopoly

Monopolies, oligopolies, acquisitions, mergers, and consolidations are all devices for avoiding destructive competition, though seldom is this acknowledged.[24, 25, p. 285] The end result may be the same, though the terms are not identical. Mergers involve both consolidations and acquisitions. Consolidations combine firms or enterprises into a single organization. In these cases, the original units disappear. Acquisitions amount to one unit purchasing another. The purchasing unit remains, and the acquired entity disappears.[22, p. 250] All these activities increase size, offer tax advantages, and are assumed to be pursued because they make companies more competitive.[26] They enlarge a company's market share. They may also ensure standardization of product design. Standardization can contribute to diffusion and adoption, something that is very beneficial in an era of new and rapid advances in technology.[27] If mergers mean that a resulting company is larger, it can, in theory, permit efficiencies and economies of scale. Cost per unit of service or product should go down, at least in theory, as volume goes up. If this were correct, then large producers, holding other things constant, would generally be more efficient than small companies. "Profits increase with both higher industry concentration and higher firm market shares."[28, p. 283] Profits are up because of the increase in volume even when prices are lower. This would benefit consumers.[25, p. 271, 29] There seems to be almost no limit as to how big is too big today. The assumption is that there is no upper limit on economies of scale.[30–32] But there is more to the story.

Mergers, consolidations, and acquisitions benefit the companies involved by helping them avoid intense competition.[33, pp. 4–6] Corporations become larger and larger though there are fewer and fewer corporate entities to "compete" in each economic sector.[34, 35] Scherer points to the problem when he asks whether it is really economies of scale that increase efficiency or whether efficiency results from "cooperation" among producers in a highly concentrated market.[36] Sometimes mergers amount to a large company acquiring smaller competitors and then closing them as a means to avoid competition.

In a market sector where only a few companies remain because of mergers and consolidations, competition still exists; but it is no longer the savage competition observed between many producers that is common to immature markets with many smaller players.[20, 35, 37, 38] It is, rather, "civilized competition," with each competitor consciously or unconsciously monitoring changes in other companies' prices before modifying its own.[39] "There are incentives for them to recognize their interdependence and to cooperate in policies that lead toward maximum group profits."[28, p. 266] Economists observe this "conscious parallelism" or "tacit collusion" in a number of other economic sectors.[40, p. 183] For example, in the airline industry, periods of routine competition are only occasionally punctuated by more strenuous competition.[41] As long as each of the major players is relatively content with profit level and market share, price increases and decreases will hold, and most players will follow the leader. In addition, in sectors where large firms emerge as price leaders, they can set prices in the sense that small competitors implicitly understand that lowering prices could unleash a price war or a struggle for market share, with dire results.[42] Such trends are global as well as national,[43] aided by the ever growing Internet.[44]

Mergers, acquisitions, and consolidations are also very effective at reducing competition that is so intense that it threatens continued existence. Businesses in a highly negative environment or declining industries are advised to cooperate by "consolidating." The strategy is one of survival—mergers and consolidations might make it possible for companies in jeopardy to avoid corporate failure.[45] "Given enough time and opportunity for adjustment and signaling, competitors in declining industries can consolidate and profitably coexist indefinitely."[46, p. 4]

If mergers, consolidations, and acquisitions help the companies involved by reducing competition, on balance, they do not do much for anyone else.[47]

Because concentration eliminates business rivals and increases the market power of those that remain, a new set of market-related dynamics emerges.[25, p. 289] When producers are so large as to be able to influence price and restrict output, then they are free to charge a higher price than can be justified under highly competitive conditions.[48, p. 542, 49, p. 84] This is especially true in those geographic areas where they control a large part of the market.[50, 51] It is the case with respect to the deregulated and increasingly concentrated local telephone market where the cost of local phone service increased 17 percent between 1996 and 2002.[52] It is also true for the college textbooks markets, for semiconductor-chip fabrication, for job recruitment companies, for the pharmaceuticals industry, and for cable television.[29, 53] The worry is always there—that in the absence of regulation, commercial enterprises will exploit their price-setting power, generate "excessive profits, or lapse into inefficient management and excessive costs."[54, p. 22]

Too much consolidation leads to the creation of oligopolies. It creates "powerful providers with little need to respond to customers."[55, p. 139, 56, 57] That is why consumer groups largely oppose them. Quality may suffer[58] because a purchaser who wants or needs a product often has no choice but to pay the price demanded. There is little alternative except to do without. Neither do mergers benefit stockholders because the vast majority of mergers—more than 80 percent—do not produce any business benefits in terms of shareholder value.[24, p. 2] Resulting oligopolies reinforce inefficiency especially when the companies receive subsidies from government, benefit from protective legislation, deliberately limit technical advances, and successfully control the agencies or commissions set up to regulate them.

Acquisitions, other forms of consolidation, vertical mergers (between producers and suppliers), and horizontal mergers (between competitors) have been increasingly tolerated since the 1960s, though this is always subject to change.[59] Republican administrations are a bit more lenient; Democratic administrations seem somewhat less so. But overall, the accepted view has come to be that competition among a few oligopolies rather than among many smaller units of production, services, and so on is acceptable. Mergers have more than doubled since the early 1990s, and there is a high tolerance for large-sized corporate entities.[29, 60]

Mergers, acquisitions, and consolidations are not the only way to avoid competition by creating monopoly-like conditions. The business community employs a number of additional strategies to achieve this situation. The development of these strategies goes back to the late nineteenth century in the United States.[42] First, corporate entities may obtain control over the supplies of raw products (cornering the market) and then raise the price of the finished product.[61] Second, they may look for a market sector, such as the water market, where the terms of doing business involve a long lease with monopoly status.[62] Third, they may seek to drive competitors from the market or discourage entry into markets where they already have a monopoly.[25] This may involve lobbying Congress, protesting government efforts to introduce competition into the marketplace, and making large payments to the campaign finance funds of friendly candidates for office.[63, p. A16] Fourth, most-favored-customer clauses, discriminating pricing arrangements, or exclusive contracts are another monopoly-linked manner to avoid competition. Such arrangements may reduce competition and encourage tacit collusion.[64] Fifth, the franchise relationship between a large company and its franchisees is basically a monopoly relationship. It leads to price inflation because no real competition is permitted. Microsoft Corporation, Coca-Cola, and others set up incentives that make it impossible for other suppliers of their products to offer these products to franchisees at a lower price.[65]

Finding a Niche

Some organizations respond to destructive competition by moving into areas, sectors, or niches where they increase their survival chances because there is less competition. Finding a niche that is not occupied by any other company is a way of achieving, at least in the short term, "monopoly status" and avoiding destructive competition.[33, p. 132] It is not about being more competitive, efficient, and so on but rather about being more adept at finding a less competitive environment. It adds predictable parameters. Bill Gates puts it nicely: "Competition is good. But you also want stability."[27, p. C2] A niche gives you that much-sought-after stability.

Niche theory comes from population biology or classic bioecology.[66] It links organization theory to modern ecological theory. It applies knowledge from environmental science to understand how organizations develop and expand.[67] If two companies "rely on completely different kinds of resources and depend on different kinds of social and political institutions, then their fundamental niches do not intersect."[68, p. 28]

"Niche competition is win-win. Everyone has a place where they can excel. No one is going to be driven out of business. Head-to-head competition . . . is win-lose."[69, p. 30] Finding a niche is especially important when innovation is high, industry standards are low, and the number of competitors is large.[20] Large corporations seek to develop strategies that bar entry into their industry[25, p. 251] and that prevent others from moving into their fundamental niche arena.[66] Small enterprises may also be very adept at creating a niche. Small drug manufacturers, for example, are very nimble, and their strategy of developing products that have fewer side effects than already existing, well-publicized pharmaceuticals is very successful.[70] Still, being first in an economic arena is the preferred strategy for companies seeking to establish themselves in a niche and protect it from intrusion.[71]

Filing Patents and Copyrights

Historically, patents and copyrights have been employed to avoid competition.[25, p. 228] They are a form of regulation designed specifically to accord a monopoly to an inventor, as an incentive to undertake and finance research that may sometimes be risky and expensive. The goal of copyrights and patents is to increase innovation, not competition. In addition, these explicit and legal mechanisms to moderate competition do not work very well anymore. More effective techniques that work better are necessarily informal.

Patents and copyrights are considered old-fashioned and not very efficient ways to reduce competition for several reasons. First, patents and copyrights are time consuming and expensive. It costs $50,000 for an initial international filing with an annual renewal fee. Processing a patent application requires, on average, two years, and this waiting puts a company at a disadvantage as competitors leapfrog ahead with new products.[72] Second, they are not very effective in a global economy where the nation granting a patent cannot always enforce it in other countries.[73] Third, they are not as useful as unofficial mechanisms in eliminating the competition in many economic sectors. Reverse engineers may be able to invent variations on a competitor's patented product and circumvent a competitor's patent.[74] Fourth, giving away some products, such as computer software, rather than limiting its distribution with a patent ensures broad adoption and gigantic market share in the long term. It guarantees future sales in a way that patent protection could not. Finally, patents are increasingly treated like any other potentially profitable commodity, capable of being traded, exchanged, or sold. This might mean cooperating with competitors by selling them information about innovations and licensing the use of copyrights and patents to them.[74, 75] Mergers are sometimes inspired by the opportunity to share patent information.[22, pp. 244–48]

In some cases, "defensive publishing" or public disclosure is replacing the patent approach to protecting intellectual property. By publishing information on a website, in a bulletin, or in a trade journal—in short, making an innovation available in the public domain—a company at least makes it impossible for competitors to win a patent on it and then charge the original "inventor" or developer a fee for using the information.

At the same time, the function of patents for those that remain committed to them has changed. Patents have become a more strategic tool with the clear goal of blocking competitors. Bronwyn Hall and Rosemarie Ham Ziedous at

Rand Corporation argue that in many cases patents no longer ensure an increase in innovation but rather slow down the development of new ideas. Companies that specialize in holding large portfolios of patents roll them out to block a competitor.[76, 77] This brings the patent full circle. Once again, it takes its place in the arsenal of techniques to avoid competition.

Opposing and Supporting Antitrust Laws

Economists generally believe that antitrust laws, a form of government regulation, ensure that increasingly large size does not end up reducing competition. In theory, antitrust laws are designed to limit market power, to prohibit business practices that permit one company (or a few) to control the market, and to discourage the misconduct associated with monopoly and oligopoly.[55] Monopoly-linked dysfunctions include price increases that are unwarranted.[64] This is why consumer groups usually support antitrust legislation,[78] arguing that profits are often higher in concentrated industries.[48] The assumption is that if no company is allowed to become too large or control too much of the market, then competition will take place among the many, smaller entities. Exemptions exist where monopoly status is not a worry: "agricultural cooperatives, sports organizations, industry export associations, insurance companies, labor unions, and closely regulated industries."[25, p. 274]

But over the last quarter of the twentieth century, economic theory on the topic of antitrust laws was increasingly called into question in America.[79, 80] In the early 1980s, the Reagan administration reduced strict enforcement of antitrust laws. Antitrust has been less of a government priority since then.[81, 82] Initially, the Clinton administration was more aggressive than Republican administrations in antitrust enforcement regarding price fixing and distinctly uncompetitive practices.[60] The Clinton administration's tough stand with regard to Microsoft Corporation is an example. Microsoft, unlike other giants, was viewed as a "predatory monopolist."[83, p. A3] Here, the problem of monopoly corporate status became intertwined with the company's "attitude" when challenged by the U.S. Department of Justice.[84] Some suggest that antitrust enforcement weakened in the last half of the 1990s, as being bigger was increasingly said to lower cost and improve quality.[85] Europeans take the exact opposite view and oppose any weakening of antitrust law.[86] But almost all the experts on the topic agree that efforts by large corporations to weaken antitrust legislation and to reduce its enforcement have been quite successful. Mergers that would have been unthinkable in the 1960s and 1970s because of resulting antitrust problems are permitted in many sectors, including aerospace, banking, health care, and telecommunications.[80] The George W. Bush administration's policies constitute a return to the Reagan years regarding antitrust policies and enforcement.[87, 88] In support of the Republican Party's approach to intellectual property is the argument that the new-economy industries function in a high-risk environment where winner-take-all results are inevitable. Winner-take-all competition, however, is likely to be short term.[89]

Companies complained during the Clinton years that while larger mergers were approved, the Federal Trade Commission and the Department of Justice often imposed intrusive settlement conditions that involved continued monitoring of the new corporate entities.[90] State-level antitrust agencies were equally likely to negotiate mergers that involved continued monitoring and oversight.[91, pt. II #2026] Beginning in 2000, a Republican in the White House made for fewer merger control features that the business community found objectionable. Antitrust cases pending from the Clinton years in office were resolved under the Bush government in favor of large-company interest at the expense of smaller competitors.[92, p. A3]

Another reason cited by the George W. Bush administration for reduced attention to antitrust legislation was the fear that rigorous enforcement might jeopardize U.S. global competitiveness. But the argument that corporations must be large to be efficient and to compete in the growing international marketplace pre-dates the election of George W. Bush.[93–95] Ironically, then, antitrust laws that were originally established to increase competition are now viewed as limiting a firm's ability to compete at the global level.[80]

Today, antitrust matters involve multinational companies. Because they are actively engaged in commerce around the world, monitoring them concerns several different countries. This makes it difficult for American-based companies to avoid competition by opposing antitrust regulation. There are more than eighty sets of antitrust legislation, called regimes, worldwide, and they do not always agree. Some of these regimes have vetoed a U.S.-based and -approved merger, arguing that the resulting corporate entity would violate antitrust requirements in these foreign markets where they expect to do business.[96, 97] There is substantial corporate pressure on antitrust regimes to cooperate and come to agreement among themselves.[98] During the Clinton administration, European officials cooperated with U.S. regulatory authorities on the Microsoft case, probably hoping to avoid the high cost of such investigations.[99] That changed when the pro-merger George W. Bush government came to power.[88] The European Antitrust Commission has maintained its case against Microsoft even as the United States resolved its problems with the company.[100] As another example, because the European Union objected, General Electric had to give up its plan to acquire Honeywell Inc.[101] Standardization efforts among countries as regards antitrust legislation are almost nonexistent, though proposed mergers are increasingly global.[102, 103]

For different reasons, many who support antitrust legislation—and some of those who oppose it—seek the same thing: to avoid too-intense competition. Competition avoidance is the underlying motive, though it may be cloaked in pro-antitrust discourse or an anti-antitrust argument. This is the case because antitrust legislation affects various players differently. The perspective defended depends on how antitrust legislation influences the business entity concerned. But no matter who is speaking, the apparently rational argument and the logic associated with it are very often camouflage for an anticompetition sentiment. In the 1940s and 1980s, companies with lower profits and generally poor performance were more likely to be involved in antitrust legal problems.[104–107]

Large entrepreneurs argue that they are opposed to antitrust laws because such laws are essentially a form of government intervention that curtails competition and hinders the development of huge and efficient corporate enterprises. Representatives of giant corporations suggest that antitrust laws interfere with laissez-faire economics, the natural working of the "invisible hand." Milton Friedman (and the whole of the Chicago School) and law professor Robert Bork (as well as many other experts) take this position.[80, 108] While granting that concentration may result, Gloria Bazzoli, a vice president at the Hospital Research and Educational Trust, an affiliate of the American Hospital Association in the mid-1990s, countered that measuring concentration is not an exact science.[109] Joe Davis, president and chief executive officer of the Medimetrix group, said that "contestability" is much more important than any simplistic measures of competition.[109]

Those of this philosophy continue that if a near monopoly imposes unreasonably high prices, the problem will be resolved because such high prices will attract new competitors to enter the sector.[110] Or, as Alan Greenspan, chairman of the U.S. Federal Reserve Board, argued, antitrust enforcement that "inhibited various types of mergers or acquisitions on the basis of some presumed projection as to how markets would evolve, how technology would evolve," is not a good idea. History, he says, "is strewn with people making projections that have turned out to be grossly inaccurate."[81, 111] Larger players are said to be good for the economy; it is assumed that there is still lots of competition even if there are only a few competitors.

Smaller companies support antitrust legislation, as do those seeking entry into markets. They see antitrust enforcement as positive because it will reduce monopoly and oligopoly power. "Most anti-trust litigation is initiated by small companies with complaints about low prices charged by competitors."[25, p. 276] Representatives of these smaller companies point out that the normative assumptions underlying antitrust legislation are centered around the virtue of individual initiative, individual freedom of choice, and the threat of large business and of activist government.[112] Small businesses do not deny that they too want to avoid competition, but they argue they do so because this kind of competition is not fair competition.

Smaller businesses also contend that antitrust enforcement is needed because large players practice predatory pricing in markets where they have a near monopoly. This practice is defined as "selling below cost with the intention of driving equally and more efficient competitors from the marketplace."[1, p. 156] For example, small airlines seeking to compete in new markets see their lower fares matched by the major airlines in the same geographic area.[113] The already established companies flood routes with so many seats that the new, smaller entrants are forced to retreat.[110, 114, p. B14, 115] Microsoft's conduct toward other players was an example of how abusive big players can be in this respect.[116]

Cooperating with One's Competitors

There are many very good reasons to cooperate with one's competitors. Some of these cooperative activities are, however legal, while others are not. Some are openly pursued; others are carried out only in secret. But after all is said and done, cooperating with one's competitors is a mixed bag. The motive may be to avoid destructive competition. This can in turn make for more constructive forms of competition, or "co-opetition."[117] But cooperating with one's competitors can also be about the far less desirable option of avoiding competition altogether.

Many justifications are offered for cooperating with one's competitors, but those offered hardly ever mention competition avoidance. For example, in the early stages of new-sector development, a company is not simply "a member of a single industry but part of a business ecosystem." In such an environment, there is said to be an important reason for companies to work together (as well as to compete) in order to "support new products, satisfy customer needs, and eventually incorporate the next round of innovations."[118, p. 76]

An argument can be made that it is logical and even profitable to cooperate with competitors. The view that one wins if one's competitors lose is said to be naive and simplistic.[117] Taking away a competitor's customer may be counterproductive if you accomplish this by offering goods or services at such a low price that you cannot make a profit, if all your existing customers now want the same low price, or if your competitors suddenly become especially aggressive and unleash a price war in which everyone loses. In these cases, "a company's move to undercut competitors could easily undercut the company itself."[117, p. 38]

Cooperating with competitors to bring new customers into the market can be a win–win situation even if the new customers end up doing business with one's competitors. This mutual gain is the case in a business sector where there is limited capacity. As soon as all enterprises are at capacity, customers lose leverage and must pay the price demanded for a product or service because the option of changing suppliers is limited if all are at full capacity.[117]

Open and public cooperation among competitors is often legal. Cross-investing is an example of open, public cooperation.[119] Cooperation by professional groups and business confederations that collectively lobby government for industry interests is another example. Cooperation here reduces "rent seeking" by individual firms and industries.[120, p. 1635] Economic rent is defined as the surplus payment to a factor (for example, land, capital, and labor) over and above what is necessary to keep it in its present use. For example, Meryl Streep is paid $15 million per movie, but she would probably make movies for $1 million if that were all that was available. Thus, $14 million is economic rent. Legal cooperation with competitors also encompasses efforts by one company to ensure that its rivals do not go out of business. In the late 1990s, Microsoft helped save Apple Computer Inc. from bankruptcy, cooperating on technology and sales matters and investing $150 million in Apple to become a nonvoting minority shareholder. This cooperation was because Apple is such an important purchaser of Microsoft's software applications that Microsoft did not wish to see its competitor fail.[121] A number of other "competitors," including computer hardware and software companies and executives and former highly placed employees from Intuit, Oracle, IBM, and Motorola, joined to assist in bringing Apple back from the edge of bankruptcy.[122, 123] Competitors in the same industrial sector also sometimes coordinate wage bargaining. Such centralized coordination with an industrywide union seems to contribute to wage restraint and reduces time lost in strikes.

When companies cooperate with their suppliers on a range of tasks from product design to performance evaluation, they abandon the spirit of destructive competition that demands buying from suppliers at the lowest price possible and selling at the highest price possible. Such cooperation involves oral agreements and long-term commitments. The goal of this legal, open cooperation is to maximize the success of all companies involved. This cooperation reduces distrust and suspicion, lowers risk, sets up a common vision, and ultimately increases profits for all.[124] It increases the willingness of suppliers to invest and raises productivity.[120, p. 1635] Toyota has historically practiced this rule of equity and distributive justice rather than destructive competition with regard to suppliers.[125]

In many cases, cooperation among competitors is not only open and legal but of substantial benefit to customers, consumers in general, other companies, and society in general. This is the case where producers work together on the research and development of products that are of social importance. For example, General Motors and Toyota worked to develop alternative-powered automobiles.[126] Pharmaceutical companies collaborated to map the human genome.[127, p. B9] Automakers who provide their employees with health insurance attempted to establish a national standard for health provider report cards.[128] Rival chip-equipment manufacturers in the semiconductor industry in several countries cooperated to develop new products.[129]

There is some evidence that in Japan, Germany, Italy, Finland, and Sweden, cooperation with competitors is more common than in the United States or the United Kingdom.[120] "Standard setting, financing, technology diffusion, design, accounting, marketing, and export promotion" among firms have, in these countries, permitted a wider range of cooperation. These practices are correlated with national economic growth.[120, p. 1639, 130] For example, small firms in Germany share state-supported technology transfers, a program to encourage exports, and technical training to reduce risk.[131]

Nations that sign agreements for monetary unions or regional trade associations or that establish common currencies are practicing a form of cooperation with their usual competitors (other neighboring countries). Again, the goal is to improve the performance of all those included by avoiding destructive competition. Regional agreements set aside external competition with neighbors in favor of cooperation. Monetary union is a similar means to bind a family of nations together. In both cases, however, competition continues and may be increased with nations that are not part of the regional agreement and with other regional unions.[130, p. 119]

Sometimes, cooperation with competitors may be practiced openly, even though it is illegal, because it is viewed as benign or even in the public interest. In these cases, it is justified on the basis that it does not injure consumers and may even benefit them. This was the case with universities competing for the best students. In the past, universities set up an elaborate public, open system of cooperation among themselves, sharing information about scholarship awards and thus preventing highly sought students from bargaining. Antitrust legislation forces them to compete today, though there is no real advantage to their doing so from society's point of view.[132, p. 225]

Cooperating with competitors may also be secret, covert, and illegal. Examples of this type of cooperation, unfortunately, involve the largest, best-known, and most respected companies. Much of this activity is an attempt to avoid price wars (destructive competition), which are counterproductive to all enterprises involved. "Once buyers, whether employers or health plans, get a taste of blood in exacting price concessions from providers, it tends to start a feeding frenzy, where buyers assume prices can be cut repeatedly. Where there might have been some slack in provider systems at first, the sharks eventually get well past eliminating waste and are still hungry."[133, p. 19] Price-fixing is one way of cooperating with competitors to avoid destructive competition. It is illegal but indirectly recommended by many market consultants through innuendo.[133]

Price-fixing carried out in secret is considered to be a conspiracy or collusion, and it is clearly illegal. For example, leaders at Sotheby's and Christie's agreed on commissions and fees charged to buyers and sellers.[134] Another example involves European and Japanese vitamin manufacturers who were fined $1 billion, the largest criminal fine in history.[135] Another billion dollars may be required to settle a class-action suit by their corporate customers who overpaid. The companies involved set up a coalition called "Vitamins, Inc." and cooperated regarding price increases. They divided up the market to avoid competition as well.[136, 137] Still another example is that of major banks from several countries forming a common online foreign currency exchange company in order to control the foreign-currency market and avoid competition.[138]

Global cartels, another form of illegal cooperation among competitors, are especially effective mechanisms for avoiding intense competition because they are difficult to uncover. In addition, guilty companies often are based in faraway locations beyond the legal control of the authorities in any single country. In many cases, companies caught violating laws find cooperating with competitors so profitable that penalties do not discourage them because the increased profits outweigh any potential downside.[139] The goal of controlling competition for mutual benefit, in these cases, harms consumer interests and those companies not included in the cooperating "community of interest." Antitrust laws were originally designed to prohibit just this type of activity.

Illegally cooperating with competitors is most likely to take place in certain, known conditions. First, it occurs with greater frequency in declining industries and during periods of crisis for the firms involved.[46] In addition, it is more likely that a firm will cooperate regarding standard setting if the size of the group is large and if that firm's close rivals are not participants.[140] Finally, the business-to-business commerce of the Internet is thought to facilitate collusion and price-fixing.[141, 142]

While the distinction between legal cooperation and illegal cooperation is analytically clear, in the real world it tends to blur. For example, Russell Coile struck an honest, refreshing note when he said, "Today's market collusions may pave the way for business collaboration tomorrow." He observed, "When competitors reach a standoff in market advantage, they can switch to cooperation to increase their mutual strengths and benefits."[143, p. 1] While situations of mutually destructive competition are not uncommon, the issue today is often how close one can come, in avoiding competition and in pursuing a win–win strategy, to the covert and illegal.

Requiring Protective Regulation

The competition paradigm criticizes government regulation for trampling freedom and suffocating business and for reducing supplies and increasing costs.[25, p. 278] For example, Enron was said to have been so effective at lobbying Washington, D.C., that Congress tailored the deregulation of the gas and oil industry to Enron's preferences, freeing the industry from certain tax burdens and reducing government oversight.[144–147]

But in some situations, regulation moves from being a tool in the enemy's arsenal to assuming a genuinely positive role for the business community.[148] When destructive competition results in chaos for consumers, business interests sometimes agree on the need for regulation and government intervention to avoid uncertainty.[149, 150] Many regulatory agencies were in fact established to benefit industry or became captives of the businesses they were supposed to regulate.[151] George Soros points out that financial markets "resent any kind of government interference, but they hold a belief that if conditions get rough, the authorities will step in."[152, p. 3]

Sometimes, regulation is explicitly requested by one sector of the business community seeking advantage over another sector. "These may well be occasions when dominant forms within an industry find it to their interests to encourage the introduction of government regulation."[1, p. 210] For example, large national insurance companies sought to have uniform national regulation established for life insurance, annuities, and disability income products. This made it easier for them to function and lift the requirements, sometimes more stringent, imposed by individual states.[153] As another example, after deregulation of utilities, many private companies entered the market, only to find that they could not make a profit. State intervention was sought to ensure essential services.[154] But this reregulation ended up also protecting business in general or some specific business sector from competition.[155, ch. 1] The deregulation of the electricity industry is an example of how specific corporations benefit while others lose out and no one-to-one relationship exists between business interests in the abstract and deregulation in the concrete.[156]

Several theories of regulation exist, but only one of the three described here, industry interest theory, accounts for its competition-avoidance qualities. The first two, public choice theory and public interest theory, disagree on many things, but they do agree that regulation is anticompetitive. Both suggest that competition and regulation are incompatible. Public choice theory opposes regulation, contending that regulations are the work of state bureaucrats who wish to enhance their own power. It argues that government should not restrain competition in this fashion. Public interest theory values regulation even if it is anticompetitive. It views regulation as protecting citizens from industry, harmful business practices, and market failure. In short, this theory sees regulation as serving the public interest.[25, pp. 281–86]

Industry-interest theory takes a different view of regulation, confirming that it is a way for business to avoid competition. It proposes that regulated businesses often lobby for regulations that protect them from competition or at least limit its impact. This theory of regulation seems counterintuitive because the business community speaks out so vehemently against government regulation.[157] George Stigler, former president of the American Economics Association and 1982 Nobel Prize winner, argues that firms seek regulations to serve their own interests.[158] He contends that government, as the source of these desired regulations, in turn receives substantial payback in the form of "lobbying or campaign contributions to policymakers who favor regulations the established firms want."[25, p. 285]

Only industry-interest theory explains why industries are sometimes unhappy when deregulation is proposed and already existing regulation is reduced. Such industries complain because they seek to avoid increased competition in their business sector. Consumer and taxpayer interests fall by the wayside as businesses struggle to preserve the regulation that protects industry from competing. Some examples illustrate the case. In the health sector, managed care plans lobbied Congress to halt the Clinton administration's demonstration project of competitive bidding for Medicare contracts.[159] Hospitals do not support the deregulation that forces them to compete.[160] Liquor producers protest efforts to deregulate the alcoholic beverage sector because regulation protects them against new competitors entering the field. Regulation may also ensure "direct subsidies to the industry, special tax breaks."[25, p. 284] As another example, tax subsidies to business are common, as are more direct subsidies from government in the form of loans, insurance, and so on.[161] In a global trade environment, U.S. tax benefits to businesses with overseas operations are viewed abroad as a violation of international trade rules.[162, 163] Finally, dairy farmers who established marketing cooperatives and received government price supports years ago went to court to obtain a restraining order when the Department of Agriculture sought to reduce milk price supports.[164]

Industry interest in regulation as a means to avoid intense competition is common in newly competitive business sectors, such as the health care sector in the United States. The same is true of markets destabilized by sudden change and in countries just beginning to establish market economies. In both situations, the rules of exchange and the governance structures necessary for routine commerce are still being established. In the absence of regulation, savage cutthroat competition threatens.[165]

An industry seeks to avoid competing with foreign companies that produce goods more cheaply and that export those goods into the industry's domestic market. To reach this goal thus-affected industries request protectionist regulations from their home country. Tariffs have historically played a protective role. Tariffs and duties have been sought and awarded to protect U.S. industries as diverse as lumber and movie production.[166] Sometimes merely the hint of a tariff is sufficient to avoid competition and protect an industry. Country-to-country voluntary restraints on exports may substitute. The fear of tariffs being levied is often sufficient to discourage foreign competitors from trying to export into a country. Toyota, for example, monitors its market share in the United States carefully to be sure it does not provoke tariff increases.[167] Self-monitoring avoids the need for more explicit regulation at a time when protecting home markets is out of favor with economists.

When an industry lobbies for protection from foreign producers, the political power of the industry requesting protection has much to do with the success achieved in avoiding competition. The rationale for protection, whether in the form of regulation or informal negotiations, is not always easy to justify and sometimes merely amounts to the fact that the offensive imports are "low priced." An example is the restriction of steel imports from Russia requested and obtained by the U.S. steel industry.[168, 169] Many U.S. allies, including Japan, Canada, and the European Union, are at odds with the United States because regulations help U.S. companies avoid competition.[170–172] Tariffs designed to help one industry in a country increasingly end up hurting industries in the same country because, in a global environment, reprisals from other countries follow the imposition of a tariff. Domestic political effects also result from what was once assumed to be exclusively an international matter. This is because tariffs increase prices internal to a country.[173] Another example of industry seeking legislation to avoid competition is AT&T's and MCI's efforts to prohibit the Mexican phone company, Telmex, from operating jointly with Sprint in the U.S. market.[174] Chrysler Corporation sought government regulation to reduce imports of Japanese cars.[151, 175]

On the domestic front, the same competition avoidance exists. When the U.S. Postal Service began acting like a competitor, private-sector players asked Congress to restrain its expansion. United Parcel Service and Federal Express sought legislation to restrain the increasingly competitive Postal Service from moving in on their markets.[176]

Avoiding competition through government intervention is sometimes the last recourse for a business. When the competition becomes so intense that it threatens the viability of companies, many look to government for assistance, often in the form of regulation or legislation as a way to avoid failure. Companies requiring bailout assistance from government in the past include Chrysler, Conrail, Lockheed, and Continental-Illinois Bank.[175, 177] The "freedom-to-farm law" of 1996 put farming on a competitive market footing, but when the Asian market suffered a downturn and demand for U.S. farm products abroad diminished, Congress adopted legislation to rescue U.S. farmers.[178] Government regulation in the form of bankruptcy laws also saves companies from disaster. Bankruptcy laws provide businesses experiencing financial problems with a period of immunity from competition—a period of time to consolidate debt and reorganize.

What Do We Do in Emergencies? Testing Discourse

Organizational behavior in situations of national emergency challenges the validity and universal applicability of the competition paradigm. How we react to emergencies demonstrates, again, that discourse and behavior diverge. Organizations do not compete but rather set aside the competition paradigm. They look to planning, regulation, and dependence on the public sector and on hierarchically organized social structures. In emergencies, organizations accept and even applaud regulation. Government assistance becomes an uncontroversial good. For example, after the September 11, 2001 terrorist attacks, all industries and economic sectors affected sought help from the government, including the insurance industry[179] and the airlines.[180]

Regulation in emergencies is the norm, not the exception. A unified effort to coordinate and cooperate takes place.[181] This appears to be the case in emergency situations ranging from wars to epidemics. It is the case with natural disasters such as earthquakes, floods, hail, wildfires, wind, hurricanes, tornadoes, and volcanic eruptions. It also holds for technological emergencies, including toxic chemical emissions and spills, massive power or water outages, telecommunications failures, explosions, airline crashes involving a large loss of life, terrorist attacks, fires, and wars.

In emergencies, destructive competition is avoided. Bids are not called for, and outsourcing is seldom contemplated. Contracting out is rare or nonexistent except when it is based on cooperative arrangements. This avoidance of destructive forms of competition should be and most often is the case at every level, from the individual to the group; the organization; the local community; local, state, and federal government; and the international level. It applies to emergencies that are both short and long term. Competitive approaches are employed only for the less critical aspects of emergency management, for example, those that do not put human life in immediate danger or those involving reconstruction and hazard assessment.

Where competition has been allowed to dominate emergency response, less-than-optimal outcomes can occur. This seems to be true whether the competition is between the private sector and the public sector or among public sector emergency responders. The interagency rivalry between the FBI and CIA is assumed to have been partly responsible for the failure of U.S. security systems to follow up appropriately to advance warnings in August 2001 of terrorist attacks employing aircraft as weapons.[182, 183] The fact that the New

York City fire and police departments had a long tradition of competing rather than cooperating made matters worse on September 11. "They did not work together that day, and they rarely did before."[184, p. A1] Feuding over which of the two should control emergency response led to tragic decisions to prohibit the police department's use of helicopters for rooftop rescue. Over the years, members of the press reported "repeated episodes of arguments, shoving matches, and even fist fights between personnel from the two services at emergency sites." The fire department did not have helicopters of its own, and it convinced the Port Authority of New York and New Jersey (the World Trade Center's owners) that the police department's efforts were merely dangerous, unnecessary, media-attention-grabbing grandstanding. They successfully argued that in the future "evacuations should be carried out by fire personnel from the ground. . . . The fire department, consistent with its focus on getting people to move down during fires, went along with the authority's policy of keeping the trade center roof exits locked." Circling helicopters on September 11 found no one on the roof to rescue.[185, p. A1]

A noncompetition approach to emergencies is not new but rather is grounded in historical experience. During World War II, the results of a cooperative approach were surprisingly positive. "The United States had wage and price controls, rationing, coerced savings, monopolistic military contracts, and a variety of other affronts to free-market pricing."[186, p. 24] There was massive state intervention throughout the economy, something entirely opposite to the approaches counseled by the competition paradigm. At the peak of World War II, "nearly 50 percent of production was in response to government procurement contracts."[186 p. 24] The government required contractors to subcontract and to cooperate with their usual competitors if they were unable, by themselves, to produce the optimal quantity of material needed for the war effort.

Under these conditions of heavy government regulation and obligatory private-sector participation in the economy, alien to the competition paradigm, the national standard of living improved, unemployment was reduced from 11 percent to full employment, and gross national product increased by nearly 50 percent.[187, ch. 6] There seems to be a consensus that includes some economists that "unified efforts to achieve clearly defined national goals are essential in times of war."[188, p. 321]

The private sector has a role to play in emergencies, though not that envisioned by the competition paradigm. The public sector participants have priority in the sense that they provide leadership and coordination.[189] The public sector is not expected to compete with the private sector. It is almost an indication that a problem is serious when the federal government assumes the principal role.[190] Private-sector agencies assist government, as do not-for-profit volunteer organizations, such as the International Red Cross. These volunteers and associated private agencies cooperate with local groups and national authorities rather than work on their own. In addition, in the postemergency planning process, the aid of private for-profit industry representatives is solicited because they are often essential in an emergency. Chemical and construction industry representatives are examples because they provide equipment and expertise in postdisaster cleanup. Private companies also increasingly play a role in disaster preparedness.[191, pp. 322–25] In California, large private-sector employers are involved in employee education and training for an earthquake emergency. As another example, the Federal Emergency Management Agency implemented a plan to encourage private-sector participation in damage control after natural disasters. The Pharmaceutical Research and Manufacturers of America took responsibility for distributing Centers for Disease Control and Prevention materials about anthrax to doctors in the wake of the mail containment in late 2001 in the United States.[192] Private companies cease to function as expected by the competition paradigm in emergencies. They set aside their self-interest to assist in resolving these crises. For example, the industrial capacity of General Motors was used to build tanks and trucks in World War II; no passenger cars were produced.

Patterns of public responsibility in periods of crisis are evident, to varying degrees, in all countries.[193] Still, the United States is more likely to include the private sector (usually private not-for-profit and voluntary organizations) in disaster response than are other countries, such as Japan and Italy.[194, p. 343, 195, 196]

Even many of those committed to the competition paradigm grant that natural hazards are not handled well by market forces. In such events, the interest of society as a whole is at stake, and it is difficult for an individual competitor to derive profits from providing the service or product in any case. Early warning about the adverse affects of El Niño is a concrete example. Assessment of a threat to the earth from possible collision with an asteroid is another example.[190, 197–199] Sandra Sutphen, California State University professor of political science and an expert in the field of emergency management, suggests that "markets will not always perform in the best interest of the community and . . . simple, inexpensive mitigation on the part of the public sector is most effective."[200, p. 1]

In emergencies, cooperation, not competition, takes over almost spontaneously, sometimes even among those divided by serious differences. This is because cooperation is more effective than competition in emergencies. For example, in the case of health epidemics (for example, cholera, meningitis, and malaria), cooperation among countries and their representative agencies is the norm, sometimes even when the countries involved are bitter enemies.[201] During the 1999 earthquake disaster in Turkey, assistance from

Greece—Turkey's historical enemy—surprised experts. This coming together in the form of spontaneous cooperation did not happen, however, with neighboring Armenia, also a historical enemy.[202] In the case of the Egypt Air crash in 1999, there was cooperation right from the beginning between the U.S. National Transportation Safety Board and Egypt despite fundamental differences between the two countries as to the suspected cause of the crash.[203]

In general, while cooperation between enemies is observed in times of emergency, clear lines of authority are essential for efficiency. The early investigation of the 1996 crash of TWA flight 800 is testimony to what takes place in the absence of a single authority assuming direction.[204] The bitter quarrels and between-agency espionage made for chaos and disarray, speculation, and counterproductive competition for information, thus jeopardizing discovery of why the crash occurred.[204]

Without cooperation and coordination, failure to adequately deal with emergencies is common. In fact, the absence of a coordinated, closely organized, noncompetitive approach is an indication of a less-than-optimal response. There was no organized, planned crisis management center in the aftermath of the 1999 earthquake in Turkey to coordinate the relief effort. This meant that "tens of thousands of volunteers from around Turkey arrived ... outnumbering residents and promptly creating bedlam. . . . The utter chaos of Turkey's rescue and relief effort is making things much worse. . . . International relief workers arrived from Israel, Russia and Western Europe, but found no one to give them any clear orders or supply translators."[205, pp. A1, A10] Volunteers and volunteer groups are sometimes more of a problem than an asset in the absence of centralized coordination.[191, p. 71]

Setting aside competition and instead planning systemically and consciously organizing means avoiding waste and duplication. "Someone working independently must spend time and skill on problems that already have been encountered and overcome by someone else."[206, p. 61] Without coordination and cooperation, an effective division of labor that saves time and resources fails to be developed.[207] Planning and cooperation are widely supported, in opposition to the competition paradigm, because the potential consequences of emergency situations are so great.[197] All of this concerns societies, nations, and cultures as much as it does organizations.

In short, competition's impact on organizations and the organizational response to avoid competition is global in the sense of being all-encompassing. At the same time, it is global in the geographic sense. This global competitive environment has an impact at the local, national, and international levels. Global markets make for a more competitive environment today. Easier international transportation of goods and the more rapid diffusion of technology have encouraged the expansion of global competition.[208] The excessively high levels of competition experienced by firms, companies, and enterprises may be due to the need to compete globally.[209, 210] Failing to meet this challenge, according to the competition paradigm, would be a recipe for disaster. But rising to the occasion may have equally dire consequences in the long run. These topics are explored in the next chapter.

Notes

1. Burke, T, Genn-Bash A, Haines B. *Competition in Theory and Practice.* London: Routledge; 1991.

2. Bryant, A. All for One, One for All and Every Man for Himself. *New York Times* (February 22, 1998) sec. 4, p. 6.

3. Eichenwald, K. Clues to Sentencing Mystery in the Archer Daniels Case. *New York Times* (July 13, 1999) C2.

4. Eichenwald, K. Three Sentenced in Archer Daniels Midland Case. *New York Times* (July 10, 1999) C1.

5. Simmons, CH, King CS, Tucker SS, Wehner EA. Success Strategies: Winning through Cooperation or Competition. *Journal of Social Psychology* 1986; 126:437–44.

6. Simmons, CH, Wehner EA, Tucker SS, King CS. The Cooperative/Competitive Strategy Scale: A Measure of Motivation to Use Cooperative or Competitive Strategies for Success. *Journal of Social Psychology* 1988;128:199–205.

7. Hogarth, RM, Einhorn HJ. Venture Theory: A Model of Decision Weights. *Management Science* 1990;36(7):780–803.

8. Smithson, M. Conflict Aversion: Preference for Ambiguity vs. Conflict in Sources and Evidence. *Organizational Behavior and Human Decision Processes* 1999;79(3):179–98.

9. King, CS, Simmons CH, Welch ST, Shimezu H. Cooperative, Competitive and Avoidance Strategies: A Comparison of Japanese and United States Motivations. *Journal of Social Behavior and Personality* 1995;10(3):807–16.

10. Ouchi, WG. *Theory Z: How American Business Can Meet the Japanese Challenge.* Reading, MA: Addison-Wesley Publishing Company; 1981.

11. Connor, RA, Feldman RD, Dowd BE, Radcliff TA. Which Types of Hospital Mergers Save Consumers Money? *Health Affairs* 1997;16(6):62–74.

12. Taylor, A. Is Jack Smith the Man to Fix GM? *Fortune* (August 3, 1998) 86–92.

13. Baron, R. Annual Report—Baron Funds 1998. New York: Baron Funds; 1998. p. 38.

14. Edgeworth, FY. *Mathematical Physics.* London: Kegan-Paul; 1881.

15. Marshall, A. *Principles of Economics.* 8th ed. London: Macmillan; 1920 (1890).

16. Bohm-Bawerk, E. *Positive Theory of Capital.* South Holland, IL: Libertarian Press; 1959 (1889).

17. Knight, FH. *Risk, Uncertainty and Profit.* Boston: Houghton Mifflin Company; 1921.

18. Clark, JM. *Studies in the Economics of Overhead Costs*. Chicago: University of Chicago Press; 1923.

19. Shellenbarger, S. Companies Are Finding It Really Pays to Be Nice to Employees. *Wall Street Journal* (July 22, 1998) B1.

20. Smith, KG, Grimm CM, Gannon MJ. *Dynamics of Competitive Strategy*. Newbury Park, CA: Sage Publications; 1992.

21. Bettis, RA, Weeks D. Financial Returns and Strategic Interactions: The Case of Instant Photography. *Strategic Management Journal* 1987;8:549–63.

22. Telser, LG. *A Theory of Efficient Cooperation and Competition*. Cambridge, U.K.: Cambridge University Press; 1987.

23. Hirschman, AO. *Exit, Voice, and Loyalty*. Cambridge, MA: Harvard University Press; 1970.

24. KPMG. Unlocking Shareholder Value: The Keys to Success. KPMG; 1999; at www.us.kpmg.com (accessed January 2, 2000).

25. Byrns, RT, Stone GW. *Microeconomics*. 6th ed. New York: HarperCollins College Publishers; 1995.

26. Danzon, PM, Boothman LG, Greenberg PE. Consolidation and Restructuring: The Next Step in Managed Care. *Health Care Management: State of the Art Reviews* 1995;2(1):221–35.

27. Guernsey, L. Gates Advocates Competition, but He Has His Doubters. *New York Times* (November 16, 1999) C2.

28. Scherer, FM. *Industrial Market Structure and Economic Performance*. 2nd ed. Boston: Houghton Mifflin Company; 1980.

29. Dreazen, YJ, Ip G, Kulish N. Big Business: Why the Sudden Rise in the Urge to Merge and Form Oligopolies? *Wall Street Journal* (February 25, 2002) A1, A10.

30. Sherer, PM. The Lessons from Chrysler, Citicorp and Mobil: No Companies Nowadays Are Too Big to Merge. *Wall Street Journal* (January 4, 1999) R8.

31. Holson, LM. Magnetic Mania: In This Merged World, Anything Goes. *New York Times* (June 26, 1998) C1, 4.

32. Frank, RH. A Merger's Message: Dominate or Die. *New York Times* (January 11, 2000) Op-ed.

33. D'Aveni, RA, Gunther R. *Hypercompetitive Rivalries: Competing in Highly Dynamic Environments*. New York: Free Press; 1995.

34. Gruley, B. A Free Hand: Why Laissez Faire Is the Washington Line on Telecom Mergers. *Wall Street Journal* (May 10, 1999) A1, A8.

35. Zuckerman, L. A New Math: Fewer Airlines + Higher Profits = More Competition. *New York Times* (June 22, 2000) 1, 8, Business.

36. Scherer, FM, Ross D. *Industrial Market Structure and Economic Performance*. 3rd ed. Boston: Houghton Mifflin Company; 1990.

37. Capon, N. Product Life Cycle. Boston: Harvard Business School; 1978.

38. Rosenau, PV. Market Structure and Performance: Evaluating the U.S. Health System Reform. *Journal of Health and Social Policy* 2001;13(1):41–72.

39. McDowell, E. 3 Airlines Reverse Course on Raising Fares, for Now. *New York Times* (November 30, 1999) C2.

40. Mobley, LR. Tacit Collusion among Hospitals in Price Competitive Markets. *Health Economics* 1996;5(3):183–93.

41. McCartney, S. Ticket Shock: Business Fares Increase Even as Leisure Travel Keeps Getting Cheaper. *Wall Street Journal* (November 3, 1997) A1, A6.

42. Fligstein, N. *The Transformation of Corporate Control.* Cambridge, MA: Harvard University Press; 1990.

43. Bradsher, K. Industry's Giants Are Carving Up World Market. *New York Times* (May 8, 1998) Business 1, 4.

44. Varian, HR. Economic Scene: When Commerce Moves Online, Competition Can Work in Strange Ways. *New York Times* (August 24, 2000) C2.

45. *The Economist.* Finance and Economics: J. P. Morgan's Uncertain Future. *The Economist* (February 14, 1998) 71–73.

46. Hambrick, DC, D'Aveni RA. Large Corporate Failures as Downward Spirals. *Administrative Science Quarterly* 1988;33(March):1–23.

47. Passell, P. When Mega-Mergers Are Mega Busts. *New York Times* (May 17, 1998) 18, Week in Review.

48. Samuelson, PA, Nordhaus WD. *Economics.* 12th ed. New York: McGraw-Hill Book Company; 1985.

49. Stiglitz, J. *Economics of the Public Sector.* New York: W. W. Norton & Company; 1986.

50. Machalaba, D, Mathews AW. Shipper Demands More Railroad Competition. *Wall Street Journal* (April 5, 1999) A2, A6.

51. Wessel, D, Harwood J. Capitalism Is Giddy with Triumph: Is It Possible to Overdo It? *Wall Street Journal* (May 14, 1998) A1, A10.

52. Young, S, Dreazen YJ, Blumenstein R. Familiar Ring: How Effort to Open Local Phone Markets Helped the Baby Bells. *Wall Street Journal* (February 11, 2002) A1, A14.

53. Schiesel, S. For Local Phone Users, Choice Isn't an Option. *New York Times* (November 21, 2000) A1.

54. Culbertson, JM. *Competition, Constructive and Destructive.* Madison, WI: Twenty-First Century Press; 1985.

55. Teisberg, EO, Porter ME, Brown GB. Making Competition in Health Care Work. *Harvard Business Review* 1994;(July–August):131–41.

56. Lohr, S. Paradox of the Internet Era: Behemoths in a Jack-Be-Nimble Economy. *New York Times* (September 12, 1999) 1, 6, Week in Review.

57. Lagnado, L. Personality Change: Old-Line Aetna Adopts Managed-Care Tactics and Stirs a Backlash. *Wall Street Journal* (July 29, 1998) A1, A6.

58. Freudenheim, M. Concern Rising about Mergers in Health Plans. *New York Times* (January 13, 1999) A1, C3.

59. Wilke, JR. FTC Weighs Stricter Policy on Mergers. *Wall Street Journal* (January 12, 2000) A3.

60. Labaton, S. Despite a Tough Stance or Two, White House Is Still Consolidation Friendly. *New York Times* (November 8, 1999) A22.

61. Perine, K. Mylan Faces Charge of Trade Restraint. *Wall Street Journal* (December 22, 1998) A3, A10.

62. Fleming, C. Sofia's Choice: Water Business Is Hot as More Cities Decide to Tap Private Sector. *Wall Street Journal* (November 9, 1998) A1, A15.

63. Ingersoll, B. Major Airlines Attack Clinton's Plan to Push Competition at Hub Airports. *Wall Street Journal* (June 19, 1998) A16.

64. Gaynor, M, Haas-Wilson D. Change, Consolidation, and Competition in Health Care Markets. *Journal of Economic Perspectives* 1999;13(1):141–64.

65. Hays, CL. When Your Bottler Is Your Rival: Vending-Machine Owners Ask Whose Side Coke Is On. *New York Times* (January 21, 1999) C1, C6.

66. Carroll, GR, Hannan MT, editors. *Organizations in Industry: Strategy, Structure, and Selection.* New York: Oxford University Press; 1995.

67. Hannan, MT, Freeman J. *Organizational Ecology.* Cambridge, MA: Harvard University Press; 1989.

68. Hannan, MT, Carroll GR. *Dynamics of Organizational Populations: Density, Legitimation, and Competition.* New York: Oxford University Press; 1992.

69. Thurow, L. *Head to Head: The Coming Battle among Japan, Europe and America.* New York: Morrow; 1992.

70. Tergesen, A. A Small Drug Maker in a Low-Risk Niche. *New York Times* (September 13, 1998) sec. 3, p. 5.

71. Anonymous. Productline Marketing: Respite Care Services. *The Home Advantage* 1999;5(1):405.

72. Milstein, S. New Economy: Many Midsize Companies Find That "Defensive Publishing" Is a Quick and Cheap Way to Protect Intellectual Property. *New York Times* (February 18, 2002) C3.

73. *The Economist.* Here, There and Everywhere. *The Economist* (June 24, 2000) 91–92.

74. Weinstein, MM. Rewriting the Book on Capitalism: Now Cooperative Innovation Steals Competition's Thunder. *New York Times* (June 5, 1999) A17, A19.

75. Baumol, WJ, Blinder AS. *Economics: Principles and Policies.* New York: Harcourt Brace College Publishers; 1999.

76. Hall, BH, Ziedonis RH. The Patent Paradox Revisited: An Empirical Study of Patenting in the U.S. Semiconductor Industry, 1979–1995. *Rand Journal of Economics* 2001;32(1):101–28.

77. *The Economist.* Patently Absurd? *The Economist Technology Quarterly* (June 23, 2001) 40–42.

78. Hershey, RD. Users Fear Higher Costs and a Loss of Competition. *New York Times* (April 7, 1998) C9.

79. Gomes, L. Economists Debate Merits of Microsoft Breakup Plan. *Wall Street Journal* (May 1, 2000) A8.

80. Lowenstein, R. Antitrust Enforcers Drop the Ideology, Focus on Economics. *Wall Street Journal* (February 27, 1997) A1, A8.

81. Sanger, DE. From Trust Busters to Trust Trusters. *New York Times* (December 6, 1998) 1, 4, Week in Review.

82. Lipin, S. Corporations' Dreams Converge in One Idea: It's Time to Do a Deal—Merger Wave Gathers Force as Strategies Demand Buying or Being Bought—"You Need to Be a Gorilla." *Wall Street Journal* (February 26, 1997) A1, A12.

83. Wilke, JR, Bank D. Microsoft Is Found to Be Predatory Monopolist. *Wall Street Journal* (November 8, 1999) A3.

84. Clark, D. Portrait of a Monopolist: Threats, Profits and Power. *Wall Street Journal* (November 8, 1999) A30.

85. Wilke, JR. New Antitrust Rules May Ease Path to Mergers. *Wall Street Journal* (April 9, 1997) A3, A4.

86. Deogun, N, Raghavan A. Antitrust Enforcers' Actions on Mergers Chill Wall Street. *Wall Street Journal* (September 6, 2000) C1.

87. Labaton, S. The World Gets Tough on Price Fixers: With Consumers Pinched at Every Turn, U.S. Leads a Crackdown. *New York Times* (June 3, 2001) sec. 3, p. 1, 7, Money and Business.

88. Sorkin, AR. U.S. Businesses Often Turn to Europe for Antitrust Help. *New York Times* (June 19, 2001) A1, C4.

89. Evans, DS, Schmalensee R. Some Economic Aspects of Antitrust Analysis in Dynamically Competitive Industries. Report No. W8268. Cambridge, MA: National Bureau of Economic Research; 2001.

90. Wilke, JR, Gruley B. Merger Monitors: Acquisitions Can Mean Long-Lasting Scrutiny by Antitrust Agencies. *Wall Street Journal* (March 4, 1997) A1, A10.

91. Hellinger, FJ. Antitrust Enforcement in the Healthcare Industry: The Expanding Scope of State Activity. *Health Services Research* 1998;33(5, Pt. 2):1477–94.

92. Wilke, JR, McCartney S. American Airlines Secures Antitrust Win. *Wall Street Journal* (April 30, 2001) A3.

93. Peters, G. *American Public Policy.* New York: Chatham House Publishers; 1996.

94. Keller, JJ, Gruley B. Is a $50 Billion Merger What Deregulation Was Really All About? *Wall Street Journal* (May 28, 1997) A1, A6.

95. D'Aveni, RD. Waking up to the New Era of Hypercompetition. *The Washington Quarterly* 1998;21(1):183–95.

96. Petersen, M. Antitrust Scrutiny Ends Plans to Merge Accounting Firms. *New York Times* (February 14, 1998) A1, B2.

97. Mitchener, B, Hehir G. Europe May Foil 3-Way Aluminum Merger. *Wall Street Journal* (March 2, 2000) A18.

98. Cowell, A. Seeking a Common Rule Book for International Mergers. *New York Times* (January 28, 2001) 4, Business.

99. Andrews, EL. Europeans Have Deferred to U.S. in Microsoft Litigation. *New York Times* (November 10, 1999) C4.

100. Mitchener, B. Microsoft Takes Steps to Address Antitrust Complaints in Europe. *Wall Street Journal* (March 12, 2002) B7.

101. Mitchener, B. Standard Bearers: Increasingly, Rules of Global Economy Are Set in Brussels. *Wall Street Journal* (April 23, 2002) A1, A10.

102. Mitchener, B. U.S. Endorses a Global Approach to Antitrust. *Wall Street Journal* (September 15, 2000) A15.

103. Meller, P. Europe Plans Full Inquiry on G.E.-Honeywell Deal. *New York Times* (May 9, 2001) 1, Business.

104. Katona, G. *Price Control and Business.* Bloomington: Indiana University Press; 1946.

105. Lane, RE. *The Regulation of Businessmen: Social Conditions of Government Control.* New Haven, CT: Yale University Press; 1954.

106. Staw, BM, Szwajkowski E. The Scarcity-Munificence Component of Organizational Environments and the Commission of Illegal Acts. *Administrative Science Quarterly* 1975;20:345–54.

107. Clinard, MB, Yeager PC. *Corporate Crime.* New York: Free Press; 1980.

108. Bork, RH. *The Antitrust Paradox: A Policy at War with Itself.* New York: Free Press; 1995.

109. Anonymous. Measuring Competition within Markets: An Elusive Topic That Merits Discussion. *Health Care Financing and Organization: News & Progress (HCFO News & Progress)* 1997(March):1–3.

110. *The Economist.* The Trustbusters' New Tools. *The Economist* (May 2, 1998) 62–64.

111. Wilke, JR. Greenspan Questions Antitrust Efforts. *Wall Street Journal* (June 17, 1998) A1, A2.

112. Patel, K. *Health Care Politics and Policy in America.* Armonk, NY: M. E. Sharpe; 1995.

113. McCartney, S, Adair B. Merger Talk Fills Skies and Airline Regulators Have a Juggling Act. *Wall Street Journal* (June 8, 2000) A1, A16.

114. Zuckerman, L. States Threaten Airlines with Antitrust Steps. *New York Times* (July 25, 1998) 1, 14, Business.

115. Zuckerman, L. How the Antitrust Wars Wax and Wane. *New York Times* (April 11, 1998) A13, A15.

116. Lohr, S. Microsoft Case May Be Prelude to a Wider Antitrust Battle. *New York Times* (February 9, 1998) C1, C8.

117. Brandenburger, AM, Nalebuff BJ. *Co-opetition: 1. A Revolutionary Mindset That Redefines Competition and Cooperation; 2. The Game Theory Strategy That's Changing the Game of Business.* New York: Currency Doubleday; 1996.

118. Moore, JF. Predators and Prey: A New Ecology of Competition. *Harvard Business Review* 1993;71(May/June):75–68.

119. Wysocki, B. Cyberspace Inc.: More Companies Cut Risk by Collaborating with Their "Enemies." *Wall Street Journal* (January 31, 2000) A1, A10.

120. Hicks, A, Kenworthy L. Cooperation and Political Economic Performance in Affluent Democratic Capitalism. *American Journal of Sociology* 1998;103(6):1631–72.

121. Markoff, J. Rival to Make $150 Million Investment. *New York Times* (August 7, 1997) A1, C6.

122. Zuckerman, L. Computer Industry in the Apple Camp. *New York Times* (August 7, 1997) 1, 7, Business.

123. Lohr, S. Jobs's Team and Name Are on the Line. *New York Times* (August 7, 1997) 1, 7, Business.

124. Dyer, JH. How Chrysler Created an American Keiretsu. *Harvard Business Review* 1996;74:42–56.

125. Fruin, WM, Nishiguchi T. Supplying the Toyota Production System: Intercorporate Organizational Evolution and Supplier Subsystems. In: Kogut B, editor. *Country Competitiveness: Technology and the Organizing of Work.* New York: Oxford University Press; 1993. p. 225–48.

126. Ball, J. To Define Future Car, GM, Toyota Say Bigger Is Better. *Wall Street Journal* (April 20, 1999) B4.

127. Langreth, R, Waldholz M, Moore SD. DNA Dreams: Big Drug Firms Discuss Linking up to Pursue Disease-Causing Genes. *Wall Street Journal* (March 4, 1999) A1, A6.

128. White, JB. Business Plan: Big Employers Are Starting to Design Their Own Report Cards on Competing HMOs. *Wall Street Journal* (October 19, 1998) R18, Health and Medicine.

129. Markoff, J. Rivals Cooperate on Chip Equipment. *New York Times* (December 12, 2000) A1.

130. Group of Lisbon. *Limits to Competition.* Cambridge, MA: MIT Press; 1995.

131. Herrigel, G. Large Firms, Small Firms, and the Governance of Flexible Specialization: The Case of Baden Wurttemberg and Socialized Risk. In: Kogut B, editor. *Country Competitiveness: Technology and the Organizing of Work.* New York: Oxford University Press; 1993.

132. Frank, RH, Cook PJ. *The Winner-Take-All Society: Why the Few at the Top Get So Much More Than the Rest of Us.* New York: Free Press; 1995.

133. MacStravic, S. Market Memo: Price Wars Are No-Win Games for Health Care Systems. *Health Care Strategic Management* 1996;14(5):1, 19–23.

134. Frantz, D, Blumenthal R, Vogel C. Ex-Leaders of 2 Auction Giants Are Said to Initiate Price-Fixing. *New York Times* (April 7, 2000) A1, C2.

135. Meller, P. Vitamin Producers Fined $752 Million. *New York Times* (November 22, 2001) W1, W7.

136. Moore, SD. Vitamin Makers Still Face EU Objections. *Wall Street Journal* (October 12, 2000) B5.

137. Marquis, C. Four Drug Companies to Pay $33 Million in Fines. *New York Times* (May 6, 2000) B2.

138. Wilke, JR. U.S. Probes whether Big Banks Stifled Rival in Currency Trading. *Wall Street Journal* (May 15, 2002) A1, A4.

139. Barboza, D. Tearing Down the Facade of "Vitamins Inc." *New York Times* (October 10, 1999) B1, B11.

140. Axelrod, R, Mitchell W, Thomas RE, Bennett DS, Bruderer E. Coalition Formation in Standard-Setting Alliances. *Management Science* 1995;41(September):1493–508.

141. Labaton, S. As Competition Heats Up, So Does the Treatment of Collusion. *New York Times* (October 25, 2000) H22.

142. Slade, M. When Competitors Are Partners, How Bare Do They Dare? *New York Times* (October 25, 2000) H24.

143. Coile, R. Concentration, Co-opetition, Consumerism . . . and Seven More "C's." *The Healthcare Strategist* 1998;2(1):1–6.

144. Cummings, J, Hamburger T. Enron's Washington Clout before Collapse Draws Scrutiny. *Wall Street Journal* (January 15, 2002) A18.

145. Schroeder, M, Ip G. Out of Reach: The Enron Debacle Spotlights Huge Void in Financial Regulation. *Wall Street Journal* (December 13, 2001) A1, A6.

146. Eichenwald, K. Audacious Climb to Success Ended in a Dizzying Plunge. *New York Times* (January 13, 2002) 1, 26.

147. Wayne, L. Enron, Preaching Deregulation, Worked the Statehouse Circuit. *New York Times* (February 9, 2002) B1, B5.

148. Wessel, D. Capital: The Market Demands Rules. *Wall Street Journal* (November 29, 2001) A1.

149. Smith, R. Gloom and Doom: New Rules, Demands Put Dangerous Strain on Electricity Supply. *Wall Street Journal* (May 11, 2000) A1, A8.

150. Smith, R, Emshwiller JR. Down to the Wire: Why California Isn't the Only Place Bracing for Electrical Shocks. *Wall Street Journal* (April 26, 2001) A1.

151. Tolchin, SJ, Tolchin M. *Dismantling America.* Boston: Houghton Mifflin Company; 1983.

152. Nutting, R. The Sky Is Falling: Soros, Gramlich Call for IMF Repairs. CBS MarketWatch; 1998.

153. Oster, C. States Seek Insurance Regulations. *Wall Street Journal* (June 10, 2002) C12.

154. Salpukas, A. Subsidizing Competition in Utilities. *New York Times* (February 1, 1997) A19.

155. Vogel, SK. *Freer Markets, More Rules: Regulatory Reform in Advanced Industrial Countries.* Ithaca, NY: Cornell University Press; 1996.

156. Berenson, A. Deregulation: A Movement Groping in the Dark. *New York Times* (February 4, 2001) sec. 4, p. 6.

157. *The Economist.* The Hidden Cost of Red Tape. *The Economist* (July 27, 1996) 13.

158. Stigler, GJ. The Theory of Economic Regulation. *Bell Journal of Economics and Management Science* 1971;2:3–21.

159. Weinstein, MM. Rebates Could Smooth the Way for a Medicare Reform Plan. *New York Times* (September 23, 1999) C2.

160. Lagnado, L. New York's Hospitals Merge, Cut and Fret as Deregulation Nears. *Wall Street Journal* (October 25, 1996) A1, A6.

161. Rosenbaum, DE. Corporate Welfare's New Enemies. *New York Times* (February 2, 1997) sec. 4, p. 1, 6.

162. *The Economist.* Transatlantic Trade: Testing Times. *The Economist* (January 19, 2002) 60.

163. McKinnon, JD. Exporters Fear Loss of Subsidy. *Wall Street Journal* (May 1, 2002) A2, A4.

164. Antosh, N. Farmers Groups File Lawsuit to Block New Milk Pricing Plan. *Houston Chronicle* (September 16, 1999) 2, Business.

165. Fligstein, N. Markets as Politics: A Political-Cultural Approach to Market Institutions. *American Sociological Review* 1996;61(August):656–73.

166. Simon, B. Using Tariffs to Discourage Movie Production outside U.S. *New York Times* (March 29, 2002) W1.

167. Reitman, V. Toyota Eases Export Throttle as Trade Tensions with U.S. Rise. *Wall Street Journal* (November 22, 1996) A12.

168. Greenberger, RS. Clinton Administration Considers Plan to Restrict Flood of Steel to U.S. *Wall Street Journal* (December 1, 1998) A4.

169. Matthews, RG, King N Jr. Breathing Room: Imposing Steel Tariffs, Bush Buys Some Time for Troubled Industry. *Wall Street Journal* (March 6, 2002) A1, A8.

170. King, N, Jr., Baghole J. Canada to Join Nations Challenging U.S. Trade Moves. *Wall Street Journal* (March 25, 2002) A2.

171. Simon, B. U.S. Will Impose 29% Tariff on Canada Building Lumber. *New York Times* (March 23, 2002) B2.

172. King, N, Jr., Zaun T. Japan Joins Forces with the EU, Escalating Steel Spat with U.S. *Wall Street Journal* (May 17, 2002) A1, A7.

173. King, N, Jr., Matthews RG. America Feels Pain of Tariffs on Steel Imports. *Wall Street Journal* (May 31, 2002) A2, A5.

174. Friedland, J. U.S., Mexico Closing in on a Telephone Deal. *Wall Street Journal* (July 16, 1998) A12.

175. Reich, RB. Bailout: A Comparative Study in Law and Industrial Structure. In: Spence AM, Hazard HA, editors. *International Competitiveness*. Cambridge, MA: Ballinger Publishing Company; 1988. p. 301–60.

176. Rogers, D. UPS Scores a Victory, as House Panel Blocks Postal Service's Growth Overseas. *New York Times* (July 30, 1997) A3.

177. Norris, F. Does the U.S. Still Trust Markets to Work? *New York Times* (October 25, 2001) C1, C8.

178. Schlesinger, JM. Possible Paths: The Embrace of Capitalism Could Be Just Beginning—Or Disappear in the Next Recession. A Case Can Be Made for Both. *Wall Street Journal* (September 27, 1999) R23.

179. Labaton, S. Bush Advisers Press for Help for Insurers. *New York Times* (October 25, 2001) 1, 7, Business.

180. Hitt, G, Cummings J. Reregulation: Terror Attack Reverses a Two-Decade Drive to Shrink Government. *Wall Street Journal* (September 26, 2001) A1, A8.

181. Gorman, JW. The Private Sector's Involvement in Preparedness Response, Recovery, and Mitigation. Paper presented at the 1997 Annual Hazards Research and Applications Workshop; July 1997; Denver, CO.

182. Van Natta, D Jr., Johnston D. Wary of Risk, Slow to Adapt, F.B.I. Stumbles in Terror War. *New York Times* (June 2, 2002) A1, A24–A25.

183. Risen, J. C.I.A. and F.B.I. Agree to Truce in War of Leaks vs. Counterleaks. *New York Times* (June 14, 2002) A1, A23.

184. Dwyer, J, Flynn K, Fessenden F. 9/11 Exposed Deadly Flaws in Rescue Plan. *New York Times* (July 7, 2002) A1.

185. Paltrow, SJ, Kim QS. No Escape: Could Helicopters Have Saved People from Trade Center? *Wall Street Journal* (October 23, 2001) A1, A14.

186. Kuttner, R. *Everything for Sale: The Virtues and Limits of Markets*. New York: Alfred A. Knopf; 1997.

187. Wilkinson, R. *Unhealthy Societies: The Afflictions of Inequality*. London: Routledge; 1996.

188. Scherer, FM, editor. *Monopoly and Competition Policy*. Aldershot, U.K.: Edward Elgar Publishing Company; 1993;Vol. 1.

189. Anonymous. The Private Sector's Involvement in Preparedness Response, Recovery, and Mitigation; 1997.

190. Broad, WJ. For Killer Asteroids, Respect at Last. *New York Times* (May 14, 1996) B5, B9.

191. Drabek, TE, Hoetmer GJ, editors. *Emergency Management: Principles and Practice for Local Government*. Washington, DC: International City Management Association; 1991.

192. Reuters. A Nation Challenged: The Bioterror Threat; Drug Makers to Help U.S. Inform Doctors. *New York Times* (April 12, 2002).

193. Mileti, DS, Drabek TE, Haas JE. *Human Systems in Extreme Environments.* Boulder: Institute of Behavioral Science, University of Colorado; 1975.

194. Drabek, TE. *Human System Responses to Disaster: An Inventory of Sociological Findings.* New York: Springer-Verlag; 1986.

195. McLuckie, BF. A Study of Functional Response to Stress in Three Societies. Dissertation. Columbus: Ohio State University; 1970.

196. Mileti, DS, Hutton JR, Sorensen JH. *Earthquake Prediction Response and Options for Public Policy.* Boulder: Institute of Behavioral Science, University of Colorado; 1981.

197. Browne, MW. Asteroid Is Expected to Make a Pass Close to Earth in 2028. *New York Times* (March 12, 1998) A1, A15.

198. Mallon, T. Coming! The Asteroids Are Coming. *New York Times Magazine* (July 28, 1996) 17–19.

199. Broad, WJ. New Asteroid That May Threaten Earth Is Found. *New York Times* (February 8, 2000) 16, col. 4.

200. Frame, D. The Economics of Disaster Management. Paper presented at the 1998 Annual Hazards Research and Applications Workshop; July 1998; Boulder, CO.

201. Samba, EM. Initiative: Great Lakes. *UN Chronicle* 1997;34(4):49.

202. Kinzer, S. A Natural Disaster Helps Draw Two Enemies Closer. *New York Times* (August 22, 1999) sec. 4, p. 3.

203. Revkin, A, Wald ML. Split over T.W.A. Crash's Cause Widens as the Inquiry Continues. *New York Times* (October 13, 1996) sec. 1, p. 1, 19.

204. Sexton, J. Daily Assurances Belie Chaos of Crash Inquiry. *New York Times* (August 23, 1996) A1, A14.

205. Andrews, E. Quake Victims Confront Chaos of Relief Effort. *New York Times* (August 20, 1999) A1, A10.

206. Kohn, A. *No Contest: The Case against Competition.* Boston: Houghton Mifflin Company; 1992.

207. Deutsch, M. *The Resolution of Conflict: Constructive and Destructive Processes.* New Haven, CT: Yale University Press; 1973.

208. Hamel, G, Prahalad CK. Strategic Intent. *Harvard Business Review* 1989;67(May–June 1989):63–76.

209. Levine, HZ. The View from the Board: The State of Compensation and Benefits Today. *Compensation & Benefits Review* 1992;24(2):24–29.

210. Cappelli, P. Rethinking Employment. *British Journal of Industrial Relations* 1995;33(December):563–602.

6

The High Cost of Competition at the Global Level for Society, Nation, and Culture

THIS CHAPTER SHOWS THAT SOME societies and cultures are extremely successful regarding the much-sought-after national competitiveness characteristic, while others are less so. Though competitiveness is not a fixed characteristic of nations, the most competitive countries tend to remain so year after year. The benefits are known, and the competition paradigm speaks to these. The costs of destructive competition at the national and global levels are generally ignored or sometimes perhaps simply unknown. The question is, Do they compromise productivity? Coming out on top, winning in the context between nations to be the most competitive, is never an unqualified victory because of the divisions that emerge and are reinforced over time at the local, national, and international levels by destructive competition. In the next-to-last section of this chapter, the self-reinforcing spiral of competition at the societal level is examined, and the gap between the rich and the poor, within and between nations, is found to be increasing. Countries are coming to be either consistent winners or chronic losers, as is the case so often at the individual, group, and organizational levels.[1] Finally, the advisability of America's sharing of its competition paradigm with other countries is critically examined.

Defining competitiveness at the level of the society, nation, or culture is difficult because there is no overall agreement as to meaning. Nation, society, and culture are not the same—they are, however, all elements in a macrolevel analysis, and this is why they are considered together here and why for stylistic reasons these terms are used almost interchangeably. The only consensus among those who write about competitiveness at the global level is that it is multidimensional and that many indicators considered in isolation are inadequate.

Trade balance, budget deficits, cheap labor supply, and bountiful natural resources are all considered poor measures of competitiveness by themselves. Productivity is commonly assumed to be better than other indicators of national competitiveness.[2] The two international organizations that spend enormous resources ranking countries on competitiveness every year employ 200 or 300 indicators to measure it.[3, 4]

Much Stability and Some Change in National Competitiveness

Some nations, societies, and cultures emphasize competition more than others; it is, however, not a universal.[5, 6, p. 261] This appears to be the conclusion of much research, whether anthropologists or economists undertook the studies or whether the research methods were quantitative or qualitative. Among the most interesting research on this topic is Margaret Mead's 1930s observational study of thirteen groups of peoples living in remote locations, relatively untouched by modern societies. She observed that there are two basic societal orientations. The first is individualistic. It values private property for individual ends and has a single scale of success. The second is a cooperatively oriented culture where "social structure does not depend upon individual initiative or the exercise of power over persons." In the second case, much importance is attached to an ordered universe. Less significance is attributed to social mobility for status, and a high value is attributed to individual security.[7, p. 511]

Countries, societies, and cultures vary with regard to the level and type of competition and cooperation that is accepted as normal. For example, some countries (not the United States) have laws that require bystanders or witnesses at the scene of an accident to come to the aid of victims. Most societies exhibit a mix of both cooperative and competitive goal orientations, with one usually being more important than the other. The particular mix influences the culture and sets the tone for social interaction.[8] Psychologists and sociologists report important differences in national competitiveness based on observational studies.[9–12] Some researchers suggest, however, that differences across cultures are overestimated.[13] Studies indicate that there is often a wide range of individual differences within even the most homogeneous culture.

Many studies of relative societal competitiveness are based on the performance of individuals from different countries in a laboratory setting; overall findings as summarized by Alfie Kohn show that Americans are more competitive than citizens of other countries.[14, pp. 33–37] British adolescents are less competitive than Americans.[15] When already ahead in a game, Americans are more competitive than Belgians.[16, 17] Studies comparing Chinese and American children report that the Chinese are more equality and group oriented over the long run.[18] Japanese, more than Americans, have an aversion to individual competition.[19, p. 807] Japanese boys are still found to be very competitive,[20] though this is with regard to intergroup competition rather than intragroup competition.[19, 21] A case study indicates that Mexican children are less competitive than American children.[22] Anglo-American children are more competitive than Mexican American children.[23] Kibbutz children in Israel are more inclined to cooperate than are individuals who live in urban, Western cultures in general.[20, p. 40] Social loafing in situations requiring group responsibility for a task is greater for managerial trainees in the United States than for those in the People's Republic of China.[24] Social loafing refers to diminished individual performance in organizations where work is carried out in groups.

Consistency of research results across many studies over time suggests that there is some truth to the view that Americans are more competitive than others. However, the participants in all these studies are not statistically representative of the national groups from which they are drawn because they are not selected by random sampling. Therefore, generalizations to the whole society are tenuous.

Despite limitations, empirical indices have been developed to systematically measure differences between countries regarding competitiveness.[25] One of the earliest was that of Farmer and Richman, who evaluated and compared countries on what they call "constraints to internal managerial effectiveness." They used a Delphi technique to assess educational, sociological–cultural, legal–political, and economic-related constraints.[26] The Delphi technique is an anonymous process designed to elicit a group decision from experts through several iterations and controlled feedback.[27, p. v] The World Bank maintains a public database of forty-nine competitiveness indicators for more than 140 countries.[28] Competitiveness data categories include overall economic performance, macro and market dynamism, financial dynamism, infrastructure and investment climate, and human resources. The World Bank does not combine the various competitiveness indicators into a single competitiveness measure, though some of its data are employed by other organizations to construct such country competitiveness ratings.

The World Economic Forum of Geneva (WEF), a private Swiss organization created in 1971, has, since the late 1980s, issued an annual competitiveness country report. The Institute for Management Development (IMD), founded in 1987 and located in Lausanne, Switzerland, is the other important private not-for-profit competitiveness rating organization. Initially, the IMD and the WEF jointly published annual competitiveness ratings on countries of the world. In 1996, the two parted company, and now each issues its own competitiveness report with somewhat different rating criteria. The WEF and IMD competitiveness ratings are proprietary products developed for sale to countries and to investors.

Critics argue about the value of country competitiveness rankings. Some suggest that comparisons of countries as diverse as those existing in the world today are necessarily imprecise. Even within a country, there may be a great variation, depending on which economic sector is being considered. Few indicators are appropriate for all countries or all economic sectors within a country; no indicator is, in every sense, the "best" indicator.[29] Other critics point out that competitiveness is between industries and companies that operate in various countries rather than between the countries themselves.[30]

The WEF's competitiveness rankings were not developed for scholarly research; they are, however, used in this chapter to assess the costs and benefits of national competitiveness. These rankings are an important, though far from perfect, measure of the degree of the stability and change of economic competitiveness within the fifty to seventy-five countries ranked since 1996. The WEF's index includes a wide array of measures of economic policies and national institutional practices that are related to midterm (defined as five years) economic growth. It is a combination of the results of executive opinion surveys and quantitative statistics. The WEF's executive survey measures corporate business leaders' perceptions of a country's competitiveness. Over the years, the WEF has increasingly made an effort to choose a representative sampling of corporate chief executive officers and senior management to fill out its questionnaires about each country's competitiveness; 4,601 responded to the WEF's 2001 survey.[31] The executive survey plays an important role in the WEF's assessment of a country because the WEF has confidence in its use in assessing "intangibles" that statistics do not capture. The quantitative indicators that go into the WEF's country competitiveness rankings are drawn from a wide variety of sources, including the World Bank, the International Monetary Fund, the Heritage Foundation, the Organization for Economic Cooperation and Development (OECD), the Inter-American Development Bank, the International Telecommunications Union, UNESCO, and the World Telecommunications Indicators.[32, pp. 317–18]

The names of the component factors included in the WEF's national competitiveness rankings and even the name of the overall ranking index itself changes year to year, but the underlying variables measured remain much the same.[33, p. 19] In 1999, the WEF included eight factors in its competitiveness rankings: openness, government, finance, infrastructure, technology, management, labor, and institutions. In 2000, they were innovation, technology, finance, and internationalization. In 2001, the variables were technology, public institutions, and macroeconomic environment.[34, p. 32] Weights assigned factor to each depended on both intellectual assessment and empirical statistical analysis.[3, 35] In 2000, the role of variables that had accurately predicted competitive national success in the period from 1992 to 1999 were increased—these included technology. More countries were added to those being ranked in 2001, and countries were divided into either core countries or non–core countries for purposes of the ranking procedures.

For the first time, different weights were assigned to the variables that are used to calculate a country's ranking depending on the country's category. "Core" was defined as a country with fifteen patents per million population.[34, pp. 39–40]

The WEF's competitiveness ratings for nations, countries, and societies are not entirely stable.[36] A few countries show dramatic changes with regard to year-to-year competitiveness rankings. While WEF discourages cross-year comparisons, it is interesting to note that some countries have become less competitive across even the short time for which the WEF national competitiveness ratings are available. For example, New Zealand's position decreased seventeen ranks between 1996 and 2000. Between 1996 and 2001, Hungary improved eighteen ranks, and Ireland, Italy, and Finland each improved fifteen ranks.

However, on balance, differences in competitiveness ranking over time are not great for most OECD countries. The year-to-year correlation (Spearman's rho) for the WEF competitiveness rankings for twenty-nine OECD countries varied since 1996 between .90 and .97. The correlation across the entire six-year period for which rankings are available (1996 and 2001) was .82. Even substantial economic crises do not necessarily change a country's competitiveness. In 1999, the Asian financial crisis brought severe economic problems to this geographic area, but Singapore and Hong Kong remained at the top of the WEF's ratings between 1996 and 1999.[32] Using other non-WEF data sources, important variations within countries as to the competitiveness of certain groups and geographic areas have been observed.[37]

The Costs and Benefits of Competition for Society

Proponents of unrestricted competition indicate that the rewards associated with societal competitiveness are many—a higher standard of living, greater per capita revenue, investor confidence, a stable currency, and increased foreign investment. In this section, in sum, we will see that the picture is far more complicated. The competition paradigm is silent about the downside of national costs of destructive, zero-sum, intense forms of national competitiveness. In this section, we see that inequality within and between nations is one such consequence. Some scholars contend that there is a trade-off between national competitiveness and inequality both between and within countries, but others deny it. This section suggests that both groups may be right. It may be that when competition is moderate, there is little trade-off with equality (1930s–1980s). But when the competitive environment becomes very intense, as has been the case since the late 1980s, then increased national competitiveness may be at the price of increased inequality and its multiple consequences.

In the last half of this section, the increased inequality that comes with destructive competition is found to negatively affect population health. Intense competition directly or indirectly threatens social capital, reduces social cohesion, and undermines trust at the community level.[38, 39] If competition leads to greater inequality, it is also linked to serious negative social repercussions. It has distressing effects when it generates political unrest.

Competition and Societal Inequality in the Industrialized Countries

The relationship between national competitiveness and equality is enormously complex. In addition, national competitiveness has not been measured systematically until very recently, and a more complete picture requires a longer time frame. If economic growth can be used as a proxy for competitiveness, more can be said about this topic. Some economists suggest that those nations with the lowest levels of inequality are the more competitive. Wealthier nations have been more egalitarian than poor nations, and increased wealth has meant increased equality; income inequality was associated with low economic growth.[40] The same has been found true within countries across time.[41] Other economists suggest that the relationship depends on whether the country is already industrialized or developing: "Higher inequality tends to retard growth in poor countries and encourages growth in richer countries."[42, p. 5]

Kuznets[43] argues differently. He says that income inequality increases during early industrialization but that it decreases as countries achieve industrialization. In short, things get worse before they get better or inequality tapers off in the industrialized world. Aghion and colleagues disagree. They say that growth leads to sustained wage inequality in most situations. But inequality does not, in turn, increase growth. They argue that reducing inequality, over time and in a sustained fashion through government redistribution, can improve productivity and growth competitiveness even in developing countries if certain market conditions exist. This is because redistribution increases the incentives for the poor to raise their output.[44, 45] Jared Bernstein of the Economic Policy Institute suggests that inequality reduces national competitiveness. He says that if "inequality leads you to underinvest in the lives of the have-nots . . . then ultimately that can be a drag on economic growth."[46, p. 3] Michael Todaro makes the same case, suggesting that in poor countries the wealthiest sector of the population does not save and reinvest. He notes that the life conditions of the poor reduce the ability of this group to contribute to societal economic productivity. And he points out that increasing the income of the poor would stimulate demand and lead to growth.[47] Alesina and Rodrik report along the same lines that "inequality in income and land distribution is negatively associated with subsequent growth." Their study covers seventy countries for the period 1960–1985.[48, p. 485]

Many economists believe, however, that policies designed to increase equality necessarily reduce national competitiveness, especially in the developing

countries. Inequalities, they argue, are the price we pay for the benefits accruing from a free-market social system. Wealth inequality is said to enhance
growth.[49] This school of thought contends that there is a trade-off between inequality and competitiveness. Research by Partridge finds that inequality may
be good for growth.[50] Both Okun and Higgins contend that if a society wants
greater equality, it must necessarily accept lower economic efficiency.[51, 52]

Using the WEF's national competitiveness data and inequality assessments
from the Luxembourg Income Study, societal inequality among OECD nations does not appear, initially, to be related to competitiveness. GINI inequality scores measured in the 1990s for each OECD country were correlated
with WEF competitiveness scores and rankings for the years from 1996 to
2001.[3, 32, 53-55] The Luxembourg Income Study data are used here because of
the high quality of data and the fact that this organization carefully verifies
data from sources.[56] Competitiveness and inequality seem to be independent
of one another for all years in which there were data available to test this association. There is simply no statistically significant association between national competitiveness score and inequality (see figure 6.1 for an example).

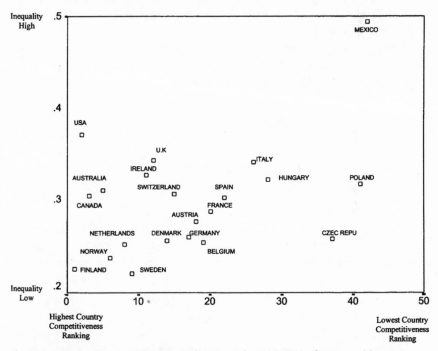

**Figure 6.1   Most Recent GINI Inequality Score by WEF Growth Competitiveness
Ranking 2001 for OECD Countries**
Note: Spearman's rho = .294 n.s.; *N* = 21.

The data needed to resolve the debate about the relationship between competitiveness and inequality, to establish the direction of casualty, and to make predictions for the future are not available. They will not be available for at least a decade, perhaps two. This is because establishing a causal connection would require comparing competitiveness ratings at one point in time and equality/inequality at a later, second point in time (five, ten, or fifteen years later). Competitiveness rankings have been calculated only since 1996; national inequality data are not made public promptly. Some countries have a policy of deliberately withholding national statistics on inequality. Japan, for example, releases inequality data only decades after they collect it. The results are then of interest more to historians than to anyone else.

Using the second-best data that are already available, it appears that increasing national competitiveness is associated with rising inequality in many of the highly industrialized OECD countries (figure 6.2). The GINI score for the mid-1980s for each country was subtracted from the most recent GINI score available from the Luxembourg Income Study data bank for the same country (see appendix 1).[54] It is plotted on the x-axis. Spain has no GINI score posted with the Luxembourg Income Study since 1990, and therefore it is not included. Changes in each country's WEF competitiveness rankings are indicated on the y-axis.

Observing that increases in national competitiveness are commonly observed in countries that have recently experienced increased GINI inequality scores is important but is also limited. It says little about a causal connection.

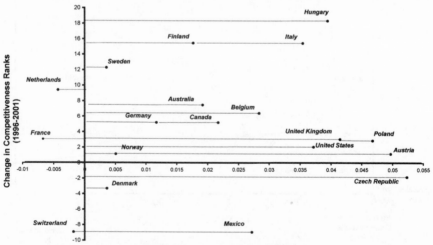

Figure 6.2   Change in Inequality by Change in National Competitiveness
Note: See appendix 1 for figure 6.2 data.

It does not prove that national competitiveness leads to inequality or vice versa. In addition, because inequality data were not available on the Luxembourg Income Study's web page for several OECD countries, the number of country cases is reduced.

Despite the limitations in these data, it is still important to ask whether there is some substance to the worry that there is a trade-off between inequality and competitiveness. From figure 6.2, it appears that the vast majority of OECD countries experienced both increasing inequality and improved national competitiveness rankings over time. Among these OECD countries, however, it cannot be said that a trade-off between national competitiveness and inequality is inevitable. There are a few cases where, as inequality is reduced, competitiveness rises. This is what has happened to France and the Netherlands. But it is also possible for inequality to increase and competitiveness to decline. This has happened in the Czech Republic and Mexico and, to a far lesser degree, Denmark. The reasons behind each of these patterns are specific to the country, its context, and its history.

Inequality Is on the Increase: Is Too Much Competition Part of the Problem?

The theories about a trade-off between equality and national competitiveness are important because there is little doubt that inequality is increasing in most Western industrialized countries, in the developing countries, and between rich and poor nations as well.[57] The fact that the industrialized countries, assumed to be immune to rising inequality, are also experiencing this trend is a surprise. In addition, the "gap between rich and poor is greater in the U.S.A. than any other industrial nation with the possible exception of Russia."[58, p. 3B]

The poor in many countries are actually earning more today than in the past. But this fact does not mean that inequality is declining. The poor can earn more and inequality can still rise because the increases the poor experience are smaller than those of the wealthiest sectors of the populations.[59] This means that inequality—the ratio of the wealth going to the rich versus the poor—is still increasing.[60, 61] Since the 1970s, income differences between the rich and the poor in many OECD countries have skyrocketed.[62–71] This constitutes a marked change from the increasing equalization of income in the United States, for example, that began in the 1930s.[72] Wage differences among occupations in the United States also increased dramatically in the 1980s.[73] The U.S. Congressional Budget Office suggests that, after inflation adjustment, four out of five Americans earned a smaller share of the national wealth in the late 1990s than they did in the mid-1970s.[74]

The last half of the 1990s was a period of high economic growth, low inflation, and low unemployment in the United States. Yet the gap between the rich and the poor failed to diminish in all but five states, even in this period of extraordinary prosperity.[75-77] The percentage of working Americans that fall below the poverty line did not decline.[78] The very poor saw their median income and net worth fall between 1995 and 1998.[46, 79, p. A10] The rise in inequality paused briefly in the late 1990s, but the gap between rich and poor is once again on the rise.[80]

This trend of increasing inequality has been documented not just in the United States but in most of the OECD countries as well.[45, 81, 82] European countries saw a larger portion of their populations living in poverty in 1985 than in 1975. France, Greece, Belgium, and West Germany were exceptions until the mid-1990s.[39, p. 77] Figure 6.2 confirms that the preponderance of OECD countries has experienced increasing inequality during the period between the mid-1980s and the mid- to late 1990s.[54]

What is true at the individual level holds for the national level as well.[83] Convergence theories that posited that the productivity differences between the rich and poor countries would diminish have not proven true in the 1990s.[84] Income inequality among countries is on the increase worldwide.[85-89] Poor countries are losing ground relative to richer countries. This trend has been in evidence for at least two decades, though it seems to be accelerating now.[85, 90, 91] While World Bank analysts argue that growth means that everyone benefits from "seeing their incomes rise simultaneously at about the same rate"[92, p. 82] and indeed while the poor countries are doing better than ever before, the disparity between the developed and the Third World countries continues to rise. The ratio was about eight to one in 1977. Today, some sources say that it is close to thirty to one, while others suggest that it is thirty-seven times higher.[93, p. 73, 94]

The exact cause of the epidemic of increasing inequality observed within modern industrialized nations and between rich and poor countries is not known. But destructive forms of national and international competition may account for it, at least in part.[95] Richard Freeman, professor of economics at Harvard University, was quoted in the New York Times as suggesting that "there is little doubt that market forces have spoken in favor of more inequality."[96, p. A17]

The purpose here is not to argue that destructive competition is the sole cause of increasing inequality in the developing countries. Scholars have suggested many reasons for increased wealth or income inequality both within countries and between nations, though few of these explanations are independent of competition. Some such variables include demographic changes,[97] economic restructurings,[72] changes in taxation policy,[98] modifications in political institutions, poor educational systems,[96] monetary policies,[99] shifts in capital/labor relations,[100] fast-moving advances in technology,[101] deunionization,[102, 103] and the process of globalization itself.[104] The effects of all these variables are consistent with those anticipated by the competition paradigm. In some cases, they may even work together in a synergistic fashion. For example, competition is increasingly intense because modern communications technology permits price and quantity information—comparative cost and price structure—to be transmitted around the world in an instant.

Resolving Different Interpretations: A Hypothesis

The possibility of a trade-off between inequality and national competitiveness cannot be rejected. But different time frames (see table 6.1) may be partly responsible for the diverging scholarly research results discussed previously.

Competition and equality may be related such that, in general, moderate levels of competition among nations are benign, while higher levels and destructive forms of competition negatively affect equality. If this hypothesis holds true, then it is unlikely that a higher national competitiveness score would have been associated with increased inequality within a country prior to the 1990s. Historically, national competitiveness has been linked to increased equality, higher rates of growth, and a positive trade balance.[45, 48] From the 1960s through the 1980s, countries with many industries practicing internal cooperation and societal neocorporatism experienced higher societal economic performance (measured by lower inflation, higher investment, increased gross domestic product, and improved trade balance) than did those that did not encourage such cooperative practices.[105] In many cases, increased conformity to the assumptions of today's competition paradigm was accompanied by reduced productivity and slowed growth in gross national product.[106, p. 23] During periods of more moderate global competition, increased inequality may not have been the price paid for national competitiveness.

TABLE 6.1
How Might the Global Context Influence the Relationship between
Equality and National Competitiveness Rankings?

In a Moderately Competitive Context (1965–1985), Constructive Forms of Competition Are Common	In a Highly Competitive Context (1990s), Destructive Forms of Competition Are Common
No trade-off:	Trade-off theory applies:
• Declining equality does not inevitably improve national competitiveness • Increased equality does not inevitably reduce national competitiveness	• Increased equality reduces national competitiveness • Declining equality increases national competitiveness

Any trade-off between inequality and competitiveness has been most evident since 1990, when destructive competition, within nations and globally, has become widespread. Today, "the new global world is dominated by the logic of economic warfare"[1, p. 49]; very few countries have been able to increase their competitiveness rankings without simultaneously increasing inequality. Phillippe Aghion and his colleagues suggest that when competition is low or moderate, increasing competition accelerates growth. But if the level of competition is already high, then increasing it further may retard growth.[107, 108]

In sum, these results call into question the all-too-easy assumption, implicit in the competition paradigm, as to the benign character of extreme competition for individual countries and the global family of nations. The possible association between increasing competitiveness and increasing inequality constitutes an important cost of destructive competition. This trade-off may not be required when competition is more restrained, as has been the case in the past.

Destructive Competition and Societal Inequality Have Population Health Consequences

If increases in national competitiveness during periods of intense global competition are related to higher inequality, then distinct population health costs result.[109] This is because increases in inequality are bad for one's health, not just at the individual level, as observed in preceding chapters, but at the societal level as well.[110] These negative health effects are cumulative over time. The "health effects of sustained economic hardship . . . have potentially important implications for public health, health care, and economic policy."[111, p. 1894] The effects are increased societal health care costs and lower societal productivity. For example, the fact that the Japanese have among the best health outcomes and the lowest health care costs of any industrialized country has been attributed to many things, including a diet high in fish. But it may also be the result of the "economic equality between social classes, and perhaps other factors such as job security."[81, p. 789]

Inequality is linked to increased morbidity and mortality at the individual level.[39, 112] People with inequality-generated disadvantage, real or perceived, are more likely to have poorer physical well-being, reduced psychological health, and problems with cognitive function. However, they are less likely to receive needed health care.[111, p. 1894] A number of studies suggest that the rich have better health outcomes than the poor across a range of morbidity measures, including coronary artery disease,[113] infant mortality,[114] and exposure to environmental hazards.[115] The relationship between health and inequality holds for the young and for adults.[116–118] In addition, inequality itself is correlated with higher mortality, even after controlling for other factors.[119, 120]

These same negative effects of inequality on health are apparent at the global level. The very poorest countries have the highest infant mortality rates, while the wealthiest countries have the lowest.[121] Though the exact mechanisms underlying these relationships are not known, the findings have held up across countries and over time.[39, 122–127] Studies suggest that the health status of the population (as measured by life expectancy) predicts subsequent national economic growth.[128] At the same time, rapid economic growth is no guarantee of improved population health. It may even increase disparities between the rich and poor regarding health.[129] While of greatest relevance for the developing countries, even with the wealthiest of countries, such as the United States, the effect of wealth or health is apparent for different geographic areas.[119]

Some societies seem to moderate or escape the effects of income inequality on health. In the United States, income inequality is closely linked to health as measured by mortality. But in Canada, between the mid-1970s and the mid-1990s, there was no relationship between health and inequality at the provincial or the metropolitan level. This difference between the United States and Canada is thought to be due to the fact that resources such as health care and quality education in Canada are publicly funded and available to all. In the United States, they are distributed as a result of competitive success, on the basis of the ability to pay.[130] It could also be because the absolute level of inequality is much lower in Canada (GINI .291 in 1997) than in the United States (GINI .372 in 1997). In Denmark as well, policies appear to moderate the influence of inequality on health.[131]

While the poor suffer the effects of inequality most, in the end the health consequences of inequality influence everyone in a society. Countries that pursue policies to reduce inequality appear to improve population health and lower mortality rates, not just for the poor but for the wealthiest as well.[114, 132, pp. 35–36, 133] In short, all benefit if inequality is reduced. This is discussed further in chapter 8, where policy solutions to destructive competition are considered.

Sometimes the connections between competition and reduced population health link microindividual experience to macrosocietal outcomes.[134] For example, intense competition supports an employment environment characterized by corporate downsizing, high job turnover, and unemployment (discussed in chapter 4) that is detrimental to population health. Employers push employees to work as hard as possible, but intense competition means that these companies are not always able to increase pay commensurate with employee effort. This results in a large gap between on-the-job effort and reward, which in turn leads to poor health.[135]

There is good reason to suspect that destructive competition increases population-level health problems. For example, as the United States has become more competitive, inequality has risen and access to health care declined.[136]

Forty-four million Americans had no health insurance in the late 1990s.[137] Lack of health insurance is linked to poor health.[138] Life expectancy is higher in countries such as Greece, Japan, Iceland, and Italy than it is in wealthier countries such as the United States and Germany,[139] and all except the United States have near-universal health insurance.[140] While it may be pure coincidence, it is interesting to note that the United States and Germany are ranked higher on national competitiveness than Greece, Japan, Iceland, and Italy.[35]

Some scholars question whether there is a relationship between inequality and health,[141, 142] but none of the debates on these matters reduces the worry that destructive competition is costly for society. The disagreements are about whether it is poverty or class rather than inequity that leads to poor population health.[143, pp. 65-68, 144] Or some researchers find that it is income level rather than inequality that leads to poor health.[145] On the other hand, it may be the lack of education[146] that is really important regarding health outcomes. Still others report that in the developed countries, it is relative rather than absolute inequality that is the problem.[147-149] Destructive competition is likely to make each of these scenarios worse no matter what the exact nature of the linkage.

Even those who argue that competition increases growth, which in turn reduces poverty by making more jobs and therefore improves population health in the long term, ground their analysis on a tenuous assumption that this book challenges, namely, that all forms of competition are the same and that they are benign. Constructive competition and destructive competition yield different results.

Anecdotes, observations, and associations are not a demonstration of cause, and they must be used with caution. The arguments presented here are suggestive. They generate hypotheses but prove little. But the purpose is not to argue that competition is the only cause of differences in health status via inequality. In fact, a range of factors are probably involved.[125, 150] But to overlook the possibility that destructive forms of competition play a role is to minimize the cost of the competition paradigm to society. It is also to ignore an aspect of the problem that can be changed through explicit policy intervention as is explained in the conclusion of this book.

Intense Competition Jeopardizes Trust and Social Capital in the Community and Society

The competition paradigm does not speak to the value of social capital and trust as societal assets. They are, however, essential to the maintenance of community life and to the context in which business itself is conducted. To the extent that destructive competition threatens social capital, it may reduce economic growth and, ironically in the long run, even national competitiveness.

"Social capital of the right sort boosts economic efficiency, so that if our networks of reciprocity deepen, we all benefit, and if they atrophy, we all pay dearly."[64, p. 325] Social capital is a synthesis of theoretical concepts from the fields of sociology and economics. It is basically a synonym for social connections. It "refers to features of social organizations such as networks, norms, and social trust that facilitate coordination and cooperation for mutual benefit."[64, 151, p. 67] Reciprocity, trust, and mutual aid are all part of social capital.[152] It is a basic human resource consisting of "obligations and expectations, information channels, and social norms."[153, pp. S95–S105, S118]

Social capital is developed in certain situations more easily than in others. Most of the time, social capital has a public good, public spirit quality about it. Families, schools, places of employment, communities, churches, social clubs, and so on are all institutions where social capital may or may not reside, depending on the circumstances. The community, rather than any specific individual, benefits from social capital. This may be why it is so difficult to develop and maintain social capital in highly individualistic societies.[154, p. 167]

The idea of interpersonal trust is central to social capital.[155–158] Trust involves two dimensions: "Trusting behavior is the willingness to risk beneficial or harmful consequences by making oneself vulnerable to another person. Trustworthy behavior is the willingness to respond to another person's risk-taking in a way that ensures that the other person will experience beneficial consequences."[159, p. 54] It "enhances individuals' willingness to engage in various forms of spontaneous sociability, but in complex and often unexpected ways."[160, p. 584] It is as important at the national and global levels as it is at the organizational level (discussed in chapter 4).

Living in a trusting community has positive life consequences. Social capital, interpersonal trust, and social cohesion mediate between inequality and health discussed previously.[161] They are correlated with lower mortality rates[162] and reductions in crime and delinquency.[163, 164] Social trust within a group or community is essential if that group or community is to be productive and attain its goals.[165] "Healthy, egalitarian countries have—or had— a sense of social cohesion and public spiritedness. Social rather than market values remained dominant in the public sphere of life."[39]

Social bonds, trust, and social capital are less vulnerable in societies where there is a sharp distinction between what is acceptable competition and what is unacceptable competition. Fair, constructive, and appropriate competition does not result in a decline of social capital and reduced trust, as would intense interpersonal or zero-sum competition.[166] Research on individuals indicates that "trust tends to be developed and maintained in cooperative situations and it tends to be absent and destroyed in competitive and individualistic situations."[159, p. 53] Experimental research suggests that a "strategy of mutual problem solving and the tactics of persuasion, openness, and mutual enhancement" associated with a cooperative orientation can create an environment where constructive competition is possible.[167, p. 365]

Social capital and trust in turn facilitate constructive competition, and business can benefit.[168, p. 23] The norms of business and all human interaction, even competition in sports encounters, require a measure of basic trust among participants. Trust is necessary for successful trade, for commercial relations between a corporation and its subcontractors, and between a business and its customers.[169] Property rights, the rule of law, and the enforceability of contracts are required for a favorable business investment climate and economic growth. Trust functions to reduce transaction costs within organizations at the national level and in global trade.

The fair exchange of goods does not jeopardize social capital; destructive competition does so. When the business environment becomes so intensely competitive that it requires an emphasis on strategies of power and the tactics of coercion, threat, and deception, there is little place for trust. Studies show that emphasis on "winning and losing and the self interest implied by that orientation" reduce trust.[170, pp. 84–85] Social capital suffers. Relationships are more hierarchical, and dominance of one over the other is the goal. This jeopardizes rather than reinforces social capital, with its requirements for an environment of reciprocity, social support, mutual sharing, and recognition of the needs of others.

Where social capital and trust are on the decline, the positive business atmosphere it supports is also in jeopardy.[158, 171, 172] The U.S. experience illustrates how the loss of trust can interrupt market relationships. The United States has the largest stock market in the world. The percentage of its citizens who have invested in the stock market is greater than that of Europe or Japan. Historically, and especially in the 1990s, investors from abroad sought to invest in the United States because of its reputation for strength, integrity, and stability. The U.S. economy benefited because this ensured access to low-cost capital. But when investors lose confidence in audits, fair account keeping, and business integrity, the environment for investing is in jeopardy.[173–175] Enron, WorldCom, and so many other companies brought distrust to the entire business community. Arthur Andersen brought scrutiny to all accounting firms with its invention of "aggressive accounting."[176] In short, a few corporate entities can destroy trust associated with social capital across a broad spectrum.

Reductions in social capital and trust may be due, in part, to the exaggerated levels of competitiveness in U.S. society. Social surveys document the increasing social isolation and the reductions in a sense of civic commitment that accompany lower levels of social capital in America today.[177] The role played by competitiveness is subtle and indirect in its effects. For example, across the whole society, the heightened employment mobility required of workers in a highly competitive economy may lead to weaker community ties. When on-the-job competition makes for less time at home, the social capital accruing from participation in parent–teacher associations, civic organizations, and church-related activities is diminished.[64, 151]

Naturally occurring experiments at the societal level provide evidence pertinent for studying the relationship between competition and social capital. The breakup of the Soviet Union constitutes one example of such an experiment. Throughout Eastern Europe, the transition from the Soviet-style bureaucratic state (with its low levels of competition) to today's high levels of market competition has resulted in decreased social capital and increased social pathology.[178] Destructive forms of competition developed in the 1990s. Social capital was jeopardized as an environment of alienation and powerlessness resulted.

In the context of destructive, zero-sum competition in Eastern Europe and Russia, social capital was in jeopardy, and civil society was on the verge of breakdown. Increases in crime were evident. The human costs of the transition to market competition were unanticipated and very high.[179, p. III] Part of the problem was that the level of system change was so great, and the population was simply not prepared. Gabor Bojar, chief executive officer of Graphisoft in Budapest, observes that personal relationships and friendships declined in Hungary.[180] "Networks, norms, and trust . . . that facilitate coordination and cooperation for mutual benefit" disappeared.[181, p. 213] An environment of alienation and powerlessness resulted where people felt that they had lost control of their lives and social support diminished.[182] "After 1989, the twin ideologies of individualism and the free market gave those at the top license to abandon those at the bottom."[181, p. 214]

A naturally occurring experiment in the opposite direction, historical in nature, is equally informative. During World War II, Britain had almost no unemployment, and there was a high sense of social cohesion. Cooperation played more of a role as market competition gave way to rationing, price controls, and subsidies. Much the same situation existed during World War I. During these periods, life expectancy increased twice as fast as during other periods in the twentieth century.[39, pp. 113–16] This could be due to many factors, but the observed absence of destructive societal competition in these historical situations might well be associated with increased social capital and improved societal health status.

Competition, Inequality, and the Negative Social Environment

Too much competition makes life unpleasant for society as a whole. It is directly and indirectly linked to a depressing and harmful social environment.

Such environments include social breakdown in the form of regional economic impoverishment, community decline, weakened family life, societal malaise, and increased crime.[183] There is evidence, however, that only extreme forms of competition lead to desperation, hostility, and aggression.[184] Yet such problems do not develop only because of competition.

George Soros says that sometimes these negative consequences of destructive competition are indirect and mediated through inequality.[185] "Too much competition and too little cooperation can cause intolerable inequities and instability."[186, pp. 47–48] This linkage has been traced to the level of human psychology. Inequality is related to higher hostility scores on the Minnesota Multiphasic Personality Inventory. Hostility is in turn associated with poorer health and higher death rates.[187, 188, p. 62] It is also linked to high coronary–artery problems, even in young adults.[189] The links between inequality and negative life circumstances, such as chronic unemployment, increased rates of imprisonment, or doing without health insurance, have also been studied.[119]

Equality is central to the development and maintenance of civic community and the public sphere. Certain patterns of inequality are associated with a poor quality of social life, with political and social violence, and with rebellion.[154, p. 105, 190] These include violent demonstrations, assassinations, coups d'état, and civil outbreaks.[191–194] Edward Muller of the University of Arizona says that "high levels of income inequality are likely to produce either high levels of rebellious political conflict . . . or else the perception among elites of a threat of rebellious political conflict and lower-class revolution."[195, p. 647]

At the societal level, inequality increases poverty. Poverty, in turn, is associated with violence and crime,[148, pp. 299, 313, 188, 196, 197] at least for a minority of those who experience markedly diminished opportunities and increased frustration.[47, 88] Increased income inequality is correlated with high arrest rates.[190] The level of homicide is related to income inequality around the world.[188] A meta-analysis of thirty-four data-based studies confirms the link between income inequality and crime, especially regarding homicide and assault.[198]

Ironically, in the long run the negative social environment that results from destructive competition may reduce a country's productivity. "To the extent that people are busy either committing crimes or trying to avoid being victims of them, they are diverted from producing legitimate goods and services."[148, p. 24] High levels of violence and crime compromise the business environment.[199] In addition, societal resources must be spent on increased security staff, on home and business monitoring systems, and on the incarceration of 1.7 million Americans. "The lower the level of trust and co-operation, the more expensive it gets."[39, p. 229] Economists estimate that spending on antiterrorist security in the United States constitutes a measurable and continuing drag on the economy.[200, 201] Anthropologists have observed that nonviolent cultures place less emphasis on destructive competition.[5] A study of fifty-eight societies indicated that societal competitiveness is directly related to psychological distress and aggression.[202]

Where there are few limits to competition, people may feel they have no choice but to pursue self-interest without regard to the consequences, especially if survival is at stake. In these cases, the weak often pay the cost. For example, an increase in destructive forms of market competition in Eastern Europe and Russia had an especially negative impact on women and children.[203] Women experienced increased unemployment, less economic independence, lower wages, poorer health outcomes, and fewer social services. They suffered higher levels of rape, prostitution, and domestic violence, concurrent with the rise of destructive forms of competition. Women and children lost many of their equity-based gains.[204]

As indicated at the beginning of this section, advocates for increasing national competitiveness point to the advantages. But any gains have to be balanced by taking into account the distribution of benefits across the population. None of these gains are necessarily an assurance of long-term success in the form of high productivity, a stable and healthy quality of life, or a civil society in which to live and raise one's children. And investors are fickle. Currencies inevitably move up and down across time. A high competitiveness ranking is no guarantee of a positive social environment.

The whole world is being brought into one global market. The no-holds-barred forms of competition central to the competition paradigm are the means; a little-regulated environment is the context. Effects are felt around the world right down to the individual worker in the industrialized countries who has experienced a decline in benefits and working conditions as part of a worldwide leveling process. The question remains, Do the costs of the competition paradigm at the global level outweigh the benefits? The answer is that constructive and appropriate competition might improve overall societal productivity if it simultaneously makes for lower inequality, improved levels of trust, increased social capital, and a more positive, less violent and hostile global environment. This challenge is discussed in chapters 7 and 8. But the assessment of the competition paradigm at the global level must first be concluded in the remainder of this chapter.

A Spiral of Self-Reinforcing Destructive Competition at the Societal Level

Competition increases inequality at the individual level,[51] and it appears to do the same between geographic regions within a country at the global level.[180] Poor countries become poorer and the better-off countries even wealthier; inequality among nations increases.[67] The self-reinforcing spiral of competition still applies, and the stakes are just as great.[1] Over time, the worry is that a permanently deprived and underproductive group of nations, societies, or regions could develop and divisions increase.[205] No matter which geographic unit is analyzed, the result is the same: a global society where the value of less intensive constructive competition may be forgotten, where the merit of cooperation is less appreciated.

The dynamics that drive the self-reinforcing spiral of destructive competition include psychological uncertainty, the economics of selective investment, and the politics of managing civil unrest. Nations that compete, as with individuals, groups, and organizations, start out with very different resources. Initial distributions matter, and economic growth will be more favorable to the poor if that distribution is more equal.[206] But the already existing allocation of resources is almost always a taken-for-granted characteristic with the poor at a substantial disadvantage. This means that the growth associated with intense global competition is likely to augment inequality.[207]

How it appears to play out is reviewed based on the previously presented dynamic. The self-reinforcing spiral of destructive competition at the societal level increases inequality within and between those countries that lose out. Internal domestic discontent, political violence, and social unrest tend to rise in these areas. This social instability leads to increased uncertainty regarding the political system, property rights, and the legal environment. Nations that lose out will subsequently be disadvantaged further by these recurring higher levels of uncertainty and lower levels of investment, escalating debt, lower productivity, and lower growth.[3, 208, 209] A study of seventy-one countries provides evidence of a vicious circle involving civic unrest that leads to reduced investment that in turn generates more unrest.[210, 211, p. 383] The risk is that the poorest countries will receive even less investment and therefore will be less competitive in the future and less able to compete effectively.[45, 61] The stability of national competitiveness rankings observed and described at the beginning of this chapter may be the result of a self-reinforcing spiral of competition at the societal level. It is very possible that the relative rankings remain the same as the distance between the rich countries and poor countries widens.

As explained previously, population health is another element in the spiral of competition. Poverty leads to inadequate food, which leads to increased disease.[39] Economic growth in developing countries and the increased national competitiveness that attracts investors can increase health disparities in the population.[129, 212] The vicious spiral influencing a country's health and disease pattern can, in turn, improve or detract from long-term economic productivity and growth by 30 to 40 percent.[213]

For example, the wealthy citizens in a country are more likely to be able to purchase medication and have access to medical care that remains unavailable to those who lose out in competitive processes. This is already occurring. Since the 1980s in Africa, fifty million people have contracted HIV/AIDS, and half have died of it.[214] In May 2000, pharmaceutical companies moved to reduce the price of AIDS medication[215, 216] prompted by President Bill Clinton's executive order indicating that patents on AIDS drugs would not be enforced in sub-Saharan Africa. George W. Bush continued the same policy. Still, existing inequality between the rich and poor nations means that the vast majority of AIDS victims in Africa will likely go untreated for many years to come.[217–222]

Regarding health, in the future the wealthiest individuals and nations are more likely than the poor to be able to afford the most sophisticated medical technologies and gene therapies for diseases such as cancer. Pharmaceuticals will be prepared somewhat differently for each individual. These "designer drugs" on the horizon have the potential to do enormous good—but only to those who have the means to purchase them. Reproductive technologies in the not-so-distant future will ensure healthier, brighter, and more handsome children—but again, only for those who have the ability to pay for these technologies. The competitive advantages, the unequal starting point for future competition, could then be passed on from generation to generation, within and among countries, even more than they are today. This would add another layer to the self-reinforcing spiral of competition, enlarging still further initial differences between competitors before the race even begins.

Going Global: Sharing an Inadequate Paradigm

The competition paradigm has now gone global. Few countries are able to disregard the recommendations inherent in it. Sharing this paradigm has become a dangerous preoccupation. However, even when the best intentions are at work, pressuring other nations, societies, and cultures to conform to paradigmatic expectations may not produce the expected changes. Experiments with increased competition often collide with societal values and thus fail. Despite broad forces for cultural homogenization around the world, value differences persist and influence the extent to which the competition paradigm can be shared.[223]

The competition paradigm does not work across the board for all economic sectors in every country. Intense competition is, for example, inappropriate where cost reduction is not the only goal, such as in the health sector.[224] In other cases, the problems may be too complex for the simple solution of more competition. To insist on it could be misguided. It is counterproductive if it increases resentment and a feeling that the United States aims to transmit not only the competition paradigm but also the value system that goes with the paradigm.[225, 226]

As Stephane Garelli of the Institute for Management Development states, in many places "the critical element in competitiveness is not found by designing competitive policies but, rather, by determining the social costs acceptable to a nation."[227, p. 7] In some cases, the programs central to the competition paradigm are politically untenable. As pointed out previously, France and the Netherlands have managed to increase their competitiveness rankings without compromising equality (see figure 6.2), thus suggesting that this is still an option. As with most industrialized countries today, these countries are making concessions to the competition paradigm, seeking to increase competitiveness ranking while at the same time pursuing policies that will not dramatically reduce equality. Labor protection laws, as in the United States and Great Britain,[228] have been sacrificed to achieve increased competitiveness. The pressure on other countries is considerable. Most have increased their competitiveness and at the same time tolerated substantial increases in inequality, but this is not the only cost.

Following the U.S. example, complying with the competition paradigm often means embracing job insecurity, lower job mobility, wage stagnation, increased individual responsibility, constrained job market mobility, corporate restructuring, and increased opportunity through risk.[229] And adopting the competition paradigm is required if a country seeks to secure the confidence of the international business community and have access to the financial investments that accompany that confidence. Countries that reject the competition paradigm find that doing so translates into ensuring employment stability, retaining unemployment benefits, maintaining wage levels, and keeping basic safety-net measures.[230] In most of Europe, ambivalence remains, if not on the part of the economic policymakers, then at least for a substantial portion of the population.[231, 232]

Overall, at the level of society, nation, and culture, there were few holdouts regarding destructive forms of competition in the 1990s. However, mechanically following the U.S. model was less in evidence after the corporate scandals of 2001–2002.[233, 234] Japanese corporations, among the last to embrace the competition paradigm, abandoned centuries of traditional organizational experience.[21] They deregulated, outsourced,[235] initiated American-style stock options for workers, and implemented incentive pay schemes for executives.[236] The Japanese reorganized their educational system along the lines of the U.S. example.[237] And even in the European Union, proposals from some sectors of the business community for economic liberalization and radical restructuring of the energy, transportation, communications, and financial markets in the direction endorsed by the competition paradigm are common.[238, 239]

Many questions regarding the competition paradigm remain unanswered. They require looking back, taking a retrospective view to better understand why the paradigm has prevailed. They also demand an appraisal of the future to ascertain the potential for paradigm change. These issues are the focus of chapter 7.

Notes

1. Group of Lisbon. *Limits to Competition.* Cambridge, MA: MIT Press; 1995.
2. Porter, ME. *On Competition.* Cambridge, MA: Harvard Business School Publishing; 1998.
3. World Economic Forum. *The Global Competitiveness Report 1999.* New York: Oxford University Press; 1999.
4. International Institute for Management Development. *The World Competitiveness Yearbook 2002.* Lausanne, Switzerland: International Institute for Management Development; 2002.
5. Bonta, BD. Cooperation and Competition in Peaceful Societies. *Psychological Bulletin* 1997;121(2):299–320.
6. Bethlehem, DW. Anthropological and Cross-Cultural Perspectives. In: Colman AM, editor. *Cooperation and Competition in Humans and Animals.* Wokingham, U.K.: Van Nostrand Reinhold; 1982.
7. Mead, M. *Cooperation and Competition among Primitive Peoples.* New York: McGraw-Hill; 1936.
8. Tjosvold, D. Power in Cooperative and Competitive Organizational Contexts. *Journal of Social Psychology* 1990;130(2):249–58.
9. McClintock, CG, Moskowitz JM. Children's Preferences for Individualistic Cooperative and Competitive Outcomes. *Journal of Personality and Social Psychology* 1976;34:643–555.
10. McClintock, CG, Moskowitz JM, McClintock E. Variations in Preferences for Individualistic, Competitive and Cooperative Outcomes as a Function of Age, Game Class and Task in Nursery School Children. *Child Development* 1977;48:1080–85.
11. McClintock, CG, Nuttin J. Development of Competitive Game Behavior in Children across Two Cultures. *Journal of Experimental Social Psychology* 1969;5:203–18.
12. Toda, M, Shinotsuka H, McClintock CG, Stech FJ. Development of Competitive Behavior as a Function of Culture, Age, and Social Comparison. *Journal of Personality and Social Psychology* 1978;36(8):825–39.
13. Lucas, JR, Stone GL. Acculturation and Competition among Mexican-Americans: A Reconceptualization. *Hispanic Journal of Behavioral Sciences* 1994;16(2):129–42.
14. Kohn, A. *No Contest: The Case against Competition.* Boston: Houghton Mifflin Company; 1992.
15. Furnham, A. The Determinants and Structure of Adolescents' Beliefs about the Economy. *Journal of Adolescence* 1987;10:353–71.
16. McClintock, CG, McNeel SP. Societal Membership, Score Status, and Game Behavior: A Phenomenological Analysis. *International Journal of Psychology* 1966; 4:263–72.

17. McClintock, CG, McNeel CP. Cross-Cultural Comparisons of Interpersonal Motives. *Sociometry* 1966;29:406–27.

18. Domino, G. Cooperation and Competition in Chinese and American Children. *Journal of Cross-Cultural Psychology* 1992;23(4):456–67.

19. King, CS, Simmons CH, Welch ST, Shimezu H. Cooperative, Competitive and Avoidance Strategies: A Comparison of Japanese and United States Motivations. *Journal of Social Behavior and Personality* 1995;10(3):807–16.

20. Pepitone, EA. *Children in Cooperation and Competition: Toward a Developmental Social Psychology.* Lexington, MA: Lexington Books; 1980.

21. Ouchi, WG. *Theory Z: How American Business Can Meet the Japanese Challenge.* Reading, MA: Addison-Wesley Publishing Company; 1981.

22. Madsen, MC. Developmental and Cross-Cultural Differences in the Cooperative and Competitive Behavior of Young Children. *Journal of Cross-Cultural Psychology* 1971;2:365–71.

23. McClintock, CG. Development of Social Motives in Anglo-American and Mexican-American Children. *Journal of Personality and Social Psychology* 1974;29:348–54.

24. Earley, PC. Social Loafing and Collectivism: A Comparison of the United States and the People's Republic of China. *Administrative Science Quarterly* 1989;34:565–81.

25. Passell, P. A New Rating of Economies Holds Some Surprises. *New York Times* (June 6, 1996) C2.

26. Farmer, RN, Richman BM. *Comparative Management and Economic Progress.* Homewood, IL: R. D. Irwin; 1965.

27. Dalkey, NC. The Delphi Method: An Experimental Study of Group Opinion. Santa Monica, CA: Rand; 1969.

28. World Bank. *World Development Indicators 1999.* Washington, DC: World Bank; 1999.

29. Marsh, IW, Tokarick SP. Competitiveness Indicators—A Theoretical and Empirical Assessment. Washington, DC: International Monetary Fund; 1994.

30. Dundass, RE. Just How Competitive Are We? *The Herald* (May 31, 1996) 24.

31. Cornelius, PK, McArthur JW. The Executive Opinion Survey. In: Schawab K, Porter ME, Sachs JD, editors. *The Global Competitiveness Report 2001–2002.* New York: Oxford University Press; 2002. p. 166–77.

32. World Economic Forum. *The Global Competitiveness Report 1998.* Geneva, Switzerland: World Economic Forum; 1998.

33. Porter, ME, Sachs JD, McArthur JW. Executive Summary: Competitiveness and Stages of Economic Development. In: Schwab K, Porter ME, Sachs JD, editors. *The Global Competitiveness Report 2001–2002.* New York: Oxford University Press; 2002. p. 16–25.

34. McArthur, JW, Sachs JD. The Growth Competitiveness Index: Measuring Technological Advancement and the Stages of Development. In: Schwab K, Porter ME, Sachs JD, editors. *The Global Competitiveness Report 2001–2002.* New York: Oxford University Press; 2002. p. 28–51.

35. World Economic Forum. *The Global Competitiveness Report 2001–2002.* New York: Oxford University Press; 2001.

36. Hui, CH, Triandis HC. Individualism-Collectivism: A Study of Cross-Cultural Researchers. *Journal of Cross-Cultural Psychology* 1986;17(2):225–48.

37. Thomas, DR. Cooperation and Competition among Polynesian and European Children. *Child Development* 1975;46:948–53.

38. Muntaner, C, Lynch J. Income Inequality, Social Cohesion, and Class Relations: A Critique of Wilkinson's Neo-Durkheimian Research Program. *International Journal of Health Services* 1999;29(1):59–81.

39. Wilkinson, R. *Unhealthy Societies: The Afflictions of Inequality.* London: Routledge; 1996.

40. Glyn, A, Miliband D, editors. *Paying for Inequality: The Economic Cost of Social Injustice.* London: Rivers Oram; 1994.

41. Corry, D, Glyn A. The Macroeconomics of Equality, Stability, and Growth. In: Glyn A, Miliband D, editors. *Paying for Inequality: The Economic Cost of Social Injustice.* London: Rivers Oram; 1994.

42. Barro, RJ. Inequality and Growth in a Panel of Countries. *Journal of Economic Growth* 2000;5:5–32.

43. Kuznets, S. Quantitative Aspects of the Economic Growth of Nations: VIII. Distribution of Income by Size. *Economic Development and Cultural Change* 1963;XI(2, Pt. II):1–80.

44. Aghion, P, Howitt P. *Endogenous Growth Theory.* Cambridge, MA: MIT Press; 1998.

45. Aghion, P, Caroli E, Garcia-Penalosa C. Inequality and Economic Growth: The Perspective of the New Growth Theories. *Journal of Economic Literature* 1999;37(December):1615–60.

46. Stevenson, RW. In a Time of Plenty, the Poor Are Still Poor. *New York Times* (January 23, 2000) 3, Week in Review.

47. Todaro, MP. *Economic Development.* 6th ed. New York: Addison-Wesley Publishing Company; 1997.

48. Alesina, A, Rodrik D. Distributive Politics and Economic Growth. *The Quarterly Journal of Economics* 1994;CIX(2):465–85.

49. Okun, A. *Equity and Efficiency: The Big Tradeoff.* Washington, DC: Brookings Institution Press; 1975.

50. Partridge, MD. Is Inequality Harmful for Growth? Comment. *The American Economic Review* 1997;87(5):1019–32.

51. Okun, AM. *Equality and Efficiency: The Big Tradeoff.* Washington, DC: Brookings Institution Press; 1975.

52. Higgins, B. Equity and Efficiency in Development. In: Savoice DJ, Breecher I, editors. *Equality and Efficiency in Economic Development.* London: Intermediate Technology Publications; 1992.

53. Havemann, J. U.S. Falls to Fifth on List of Best Competitors. *Los Angeles Times* (June 22, 1992) Business D1, col. 5, Financial Desk.

54. Luxembourg Income Study. LIS Information Server: Income Inequality Measures. Luxembourg: Luxembourg Income Study; updated November 26, 2001; at www.lisproject.org/keyfigures/ineqtable.htm (accessed May 23, 2002).

55. World Economic Forum. *The Global Competitiveness Report 2000*. New York: Oxford University Press; 2000.

56. Smeeding, TM, O'Higgins M, Rainwater L, editors. *Poverty, Inequality, and Income Distribution in Comparative Perspective: The Luxembourg Income Study (LIS)*. Washington, DC: Urban Institute; 1990.

57. Stewart, F, Berry A. Globalization, Liberalization, and Inequality: Expectations and Experience. In: Hurrell A, Woods N, editors. *Inequality, Globalization and World Politics*. New York: Oxford University Press; 1999.

58. Overberg, P. Taking a World View for Keys to Income Inequality. *USA Today* (September 23, 1996) B3.

59. Warner, AM. Income Distribution and Competitiveness. In: World Economic Forum, editor. *The Global Competitiveness Report 1998*. Geneva, Switzerland: World Economic Forum; 1998. p. 30–37.

60. Mishel, L, Bernstein J, Schmitt J. Wage Inequality in the 1990s: Measurement and Trends. Washington, DC: Economic Policy Institute; 1998.

61. Bernstein, J. Widening Gap a Threat to Future. *Baltimore Sun* (February 14, 2000); at http://epinet.org/webfeatures/viewpoints/gap.html (accessed February 17, 2000).

62. Wolff, EN. *Top Heavy: A Study of the Increasing Inequality of Wealth in America and What Can Be Done about It*. New York: New Press; 1995.

63. Fieleke, NS. Is Global Competition Making the Poor Even Poorer? *New England Economic Review* 1994;November:3–16.

64. Putnam, RD. *Bowling Alone: The Collapse and Revival of American Community*. New York: Simon & Schuster; 2000.

65. U.S. Census Bureau. Measuring 50 Years of Economic Change. Current Population Reports P60-203 ed. Washington, DC: U.S. Census Bureau; 1998.

66. Kilborn, PT, Clemetson L. Gains of 90's Did Not Lift All, Census Shows. *New York Times* (June 5, 2002) A1.

67. Thurow, LC. *The Future of Capitalism: How Today's Economic Forces Shape Tomorrow's World*. New York: William Morrow and Company; 1996.

68. Miringoff, M, Miringoff M-L. *The Social Health of the Nation: How America Is Really Doing*. New York: Oxford University Press; 1999.

69. Harrison, B, Bluestone B. *The Great U-Turn: Corporate Restructuring and the Polarizing of America*. New York: Basic Books; 1988.

70. Levy, F, Michel RC. *The Economic Future of American Families: Income and Wealth Trends*. Washington, DC: Urban Institute; 1991.

71. Galbraith, JK. By the Numbers. *Foreign Affairs* 2002(July/August) 178–83.

72. Morris, M, Western B. Inequality in Earnings at the Close of the Twentieth Century. *Annual Review of Sociology* 1999;23:623–57.

73. Cappelli, P. Rethinking Employment. *British Journal of Industrial Relations* 1995;33(December):563–602.

74. Jaffe, J, Bazie M, Kayatin T. Gaps between High-Income and Other Americans Will Reach Record Level in 1999, Analysis Finds. Washington, DC: Center on Budget and Policy Priorities; 1999.

75. Schlesinger, JM, Mabry T, Lueck S. Charting the Pain behind the Gain. *Wall Street Journal* (October 1, 1999) B1, B4.

76. Johnston, DC. More Get Rich and Pay Less in Taxes. *New York Times* (February 7, 2002) A17.

77. Bernstein, J, McNichol EC, Mishel L, Zahradnik R. Pulling Apart: A State-by-State Analysis of Income Trends. Washington, DC: Center on Budget and Policy Priorities and Economic Policy Institute; 2000.

78. Barrington, L. A Rising Economic Tide Isn't Lifting All Boats. New York: The Conference Board; 2000.

79. Dreazen, YJ. Stock Gains Help to Propel U.S. Wealth: Nearly Half of Americans from All Income Levels Own Shares, a Record. *Wall Street Journal* (January 19, 2000) A10.

80. Uchitelle, L. After Pausing, Income Gap Is Growing Again. *New York Times* (June 23, 2002) sec. 3, p. 4, col. 5.

81. Poland, B, Coburn D, Robertson A, Eakin J. Wealth, Equity and Health Care: A Critique of a "Population Health" Perspective on the Determinants of Health. *Social Science and Medicine* 1998;46(7):785–98.

82. Smeeding, TM, Gottschalk P. Cross-National Income Inequality: How Great Is It and What Can We Learn from It? *International Journal of Health Services* 1999;29(4):733–41.

83. Bergesen, AJ, Bata M. Global and National Inequality: Are They Connected? *Journal of World-Systems Research* 2002;8(1):130–44.

84. Baumol, WJ, Nelson RR, Wolff EN, editors. *Convergence of Productivity: Cross-National Studies and Historical Evidence.* New York: Oxford University Press; 1994.

85. Park, D. An Alternative Examination of Intercountry Income Inequality and Convergence. *Comparative Economic Studies* 1997;39(3/4):53–65.

86. Faux, J, Mishel L. Inequality and the Global Economy. In: Hutton W, Giddens A, editors. *Global Capitalism.* New York: New Press; 2001. p. 256.

87. International Monetary Fund Expenditure Policy Division. IMF Conference on Economic Policy and Equity. Washington, DC: International Monetary Fund; 1998.

88. Sachs, J. Sachs on Development: Helping the World's Poorest. *The Economist* (August 14, 1999) 17–20.

89. United Nations Development Programme. *Human Development Report.* Oxford: Oxford University Press; 1997.

90. Bairoch, P. The Main Trends in National Economic Disparities since the Industrial Revolution. In: Bairoch P, Levy-Leboyer M, editors. *Disparities in Economic Development since the Industrial Revolution.* London: Macmillan; 1981. p. 3–17.

91. Bairoch, P. *Economics and World History: Myths and Paradoxes.* Chicago: University of Chicago Press; 1993.

92. *The Economist.* Growth Is Good. *The Economist* (May 27, 2000) 82.

93. Mueller, J. *Capitalism, Democracy, and Ralph's Pretty Good Grocery.* Princeton, NJ: Princeton University Press; 1999.

94. Seib, GF. World Disorder: Can U.S. Thrive if It's the Norm? *Wall Street Journal* (February 27, 2002) A22.

95. Levinson, M. Capitalism with a Safety Net? *Harvard Business Review* 1996;74:173–80.

96. Stille, A. Grounded by an Income Gap. *New York Times* (December 15, 2001) A15, A17.

97. Keister, LA, Moller S. Wealth Inequality in the United States. *Annual Review of Sociology* 2000;26:63–81.

98. Krueger, AB. Economic Scene: When It Comes to Income Inequality, More Than Just Market Forces Are at Work. *New York Times* (April 4, 2002) C2.

99. Kahn, J, Weiner T. World Leaders Rethinking Strategy on Aid to Poor. *New York Times* (March 18, 2002) A3.

100. Beer, L, Boswell T. The Resilience of Dependency Effects in Explaining Income Inequality in the Global Economy: A Cross-National Analysis, 1975–1995. *Journal of World-Systems Research* 2002;8(1):30–59.

101. Wade, R. Winners and Losers. *The Economist* (April 28, 2001) 72–75.

102. Acemoglu, D, Aghion P, Violante GL. Deunionization, Technical Change and Inequality. *Carnegie-Rochester Conference on Public Policy* 2001;55:229–64.

103. Cowell, A. Davos Forum Opens with Qualified Exuberance. *New York Times* (January 28, 2000) C4.

104. Ross, RJS. *Global Capitalism: The New Leviathan*. Albany: State University of New York Press; 1990.

105. Hicks, A, Kenworthy L. Cooperation and Political Economic Performance in Affluent Democratic Capitalism. *American Journal of Sociology* 1998; 103(6):1631–72.

106. Etzioni, A. *The Moral Dimension: Toward a New Economics*. New York: Free Press; 1988.

107. Aghion, P, Harris C, Howitt P, Vickers J. Competition, Imitation and Growth with Step-by-Step Innovation. *Review of Economic Studies* 2001;68(3):467–92.

108. Aghion, P, Bloom N, Blundell R, Griffiths R, Howitt P. Competition and Innovation: An Inverted U Relationship. NBER Report No. W9269. October 2002. Cambridge, MA: National Bureau of Economic Research; available at http://papers.nber.org/papers/w9269.

109. Daniels, N, Kennedy B, Kawachi I. *Is Inequality Bad for Our Health?* Boston: Beacon Press; 2000.

110. Coburn, D. Income Inequality, Social Cohesion and the Health Status of Populations: The Role of Neo-Liberalism. *Social Science and Medicine* 2000;51:135–46.

111. Lynch, JW, Kaplan GA, Shema SJ. Cumulative Impact of Sustained Economic Hardship on Physical, Cognitive, Psychological, and Social Functioning. *New England Journal of Medicine* 1997;337(26):1889–95.

112. Evans, RG, Stoddart GL. Producing Health, Consuming Health Care. *Social Science and Medicine* 1990;31(12):1347–63.

113. Williams, RB, Barefoot JC, Califf RM, Haney TL, Saunders WB, Pryor DB, et al. Prognostic Importance of Social and Economic Resources among Medically Treated Patients with Angiographically Documented Coronary Artery Disease. *Journal of the American Medical Association* 1992;267(4):520–24.

114. Hales, S, Howden-Chapman P, Salmond C, Woodward A, Mackenbach J. National Infant Mortality Rates in Relation to Gross National Product and Distribution of Income. *The Lancet* 1999;354(9195):2047.

115. Blane, D, Bartley M, Smith GD. Disease Aetiology and Materialist Explanations of Socioeconomic Mortality Differentials. *European Journal of Public Health* 1997;7:385–91.

116. West, P. Health Inequalities in the Early Years: Is There Equalisation in Youth? *Social Science and Medicine* 1997;44(6):833–58.

117. Lundberg, O. Childhood Conditions, Sense of Coherence, Social Class and Adult Ill Health: Exploring Their Theoretical and Empirical Relations. *Social Science and Medicine* 1997;44(6):821–31.

118. Dahl, E, Birkelund E. Health Inequalities in Later Life in a Social Democratic Welfare State. *Social Science and Medicine* 1997;44(6):871–81.

119. Kaplan, GA, Pamuk ER, Lynch JW, Cohen RD, Balfour JL. Inequality in Income and Mortality in the United States: Analysis of Mortality and Potential Pathways. *British Medical Journal* 1996;312(April 20):999–1003.

120. Williams, RB. Lower Socioeconomic Status and Increased Mortality: Early Childhood Roots and the Potential for Successful Interventions. *Journal of the American Medical Association* 1998;279(21):1745–46.

121. Young, TK. *Population Health: Concepts and Methods.* New York: Oxford University Press; 1998.

122. Doorslaer, E, Wagstaff A, Bleichrodt H, Calonge S, Gerdtham U-B, Gerfin M, et al. Income-Related Inequalities in Health: Some International Comparisons. *Journal of Health Economics* 1997;16:93–112.

123. Mackenbach, JP, Kunst AE. Measuring the Magnitude of Socio-Economic Inequalities in Health: An Overview of Available Measures Illustrated with Two Examples from Europe. *Social Science and Medicine* 1997;44(6):757–71.

124. Fox, J, editor. *Health Inequalities in European Countries.* Aldershot, U.K.: Gower; 1989.

125. Kunst, AE. *Cross-National Comparisons of Socio-Economic Differences in Mortality.* The Hague: cip-gegevens Koninklijke Bibliotheek; 1997.

126. Chiang, T-L. Economic Transition and Changing Relation between Income Inequality and Mortality in Taiwan: Regression Analysis. *British Medical Journal* 1999;319:1162–65.

127. Acheson, SD. Independent Inquiry into Inequalities in Health Report. London: The Stationery Office; 1998.

128. Bloom, DE, Canning D. The Health and Wealth of Nations. *Science* 2000;287(5456):1207–9.

129. Hsiao, WCL, Liu Y. Economic Reform and Health—Lessons From China. *New England Journal of Medicine* 1996;335(6):430–32.

130. Ross, NA, Wolfson MC, Dunn JR, Berthelot J-M, Kaplan GA, Lynch JW. Relation between Income Inequality and Mortality in Canada and in the United States: Cross-Sectional Assessment Using Census Data and Vital Statistics. *British Medical Journal* 2000;320:898–902.

131. Osler, M, Prescott E, Gronbaek M, Christensen U, Due P, Engholm G. Income Inequality, Individual Income, and Mortality in Danish Adults: Analysis of Pooled Data from Two Cohort Studies. *British Medical Journal* 2002;324:13–25.

132. Vagero, D, Lundberg O. Health Inequalities in Britain and Sweden. *The Lancet* 1989(July 1):35–36.

133. Wilkinson, RG. Socioeconomic Determinants of Health: Health Inequalities: Relative or Absolute Material Standards? *British Medical Journal* 1997;314 (7080)(22 February 1997):591–95.

134. Marmot, M. Multilevel Approaches to Understanding Social Determinants. In: Berkman LF, Kawachi I, editors. *Social Epidemiology*. New York: Oxford University Press; 2000. chap. 15.

135. Siegrist, J. Adverse Health Effects of High-Effort/Low Reward Conditions. *Journal of Occupational Health Psychology* 1996;1:27–41.

136. Blumenthal, D. Health Care Reform at the Close of the 20th Century. *New England Journal of Medicine* 1999;340(24):1916–20.

137. Light, DW. Good Managed Care Needs Universal Health Insurance. *Annals of Internal Medicine* 1999;130(April 20):686–89.

138. American College of Physicians—American Society of Internal Medicine. No Health Insurance? It's Enough to Make You Sick—Scientific Research Linking the Lack of Health Coverage to Poor Health. Philadelphia: American College of Physicians—American Society of Internal Medicine; 2000.

139. Anderson, GF, Poullier JP. Health Spending, Access, and Outcomes; Trends in Industrialized Countries. *Health Affairs* 1999;18(3):178–92.

140. Rice, T. *The Economics of Health Care Reconsidered*. 2nd ed. Chicago: Health Administration Press; 2002.

141. Mellor, JM, Milyo J. Reexamining the Evidence of an Ecological Association between Income Inequality and Health. *Journal of Health Politics, Policy and Law* 2001;26(3):487–541.

142. Mellor, JM, Milyo J. Income Inequality and Health Status in the United States: Evidence from the Current Population Survey. *Journal of Human Resources* 2002;37(3):510–39.

143. Wilkinson, R. *Mind the Gap*. New Haven, CT: Yale University Press; 2001.

144. Angell, M. Pockets of Poverty. *Boston Review* 2000;25(1):11–12.

145. Mackenbach, JP. Income Inequality and Population Health. *British Medical Journal* 2002;324:1–2.

146. Muller, A. Education, Income Inequality, and Mortality: A Multiple Regression Analysis. *British Medical Journal* 2002;324:1–4.

147. Deaton, A. Relative Deprivation, Inequality, and Morality. Cambridge, MA: National Bureau of Economic Research; 2001.

148. Frank, RH. *Luxury Fever: Why Money Fails to Satisfy in an Era of Excess*. New York: Free Press; 1999.

149. Marmot, M, Wilkinson RG. Psychosocial and Material Pathways in the Relation between Income and Health: A Response to Lynch et al. *British Medical Journal* 2001;322:1233–36.

150. Tarlov, AR. Coburn's Thesis: Plausible, but We Need More Evidence and Better Measures. *Social Sciences & Medicine* 2000;51(7):993–95.

151. Putnam, RD. Bowling Alone: America's Declining Social Capital. *Journal of Democracy* 1995;6(1):65–78.

152. Kawachi, I. Social Capital and Community Effects on Population and Individual Health. In: Adler NE, Marmot M, McEwen BS, Stewart J, editors. *Socioeconomic Status and Health in Industrial Nations.* New York: New York Academy of Sciences; 1999. p. 120–30.

153. Coleman, JS. Social Capital in the Creation of Human Capital. *American Journal of Sociology* 1988;94(Suppl.):S95–120.

154. Putnam, RD. *Making Democracy Work: Civic Traditions in Modern Italy.* Princeton, NJ: Princeton University Press; 1993.

155. Barber, B. *The Logic and Limits of Trust.* New Brunswick, NJ: Rutgers University Press; 1988.

156. Seligman, AB. *The Problem of Trust.* Princeton, NJ: Princeton University Press; 1997.

157. Kramer, RM, Tyler TR, editors. *Trust in Organizations: Frontiers of Theory and Research.* Thousand Oaks, CA: Sage Publications; 1996.

158. Fukuyama, F. *Trust: The Social Virtues and the Creation of Prosperity.* New York: Free Press; 1995.

159. Johnson, DW, Johnson RT. *Learning Together and Alone: Cooperative, Competitive, and Individualistic Learning.* 4th ed. Boston: Allyn & Bacon; 1994.

160. Kramer, RM. Trust and Distrust in Organizations: Emerging Perspectives, Enduring Questions. *Annual Review of Psychology* 1999;50:569–98.

161. Kawachi, I, Kennedy BP, Lochner K, Prothrow-Stith D. Social Capital, Income Inequality, and Mortality. *American Journal of Public Health* 1997;87(9):1491–98.

162. Kawachi, I, Kennedy BP, Lochner K. Long Live Community: Social Capital as Public Health. *The American Prospect* 1997;35(November/December):56–59.

163. Sampson, RJ, Groves WH. Community Structure and Crime: Testing Social Disorganization Theory. *American Journal of Sociology* 1989;94:774–802.

164. Sampson, RJ, Raudenbush SW, Earls F. Neighborhoods and Violent Crime: A Multilevel Study of Collective Efficacy. *Science* 1997;277:918–24.

165. Coleman, JS. *Foundations of Social Theory.* Cambridge, MA: Belknap Press; 1994.

166. Nye, JS. The Decline of Confidence in Government. In: Nye JS, Zelikow PD, King DC, editors. *Why People Don't Trust Government.* Cambridge, MA: Harvard University Press; 1997.

167. Deutsch, M. *The Resolution of Conflict: Constructive and Destructive Processes.* New Haven, CT: Yale University Press; 1973.

168. Arrow, KJ. *The Limits of Organization.* New York: W. W. Norton & Company; 1974.

169. Lorenz, EH. Neither Friends nor Strangers: Informal Networks of Subcontracting in French Industry. In: Gambetta D, editor. *Trust: Making and Breaking Cooperative Relations.* Cambridge, MA: Basil Blackwell; 1988.

170. Cappella, JN, Jamieson KH. *Spiral of Cynicism: The Press and the Public Good.* New York: Oxford University Press; 1997.

171. Persson, T, Tabellini G. Is Inequality Harmful for Growth? *The American Economic Review* 1994;84(3):600–21.

172. Benabou, R. Inequality and Growth. *BER Macroeconomics Annual* 1996;11:11–74.

173. Weil, J, Barrionuevo A, Bryan-Low C. Auditor's Ruling: Andersen Win Lifts U.S. Enron Case. *Wall Street Journal* (June 17, 2002) A1, A10.

174. Rhoads, C. Funds Flow Back to Europe as Mistrust in Wall Street Mounts with Each Day. *Wall Street Journal* (June 28, 2002) A10, A11.

175. Andrews, EL. U.S. Businesses Dim as Models for Foreigners. *New York Times* (June 27, 2002) sec. 1, p. 1, col. 5.

176. Harwood, J. Americans Distrust Institutions in Poll. *Wall Street Journal* (June 13, 2002) A4.

177. Yankelovich, D. *The Magic of Dialogue: Transforming Conflict into Cooperation.* New York: Simon & Schuster; 1999.

178. Tarkowska, E, Tarkowski J. Social Disintegration in Poland: Civil Society or Amoral Familism? *Telos* 1991;89:103–9.

179. Griffin, K, Scott W, McKinley T, Hage J, Silovic D, Tadjbaksh S, et al. Human Development Report for Central and Eastern Europe and the CIS 1999. New York: United Nations Development Programme; 1999.

180. Hofheinz, P. What Now? That's What We Asked Economics, Business Executives and Others. Here's What They Said. *Wall Street Journal* (September 27, 1999) R25, R27.

181. Hertzman, C, Marmot M. The Leading Hypothesis and Its Discontents: A Synthesis of Evidence and Outstanding Issues regarding the East-West Life Expectancy Gap. In: Hertzman C, editor. *East-West Life Expectancy Gap in Europe.* Dordrecht, Netherlands: Kluwer Academic Publishers; 1996.

182. Barer, ML, Evans RG, Hertzman C, Johri M. Lies, Damned Lies, and Health Care Zombies: Discredited Ideas That Will Not Die. Houston: Health Policy Institute, University of Texas, Houston Health Science Center; 1998.

183. Luttwak, E. *Turbo-Capitalism: Winners and Losers in the Global Economy.* New York: HarperCollins Publishers; 1999.

184. Gordon, FM, Welch KR, Offringa G, Katz N. The Complexity of Social Outcomes from Cooperative, Competitive, and Individualistic Reward Systems. *Social Justice Research* 2000;13(3):237–69.

185. Bank, D. The Man Who Would Mend the World. *Wall Street Journal* (March 14, 2002) B1.

186. Soros, G. The Capitalist Threat. *The Atlantic Monthly* (February 1997) 45–58.

187. Williams, RB, Feagares J, Barefoot JC. Hostility and Death Rates in 10 U.S. Cities. Unpublished manuscript cited in Wilkinson RG, Health, Hierarchy, and Social Anxiety. In: Adler NE, Marmot M, McEwen BS, Stewart J, editors. *Socioeconomic Status and Health in Industrial Nations.* New York: New York Academy of Sciences; 1999, p. 48–63.

188. Wilkinson, RG. Health, Hierarchy, and Social Anxiety. In: Adler NE, Marmot M, McEwen BS, Stewart J, editors. *Socioeconomic Status and Health in Industrial Nations: Social, Psychological, and Biological Pathways.* New York: New York Academy of Sciences; 1999. p. 48–63.

189. Iribarren, C, Sidney S, Bild DE, Liu K, Markovitz JH, Roseman JM, et al. Association of Hostility with Coronary Artery Calcification in Young Adults. *Journal of the American Medical Association* 2000;283(19):2546–51.

190. Midlarsky, MI, editor. *The Evolution of Inequality: War, State Survival, and Democracy in Comparative Perspective.* Stanford, CA: Stanford University Press; 1999.

191. Alesina, A, Ozler S, Roubini N, Swagel P. Political Instability and Economic Growth. *Journal of Economic Growth* 1996;1:193–215.

192. Hibbs, D. *Mass Political Violence: A Cross-Sectional Analysis.* New York: Wiley; 1973.

193. Venieris, Y, Gupta D. Socio-Political Instability and Economic Dimensions of Development: A Cross-Sectional Model. *Economic Development and Cultural Change* 1983;31:727–56.

194. Venieris, Y, Gupta D. Income Distribution and Socio-Political Instability as Determinants of Savings: A Cross-Sectional Model. *Journal of Political Economy* 1986;96:873–83.

195. Muller, EN, Seligson MA. Civic Culture and Democracy: The Question of Causal Relationships. *American Political Science Review* 1994;88(3):635–52.

196. Curry, GD, Spergel I. Gang Homicide, Delinquency, and Community. *Criminology* 1988;26:381.

197. Taylor, R, Covington J. Neighborhood Changes in Ecology and Violence. *Criminology* 1988;26:553.

198. Hsieh, C-C, Pugh MD. Poverty, Income Inequality, and Violent Crime: A Meta-Analysis of Recent Aggregate Data Studies. *Criminal Justice Review* 1993;18(2):182–202.

199. Barrionuevo, A, Herrick T. Wages of Terror: For Oil Companies, Defense Abroad Is the Order of the Day. *Wall Street Journal* (February 7, 2002) A1, A12.

200. Rhoads, C. Long-Term Economic Effects of September 11 May Be More Costly. *Wall Street Journal* (June 7, 2002) A2.

201. Organization for Economic Cooperation and Development. Economic Consequences of Terrorism. In: OECD, editor. *OECD Economic Outlook No. 71.* E-book ed. Paris: OECD; 2002. p. 117–40.

202. Gorney, R, Long JM. Cultural Determinants of Achievement, Aggression, and Psychological Distress. *Archives of General Psychiatry* 1980;37:452.

203. The Economist. Trafficking in Women: In the Shadows. *The Economist* (August 26, 2000) 38–39.

204. UNICEF. Women in Transition. Florence: UNICEF–International Child Development Centre; 1999. p. 161.

205. United Nations Secretariat, DoEaSA-PD. Concise Report on World Population Monitoring, 2001: Population, Environment and Development. New York: United Nations Economic and Social Council; 2001. p. 58.

206. Bruno, M, Ravallion M, Squire L. Equity and Growth in Developing Countries: Old and New Perspectives on the Policy Issues. In: Tanzi V, Chu K-y, editors. *Income Distribution and High-Quality Growth.* Cambridge, MA: MIT Press; 1998. p. 117–41.

207. Taylor, L, editor. *External Liberalization, Economic Performance, and Social Policy.* New York: Oxford University Press; 2001.

208. Stiglitz, JE. *Economics.* 2nd ed. New York: W. W. Norton & Company; 1997.

209. Perotti, R. Growth, Income Distribution, and Democracy: What the Data Say. *Journal of Economic Growth* 1996;1(June):149–87.

210. Alesina, A, Perotti R. Income Distribution, Political Instability, and Investment. *European Economic Review* 1996;40(6):1203–28.

211. Yergin, D, Stanislaw J. *The Commanding Heights: The Battle between Government and the Marketplace That Is Remaking the Modern World.* New York: Simon & Schuster; 1998.

212. Kim, JY, Irwin A, Millen J, editors. *Dying for Growth: Global Inequality and the Health of the Poor.* Monroe, ME: Common Courage Press; 2000.

213. Arora, S. Health, Human Productivity, and Long-Term Economic Growth. *Journal of Economic History* 2001;61(3):699–750.

214. Sachs, JD. Investing in Health for Economic Development: Time for U.S. Action. *Global Health Link* (March–April 2002); at www.globalhealth.org/assets/publications/HL114.pdf.

215. McNeil, DG. Companies to Cut Cost of AIDS Drugs for Poor Nations. *New York Times* (May 12, 2000) A1, A12.

216. Lewis, NA. Clinton Tries to Expedite AIDS Drugs into Africa. *New York Times* (May 11, 2000) A7.

217. Woods, L. Government AIDS Efforts Target Drug Makers. *Corporate Legal Times* (August, 2000) 18.

218. McNeil, DG. Prices for Medicine Are Exorbitant in Africa, Study Says. *New York Times* (June 17, 2000) A6.

219. *The Economist.* A War over Drugs and Patents. *The Economist* (March 10, 2001) 43.

220. Stolberg, SG. Bush Offers Plan to Help Mothers Avoid Passing H.I.V. to Babies. *New York Times* (June 20, 2002) A5.

221. Winestock, G, King N Jr. Patent Restraints on AIDS Drugs to Be Eased for Developing World. *Wall Street Journal* (June 25, 2002) A8.

222. De Cock, KM, Janssen RS. An Unequal Epidemic in an Unequal World. *Journal of the American Medical Association* 2002;288(2):236–39.

223. Alesina, A, Di Tella R, MacCulloch R. Inequality and Happiness: Are Europeans and Americans Different? NBER Report No. W8198. April 2001. Cambridge, MA: National Bureau of Economic Research; at http://papers.nber.org/papers/w8198.

224. Rosenau, PV. Market Structure and Performance: Evaluating the U.S. Health System Reform. *Journal of Health and Social Policy* 2001;13(1):41–72.

225. Daley, S. More Vehemently than Ever, Europe Is Scorning the U.S. *New York Times* (April 9, 2000) A1, A8.

226. Sanger, DE. All the World's a Mall. *New York Times Book Review* (April 30, 2000), 13.

227. Garelli, S. The Fundamentals of World Competitiveness. In: *World Competitiveness Yearbook 1996.* Lausanne, Switzerland: International Institute for Management Development; 1996. p. 10–17.

228. Cooper, H, Kamm T. Loosening Up: Much of Europe Eases Its Rigid Labor Laws, and Temps Proliferate. *Wall Street Journal* (June 4, 1998) A1, A8.

229. Mishel, L, Bernstein J, Schmitt J. *The State of Working America, 2000–2001.* Ithaca, NY: Cornell University Press; 2001.

230. Nassar, S. Where Joblessness Is a Way of Making a Living. *New York Times* (May 9, 1999) WK 5.

231. Tagliabue, J. Resisting Those Ugly Americans. *New York Times* (January 9, 2000) sec. 3, p. 1, 10.

232. Kamm, T. Continental Drift: Europe Marks a Year of Serious Flirtation with the Free Market. *Wall Street Journal* (December 30, 1999) A1.

233. *Wall Street Journal.* U.S. Loses Sparkle as Icon of Marketplace. *Wall Street Journal* (June 28, 2002) A10, A11.

234. Erlanger, S. America the Invulnerable? The World Looks Again. *New York Times* (July 21, 2002) sec. 4, p. 3, col. 1.

235. Landers, P. Japan's Local Drug Makers to Outsource to Suppliers. *Wall Street Journal* (March 26, 2002) A20.

236. Belson, K. Learning How to Talk about Salary in Japan. *New York Times* (April 7, 2002) 12, Business.

237. Ono, Y. Rethinking How Japanese Should Think. *Wall Street Journal* (March 25, 2002) A12, A14.

238. Daly, E. European Meeting Will Focus on Freer Rein for Economy. *New York Times* (March 15, 2002) W1.

239. Baker, G, Crooks E. Keynes Revisited. *Financial Times* (October 6–7, 2001).

7

The Need for Paradigm Change and Why It Is So Slow in Coming

ADOPTING THE COMPETITION PARADIGM WAS never a consciously thought-through policy decision in America. It just happened little by little. In the end, it was a gamble based on untested assumptions. There was little or no evidence to support taking such a chance and much to warn against it.[1] Even those who have experienced enormous success within the framework of the competition paradigm are coming to recognize that destructive competition needs to be managed, that the competition paradigm should be modified.[2]

The reasons for the United States to revise the competition paradigm go beyond national interest. It is not just because it would reduce global poverty and lessen the threats of terrorism. Nor is it to protect society's losers in some abstract sense. Neither is it to advance some bleeding-heart do-good philosophy, though those of a liberal orientation may welcome the policies required to manage the problems associated with the competition paradigm. It is, rather, essential because amending it benefits us all. If destructive competition is rewarded and the value of constructive competition and cooperation are unacknowledged, everyone, at each and every level assessed in this book, is worse off.

This chapter addresses why paradigm change is best for all and why it is so slow in coming. It examines the obstacles to modifying the competition paradigm and how these can be addressed. In fact, the potential for paradigm change is substantial at the same time that the barriers to paradigm change are everywhere. One such obstacle is particularly worrisome and in need of assessment: Pursuing constructive competition and cooperation, in isolation, without regard to what other individuals, groups, organizations, and countries are doing can be self-defeating because it may make one vulnerable. The extent to which the vulnerability problem can be avoided is also discussed in this chapter. The question of how paradigm change can best be accomplished is the topic of the next and final chapter.

Why Paradigm Change Is Best for All

The competition paradigm is assumed to hold the promise of improved performance for all economic sectors, for every organization, and for each society with a problem. The proposed solution to the problems is a simple one—more competition. But this is not a thought-through solution. The consequences play out for each level discussed in this book, and they are interactive across levels. The competition paradigm leads to a situation where there is too little of the best forms of competition.

Every underperforming individual diminishes the quality of life of every other member of society, so it is in the interest of all that destructive forms of competition that contribute to such a situation be minimized. In the absence of success and recognition, many individuals lower their effort. If enough people do so, the result is decreased societal productivity. The failure of any individual has an impact, however small, on all of us. Each child who fails to develop intellectually and physically is a missed opportunity.[3] Every high school dropout diminishes society's productivity in the long run. The causal connections between the global costs of competition and each individual's well-being may appear temporally and geographically remote. But they are linked, even if in a roundabout and not immediately obvious way.

The same is true at the level of the organization, where failure results in bankruptcy and "success" leads to oligopoly (explained in chapters 4 and 5). The market fundamentalism associated with the competition paradigm makes for dysfunctional organizations where performance is less than optimal from the perspective of that organization or the society as a whole.

The city of Houston, the home of Enron Corporation, is an example of how reining in the competition paradigm would be best for all at the municipal level. Houston "was a place where you could make a lot of money, a place where the entrepreneurial spirit was unmolested."[4, p. 21] Self-interest, the unlimited pursuit of individual gain, was the dynamic that drove the city's development and sustained growth. Public support for this orientation was broad and deep. But much has changed. Competition with little interference—destructive competition—has meant that Houston has come to have one of the highest levels of air pollution in the United States today. As a result, that city's image is suffering, the health status of residents has been affected, businesses are less interested in locating in the Houston area, and the Environmental Protection

Agency is considering sanctions against it. The short-term gain, immediate prosperity, which resulted from ignoring competition-generated pollution, turns out to have been a recipe for long-term pain.

The same is true for the family of nations. Here, too, revising the competition paradigm is best for all. The competition paradigm leaves no room for redistributing wealth from the poor nations to the rich nations, which would be best for all, as explained in chapter 6. With the rise of the competition paradigm, foreign aid has declined.[5, 6, p. 833, 7, p. 801] Cooperation in the form of a package of public health and population health benefits costing $10 billion a year from the First World countries would save millions of lives in the Third World countries.[8] If just $34 of each First World nation's per person health care spending were redistributed to the world's poorest countries, eight million lives per year would be saved. Productivity of the recipient countries would increase; in some cases, benefits would be fivefold the cost.[9] It would be best for all because each and every underperforming nation reduces the quality of our international life.

It is best for all countries if changing the competition paradigm makes it more likely that every nation has effective government and produces to capacity. "Hungry, sick homeless, and illiterate people cannot contribute to economic development and technological and industrial modernization."[10, p. 172] Those nations already producing to capacity will find that their responsibilities increase and their burdens enlarge until the situation of the lesser-developed countries improves. In the long run, the world is a more dangerous and less healthy place unless steps are taken to achieve these goals. Neither crime nor disease, for example, respects national boundaries.[11] The weakest member of the global society of nations establishes, directly or indirectly, the security level with which all must live. Controlling destructive competition may appear to be a form of altruism at first glance, but it is at the same time extraordinarily self-interested.[12]

The competition paradigm underestimates the value of cooperation, and changing it reopens these opportunities. Cooperation can have positive value at each level considered in this book, from the biological to the organizational and societal levels. For example, cooperation for the good of the species is as evident for human beings as it is for self-sacrificing parasites or community-oriented colony-residing insects.[13, 14] The theory of "mutualism" within a species proposes that individuals must cooperate to enhance the survival of one another.[15–17]

The competition paradigm instead emphasizes that Darwinian competitiveness of the most ferocious forms at every level is what it takes to ensure the continued existence of the human race. It assumes that uninhibited competition will guarantee that only the healthiest and most fit (organizations, individuals, or countries) survive from one period to the next. Many sociobiologists suggest, on the basis of primate research, that evolution advantages those in modern industrialized society who strive to maximize individual gain.[18, 19]

The opposite argument is also plausible. Darwinian assumptions, commonly understood, may be counterproductive and may not contribute to the survival of the human species at all.[20, p. 256] George Soros makes this case: "There is something wrong with making the survival of the fittest a guiding principle of civilized society. The main point I want to make is that cooperation is as much a part of the system of competition, and the slogan 'survival of the fittest' distorts this fact."[2, p. 55] A survival-of-the-fittest philosophy means that there is no global society within the global economy.[21]

In addition, there is a second interpretation of Darwin. This Darwin does not place competition above all else. Rather, this reading of Darwin looks to endless examples of cooperation between species, mutual interdependence, and synergistic relationships that contribute to the continued existence of a species. Some studies of primate behavior indicate that moderating and controlling competition permits the peaceful sharing and trading required for group survival.[22] In addition, altruists make better parents, and their offspring are more likely to survive, which is essential from an evolutionary point of view.[13] Simply put, "groups with altruists in them leave more successors than groups of selfish creeps."[23, p. B7] Over time, the altruistic and trustworthy come to have a reputation for their other-oriented contribution to the community. They can be counted on when they are not being watched or monitored to act in the interest of the group as a whole. Once this character trait or personality attribute is recognized in a long-term relationship among individuals in groups or organizations, it makes for new possibilities that are of benefit to all within a group, organization, or society.[24] Cooperation is more than its own reward. There is good evidence based on magnetic resonance imaging studies of the brain that many human beings are innately "wired" to cooperate, trust, and choose generosity over selfishness.[25] When cooperation generates reciprocity, people feel good about it, and all benefit because of the less stressful quality of life in such a society and the overall improved population mental health that accompanies it.[14]

To pursue policies that benefit all, the United States must look beyond "winning" at the global level without regard to other things. For example, it is in the interest of the United States to do everything possible to promote worldwide population health and wealth. Only if there is a global community free of disease, poverty, and warfare can the United States avoid the costly side effects resulting from pollution, global warming, terrorism, unprecedented human migration, and the uncontrollable spread of disease.[26, 27] In the end, winning by means of destructive competition is a short-term victory if the social, psychological, and economic environment is sacrificed. Future opportunities for constructive forms of competition disappear.

The competition paradigm contains another internal contradiction that in the long term not only is likely to undermine it but at the same time supports changing it. The story of the tragedy of the commons illustrates how each individual organization or nation aggressively pursuing his or her short-term interest may not always serve society's best interest. Society's "best interest" is, of course, a contentious issue. It is often difficult to identify because it is so subjective and dependent on one's point of view. But in other cases it is uncontroversial. When each farmer was free to run as many of his own sheep as possible on the community–commons grassland, overgrazing resulted. The commons were destroyed. The unrestrained pursuit of individual self-interest leads to collective disaster in the long term.[28, pp. 171–72] In a similar manner, the unrestricted, self-reinforcing spiral of too-intense competition functions at every level studied here to reinforce the competition paradigm. It simultaneously initiates a process of self-destruction.

The Power of a Paradigm: Why No Change?

If changing the competition paradigm is best for all, why does it remain so resistantly in place? Despite the rising costs of the competition paradigm— some clear and evident and others less obvious—there is only a limited worry about it in the United States.[29] The need for change is generally unappreciated, and the constituency interested in it in the United States is very small. Paradigm change has been postponed for a long time.

In this section, we will see that a specific, too narrow, often superficial social and intellectual focus and an oversimplified view of America's own success shelters the competition paradigm in the face of substantial counterevidence. Many factors account for the force of the competition paradigm and why it goes unchallenged. But three explanations are especially important. First, a short-term focus diminishes the awareness or visibility of the long-term consequences of the competition paradigm. Second, the costs of destructive competition are largely indirect rather than direct, and they are therefore difficult to discern. Because they escape attention, the competition paradigm is less likely to be subject to serious scrutiny. Third, America's global superiority in the 1990s is regarded as proof of the validity of the competition paradigm. But only the narrowest of perspectives can sustain this singular understanding of U.S. accomplishments. In any case, alternative explanations as to why the United States did so well in the 1990s are as likely to be true as those offered by the competition paradigm.

Focusing on the Short Term Rather Than the Long Term

The competition paradigm focuses on the immediate, and this diverts attention from the need for change. The most serious problems related to the competition paradigm may not be evident in the short term because they are long term in character. In situations of intense competition, short-term survival is critical.[30] This is the case for every level of analysis considered here. What counts most are instantaneous biological responses, guaranteed individual wins, quick organizational profits, and high national competitiveness ratings. Focusing on the short term may permit the mistaken conclusion that destructive competition pays off. A long-term analysis reveals that the inadequacies of the competition paradigm are substantial.[31, p. 173, 32]

At the level of the individual, the competition paradigm encourages the "me now" culture of personal gratification. Attention is riveted on this instant, on the quick fix. In the United States, a short-term orientation translates into historic lows regarding the percentage of earned income that is saved. Record-high individual credit card debt is not criticized. In the late 1990s, day traders were concerned with getting out of the market before the close of the stock exchange. A buy-and-hold investment strategy was considered passé. These and other short-term preoccupations made for a climate where worrying about the long term regarding the competition paradigm or anything else was less compelling than glorying in the here and now. Repeated winners are still honored with ever greater rewards. Persistent losers experience an increased sense of deprivation in the long term and a diminished sense of why they should strive and work to their full ability.

At the level of the organization, destructive competition puts enormous short-term demands on corporate leaders. This was especially clear in the late 1990s. Paying out dividends was less important than generating an increase in corporate stock price. If this meant sacrificing the company's future interest to increase current profits, then so be it.[33] This philosophy was not good for business.[34] Still, some business consultants argue that long-term business planning is futile and that short-term advantage is more important.[35, p. 164] This perspective translates into "a steady decrease in amortization time . . . an increased concern with short-term profit."[36, p. 190] Neither is it good for the individuals who work in these commercial enterprises as discussed in chapters 3 and 4.[37, p. 306]

At the societal level, the competition paradigm's short-term perspective fails to consider future generations and their needs. But they must be part of the equation if the human species is to survive.[38] This is because the future of the human race is far from certain. We are a small and fragile development in a universe that is large and forbidding. Our survival is far from assured in the long term; the human situation is more an emergency than a simple routine affair. As David and Roger Johnson, who researched the topic for more than twenty-five years, suggest, "Humans do not have a choice; we have to cooperate."[39, p. 15]

The Costs of Destructive Competition Are Indirect Rather Than Direct

Because the costs of the competition paradigm are often indirect rather than direct, they go unnoticed. As a result, the competition paradigm is difficult to challenge because its inadequacies are hidden rather than immediately obvious. Probing below the surface, searching for the less immediately apparent, reveals that the problems resulting from too much competition are great and are likely to become more so in the future.

At the biological level, the costs of destructive competition are largely poor health. But this appears to be due not as much to competition as to stress and anxiety. The extent to which stress results from competition is overlooked. At the individual level, competition reduces individual productivity in many situations. It does not do so for every individual, however. Competition may even mean increased productivity for some. The extent to which this is the case for any specific individual is largely unknown. It probably does so for winners, but this is certainly not always the case. But the mechanisms by which competition works its effects on individuals are complex and, again, indirect.

Because the costs of competition for organizations are indirect, they too often go undetected. The fact that competition internal to the group interferes with productivity is seldom noticed. The improved performance accruing from internal cooperation is overlooked, perhaps because it is inconsistent with the competition paradigm. Less attention to business ethics and higher bankruptcy rates do not appear on the surface to be related to a rise of destructive competition, but they too are part of the indirect costs to society of too much competition of the wrong kind. In the short term, destructive competition rewards the least honest and those corporations most willing to cut corners. Often this takes place at the expense of more efficient organizations. But on the surface of it all, none of this appears to be directly related to the competition paradigm. After all, there are other explanations, for example, for fraud and dishonesty.

The indirect costs of destructive competition among nations or among multinational corporations is great though, again, not at once evident. Any causal connection between destructive competition and societal-level dysfunction seems weak. The potential problems reviewed in chapter 6 include increasing inequality and sacrificing population health. Too much competition may be responsible, in good part, for a decline in trust, a reduction in social capital, and damage to the social fabric. If productivity is reduced, no one considers that destructive competition may be part of the problem. The linkages between the two are so intertwined and complex as to defy direct causal attribution. In the end, no one appears to be responsible for societal needs because fulfilling them is not a means to improve one's competitive position in the marketplace in the short term. The consequences constitute an indirect cost of competition, but the competition paradigm escapes responsibility.

A case study of an increasingly competitive health market sector in the United States itself illustrates how cooperative societal functions are indirectly threatened by competition gone awry. The for-profit sector gains market share even though the nonprofit providers, in general, cost less and offer better quality.[40] Competition is allowed to drive out cooperation, but the competition paradigm escapes question. As the health system in the United States has become more competitive over the past decade, previously cooperative responsibilities are no longer ensured.[41] As the number of uninsured grows, charity care has diminished.[42, 43] In a highly competitive market, medical institutions reduce subsidies to academic research.[44, 45] Even the commitment to spend societal resources on the teaching of medicine is at risk.[46–48]

An Oversimplified Understanding of U.S. Success:
Some Alternative Explanations

America's successes, especially its economic performance in the late 1990s, are believed to be testimony to the validity of the competition paradigm. Paradigm change is delayed or permanently deferred because of the strong support it receives from American excellence and accomplishments, however they may be defined and measured (high growth, low inflation, high employment, or international military power). The market is said to have made America great. Many conclude, therefore, that unrestricted competition is the way to go, politically, socially, and economically, in every sphere from business to education to the sports field and in the health services sector as well. But the exact causal mechanisms that link competition and American macroeconomic success have not yet been documented and remain a matter of faith as much as anything else.[49] There is no reason to assume that America's achievements are solely attributable to any national commitment to the competition paradigm. There is simply too little scientific evidence to sustain this singular accounting. Simultaneity does not necessitate causality.

There are other, equally plausible explanations of America's prosperity. It may result from, for example, the fact that the United States has a common language and currency. It could be because the United States was the first country to benefit from a large regional common market without burdensome customs or tariffs. This encouraged the development of huge industries and permitted them to relocate easily. America's accomplishments may be due to specific and particularly fortunate political cycles.[50, p. 28, 51] Perhaps it is because the United States is rich in natural resources[52] and had abundant land.[53] Climate may also play a role, though it is often overlooked. Weather patterns, according to the World Health Organization, have a substantial effect on health,[54] and population health is related to national productivity. Historically, the United States may have been among the first countries to experience the virtuous spiral of health-promoting economic growth that in turn improves population health and so on.[53, 55] Higher U.S. productivity may also result from advances in information technology as much as from a dedication to destructive competition.[56, p. A1, C14, 57]

Being "best" is sometimes a matter of good fortune, and luck is often a factor. Random, idiosyncratic events play a role.[50, p. 28, 51] "Luck works cumulatively, so that those that do well in the early rounds gain progressively and differentially as the game proceeds, while those who do badly may not even remain in the game. To do well it is imperative to get a good start, either by luck or through initial endowments."[58, p. x] The United States may be ahead of other countries because it had such a good head start in terms of the gross domestic product (GDP). Several studies suggest that historical and geographic opportunities are more important in predicting national achievement than is competition.[1] Some experts suggest that location may be destiny, and the United States is especially lucky in this respect as well.[59] A country poor in natural resources, with limited access to transportation and located in a fragile ecological area such as the tropics, will have less chance at success.[60] Prevalence of infectious diseases has a tremendous impact on productivity. One study suggests that sub-Saharan Africa's GDP would be a third greater today if a single infectious disease, malaria, had been eliminated in 1965.[61, 11] The impact of AIDS on GDP in this geographic area is probably as great.

Some argue that U.S. success is all a matter of culture: The United States does well because its cultural values emphasize work, thrift, honesty, effort, and patience.[62] Aspects of culture such as religion have much to do with how a country gets things done and its level of democracy.[63] Max Weber developed this perspective. There is agreement across the political spectrum that culture influences national economic success, though the policy conclusions drawn from this view differ for the left and the right.[64]

America's recent success in the last decades of the twentieth century has been attributed to government policy. Joseph Stiglitz suggests that fortuitous "mistakes" contributed to economic growth in the United States in recent decades.[65] According to Michael Meerpool, decisions not to intervene to slow growth at too early a point in the economic cycle when unemployment first hit record lows, to increase the minimum wage, and to pursue redistributive economic policies were all important.[66] America's achievements may be due to a rather stable economic environment brought on by the good fortune of low inflation in the late 1980s and the 1990s. Economists believe that this low inflation was due to the coming together of several factors: the Asian crisis that made imports inexpensive, the availability of inexpensive oil for much of the 1990s, low health care cost increases during the same period, and the initiation of new ways to measure inflation that made it look lower.

No one really knows why the United States did so well in the last half of the twentieth century. There is simply very little evidence as to which of the previously mentioned explanations is superior to any other. It is likely that many, perhaps all, played some small part in it. To accept U.S. success as a basis for validating the competition paradigm is too simple. Ironically, if together these alternatives to competition account for America's success in the past, then the United States did as well as it did not because of, but rather despite, the competition paradigm.

Recognition that U.S. prosperity—all its accomplishments—may be due to something other than the competition paradigm opens up the possibility of paradigm change. Moving beyond the simplistic assumption of a singular causal link undermines resistance to revising the competition paradigm, to examining its latent indirect costs and its evident long-term disadvantages. It opens up a context in which paradigm change is possible and the true-believer paradigm-affirming mentality can be questioned.

The Forces for Paradigm Change

If the obstacles to paradigm change are understandable, the potential for paradigm change at every level, from the individual to the national, is more and more evident. Taken together, the power of these sources of change is impressive. The most important has to do with the possibility that America's success is, at least in part, a myth. The possibility that America's success going forward is not assured is another reason to question the integrity of the competition paradigm. Those who advance this view argue that the United States is in decline[67] and that its experience does not provide much support for the competition paradigm.[68] They question whether America's romance with competition has been effective and ask whether it can sustain growth and productivity or whether it will falter. They point to America's domestic problems with corporate responsibility in the wake of accounting scandals in 2000–2002.

Those challenging the competition paradigm on the basis of America's evident problems ask about the volatility of the U.S. dollar, America's huge foreign trade deficits, its low savings rate, its inability to consistently achieve a balanced budget, its failure to provide responsible leadership at the international level, its periodic retreat into isolationism and unilateralism, and the gap between its practice and its principles regarding free trade.[65, 69, 70] U.S. foreign policy periodically alienates its allies in Europe and abroad.[71] For example, the United States has refused to sign international treaties, withdrawn from treaties it signed in the past, or undermined efforts to formulate new treaties of substantial importance to its allies.[72] The list is long and includes the Kyoto Treaty on Climate, the Anti-Ballistic Missile Treaty, the Land Mine Treaty, the Biodiversity Treaty, the treaty to establish a verification mechanism on biological weapons (Biological Weapons Convention Compliance Protocol), a comprehensive test ban treaty (Comprehensive Nuclear Test Ban Treaty), the UN efforts to reduce small-arms exports (Illicit Trade in Small Arms and Light Weapons in All Its Aspects Conference), and the 1989 UN Basel Convention to limit hazardous exports (Basel Convention on the Control of Transboundary Movements of Hazardous Wastes and Their Disposal). The United States refused to participate with its allies to protect international human rights standards when it rejected establishment of an International Criminal Court.[73] It opposed implementation of the 1989 UN Convention on Torture.[74] The Council on Foreign Relations concludes that the United States had a significant image problem and that many see it as "arrogant, self-indulgent, hypocritical, inattentive, and unwilling or unable to engage in cross-cultural dialogue."[75]

Other forces for paradigm change are also evident at each level analyzed in previous chapters. At the individual level, too much competition is one important source of individual tension and anxiety; awareness of the problem legitimizes the need for paradigm change. Self-help guides to stress reduction are everywhere. Medication can calm the effects of competition-generated stress for individuals and diminish the impact of the destructive biological mechanisms involved in the process. But the underlying dynamics of the problem remain.[76] Direct intervention at the level of competition could be of more value than merely medicating the symptoms.

Overall, if there is the will to control destructive competition at the individual level, it seems quite likely that it could be accomplished. Differences among individuals exist; to a large extent, competition is learned, not inherent.[77, 78] Research suggests that in general it is easier to teach people with cooperative personalities to compete than it is to convince those with individualist personalities to cooperate, at least in the United States.[79] At the same time, individualist, competitive personalities are found to adapt and to become more cooperative if the larger culture is essentially cooperative.[80] Still, learning to cooperate in an already overly competitive world, one in which the competition paradigm is so central, is not easy for individuals. Competition that is too intense may remove the opportunity to acquire, early in life, the basic skills needed for appropriate competition and cooperation.[81] It involves unlearning what is already taken for granted. But if a policy to control destructive competition becomes a priority, research suggests that early-life intervention would be effective.[82]

Evidence is mixed regarding paradigm change at the group and organizational levels. Destructive competition among groups appears to drive out cooperation[83, pp. 142–43] and more benign forms of competition. But at both the group and the organizational level, there is some evidence that cooperative or competitive environments are open to modification. When competing groups are required by circumstance to work together in order to accomplish superordinate goals, they set aside competition and they cooperate.[84] An example is how New York City's residents rallied together after the September 11, 2001 terrorist attacks. Gradually and over time, group cooperation regains a place in what was a predominantly competitive social situation.[85] The competitive styles of corporate cultures are similarly open to modification.[86]

As with most social phenomena, exceptions apply, and the same is true for learning to cooperate. In some situations, learning to be less competitive may be undesirable and inappropriate. This is the case discussed in chapter 5 for corporations that are too willing to develop cooperative strategies among themselves. Such forms of cooperation between organizations, if they are designed to limit competition entirely and dominate an economic arena, are often counterproductive. Such efforts might well reduce the potential for constructive and appropriate competition.

At the societal or national level, there is almost no solid information as to what makes some more competitive than others and whether it is possible to control destructive competition within and between countries. The once-vibrant field of peace research has been eclipsed in recent decades. Research at the individual and group levels is of some help because societies are made up of individuals and groups. And the fact that at least a few countries have seen their national competitiveness change across time suggests that levels of societal competitiveness might be open to modification.

At the international level, organizational and institutional policies for managing destructive competition are embryonic at best.[87] Foreign aid and foreign investment are uncoordinated and cannot be depended on. Solutions rest on the initiative of individual nations, but the problems are beyond the control of any single nation acting by itself. Strong international institutions are needed to address the issues, though they are almost absent today. The World Trade Organization, the International Monetary Fund, the World Bank, and the United Nations are potentially useful. But none has the authority to manage destructive competition or strive for balance between competition and co-operation. Among them, only the United Nations has a large, economically diverse constituency. Legitimate global, citizen-based governance could make a difference,[88, 89] but none exists at the moment. And part of the problem is U.S. opposition, in conformity with the competition paradigm, to global governance that in any way limits its authority.[90]

Managing destructive competition and moderating the extremes inherent in the competition paradigm at all these levels is desirable and can be accomplished. But can it be ensured without the risk of increased vulnerability to the initiators of such an approach, be they individuals, organizations, or nations? Until now, the forces for change have been few, and this has not been a worry. Too much competition has not been understood to be a problem. However, if managing destructive competition were to become a priority, working to achieve an environment safe for constructive competition and cooperation would be equally important.

The Vulnerability Problem

Controlling the effects of the competition paradigm raises the question of balancing defense with exposure. It is extremely difficult for a single individual, organization, or nation to move beyond the competition paradigm independently and without regard to what all the others are doing. The substitution of constructive competition or cooperation for destructive competition is not a reasonable proposal if it makes for vulnerability, as it well might.[14, 91] Such a reorientation would be extremely unwise if there were no protective mechanisms of any kind in place. Such protections may be moral, social, or legislative. In each case, the goal is the same: to keep competition in balance. In the absence of such mechanisms, the costs of independent action to control competition cannot be anticipated. In the context of the competition paradigm, a defensive policy of "safety first" results, and this biases decisions and actions in an antisocial direction.[92] It remains the logical choice, however, if forgoing destructive competition translates into vulnerability.

Societies that emphasize cooperation are open to exploitation by the selfish individual within the group or by aggressive neighboring states. Destructive competition often drives out cooperation at the level of individuals in the workplace, at the level of organizations, within society, and among nations.[92–94] This has been documented in the aptly named prisoner's dilemma experiments in the laboratory setting where the structure of incentives encourages cooperation but only if both sides practice the same level of collaboration. There is a sense in which global society approximates this situation. We are all on the planet together, and while each (individual, organization, or nation) may have a clear self-interest at stake, in the end cooperation makes sense. Still, it takes only one "defector" to call into question the gains achieved by the others. Any understanding of their mutual dependence does not come immediately. In general and across many prisoner's dilemma experiments, Anatol Rapport discovered that "first the subjects learn not to trust each other; then they learn to trust each other."[95, p. 201] Is this the process at work in the family of nations at the global level today? If so, how long might such a process take?

There are mechanisms that offer some protection and create a safe space for initiating constructive competition and avoiding vulnerability. But research on these topics is based largely on experimental laboratory evidence; while promising, such research needs more testing in the real world. Given these limitations, it still appears that insisting that generosity and altruism be reciprocal works best. Axelrod suggests that at every level, from the individual to that of international relations, a "tit-for-tat" strategy may be protective.[96] This amounts to practicing cooperation in a newly established relationship but meeting each subsequent negative or hostile gesture in kind. "Retaliation discourages the other side from persisting whenever defection is tried. Its [tit-for-tat's] forgiveness helps restore mutual cooperation. And its clarity makes it intelligible to the other player, thereby eliciting long-term cooperation."[31, p. 54] The daily life context introduces substantial complexity to these generalizations. Misunderstanding as to what constitutes a "negative or hostile gesture" can cause the entire framework to collapse.[97] It is also important to note that a tit-for-tat strategy works only in situations where relationships are stable and ongoing.

Vigilant sharing is a second means to control the vulnerability problem associated with moving away from destructive competition and toward constructive competition and cooperation. Vigilant sharing—thought to have been practiced by early hunter–gatherer societies especially with respect to food—appears to have survival value under difficult conditions. It consists of the group acting on the basis of a shared sense of fairness—a collective belief that others should not get more than their share. Sharing is emphasized over dominance. It is insisted on even though some members of the group or organization accept it with reluctance.[98]

Altruistic punishment is a third technique for protecting against vulnerability under conditions of destructive competition. It "means that individuals punish, although the punishment is costly for them and yields no material gain."[99, p. 137] Punishment is an altruistic act when its sole function is to socialize the extremely self-interested individual, organization, or nation into a new mental frame of reference that is less selfish and therefore more in line with the collective interest. It is altruistic when punishing someone else costs the punisher substantial resources. In this situation, those who do not punish are, in a sense, free riders.

In social systems where altruistic punishment is available and actually carried out, cooperation is observed to flourish. Where it is precluded, cooperation is compromised. Generous social security programs are more likely where people are confident that there will be few cheaters.[100] To be unselfish rather than self-interested would make one vulnerable if there were no possibility of altruistic punishment. Urs Fischbacher, Simon Gachter, and Ernst Fehr estimate that about one-third of the population have to be coerced by punishment to be cooperative—they are, in short, chronic free riders.[101] But where unfair behavior generates revenge at an early opportunity from others in the group, then being very selfish brings only short-term gain. Altruistic punishment explains why an individual, group, organization, or nation is more generous than predicted—why the opportunity to maximize personal gain at every occasion is not always observed.[13, 99, 102, 103]

All these strategies encourage a balance between cooperation and competition, something not easily achieved or maintained in the presence of destructive competition. Research to develop more such devices for managing destructive competition is critical. But legislative and regulative mechanisms are also effective devices for protecting against vulnerability. They are at the same time more controversial than a simple call for research. The competition paradigm gives little place to these public policy–oriented approaches, which are the topic of the next chapter.

Notes

1. Gorney, R, Long JM. Cultural Determinants of Achievement, Aggression, and Psychological Distress. *Archives of General Psychiatry* 1980;37:452.

2. Soros, G. The Capitalist Threat. *The Atlantic Monthly* (February 1997) 45–58.

3. Working Group on the National Strategy on Healthy Child Development. Building a National Strategy for Healthy Child Development. Ottawa: Federal/Provincial/Territorial Advisory Committee on Population Health, Minister of Public Works and Government Services Canada; 1998.

4. Yardley, J. Houston, Smarting Economically from Smog, Searches for Remedies. *New York Times* (September 24, 2000) A21.

5. *The Economist.* Gifts with Strings Attached: Donors Should Help Those in Need, Not Themselves. *The Economist* (June 17, 2000) 21.

6. U.S. Census Bureau. *Statistical Abstract of the United States.* 115th ed. Washington, DC: U.S. Government Printing Office; 1995.

7. U.S. Census Bureau. *Statistical Abstract of the United States.* 119th ed. Washington, DC: U.S. Government Printing Office; 1999.

8. Sachs, J. Sachs on Globalisation: A New Map of the World. *The Economist* (June 24, 2000) 81–83.

9. Sachs, J. Macroeconomics and Health: Investing in Health for Economic Development. Geneva, Switzerland: World Health Organization; 2001. p. 213.

10. Silk, L, Silk M. *Making Capitalism Work*. New York: New York University Press; 1996.

11. Angier, N. Together, in Sickness and in Health. *New York Times Magazine* (May 6, 2001) 67–69.

12. Yach, D, Bettcher D. The Globalization of Public Health, II: The Convergence of Self-Interest and Altruism. *American Journal of Public Health* 1998;88(5):738–41.

13. Sober, E, Wilson DS. *Unto Others: The Evolution and Psychology of Unselfish Behavior*. Cambridge, MA: Harvard University Press; 1998.

14. Ridley, M. *The Origins of Virtue: Human Instincts and the Evolution of Cooperation*. New York: Viking; 1996.

15. Wrangham, RW. Mutualism, Kinship and Social Evolution. In: King's College Sociobiology Group, editor. *Current Problems in Sociobiology*. Cambridge, U.K.: Cambridge University Press; 1982. p. 269–89.

16. West-Eberhardt, MJ. The Evolution of Social Behavior by Kin-Selection. *Quarterly Review of Biology* 1975;50:1–33.

17. Melotti, U. Competition and Cooperation in Human Evolution. *The Mankind Quarterly* 1985;25(4):323–51.

18. Byrne, RW, Whiten A, editors. *Machiavellian Intelligence: Social Expertise and the Evolution of Intellect in Monkeys, Apes, and Humans*. New York: Oxford University Press; 1990.

19. Byrne, RW, Whiten A, editors. *Machiavellian Intelligence II: Extensions and Evaluations*. New York: Cambridge University Press; 1997.

20. Etzioni, A. *The Moral Dimension; Toward a New Economics*. New York: Free Press; 1988.

21. Soros, G. *Open Society: Reforming Global Capitalism*. New York: Public Affairs; 2000.

22. de Waal, FBM. The Reconciled Hierarchy. In: Chance MRA, editor. *Social Fabrics of the Mind*. London: Lawrence Erlbaum Associates; 1989. p. 105–35.

23. Berreby, D. Enthralling or Exasperating: Selecting One. *New York Times* (September 24, 1996) B2, B7.

24. Frank, RH. *Passions within Reason: The Strategic Role of the Emotions*. New York: W. W. Norton & Company; 1988.

25. Rilling, JK, Gutman DA, Zeh TR, Pagnoni G, Berns GS, Kilts CD. A Neural Basis for Social Cooperation. *Neuron* 2002;35(2):395–405.

26. Institute of Medicine. *America's Vital Interest in Global Health—Protecting Our People, Enhancing Our Economy, and Advancing Our International Interests*. Washington, DC: National Academy Press; 1997.

27. Kassalow, JS. *Why Health Is Important to U.S. Foreign Policy*. New York: Council on Foreign Relations and Milbank Memorial Fund; 2001.

28. Schwartz, B. *Costs of Living: How Market Freedom Erodes the Best Things in Life*. New York: W. W. Norton & Company; 1994.

29. Kohut, A. Retropolitics: The Political Typology: Version 3.0. Washington, DC: Pew Research Center for the People and the Press; 1999. p. 163.

30. Wysocki, B. Where We Stand: Capitalism May Appear to Have Won the Global Ideological War. But Plenty of Battles Remain. *Wall Street Journal* (September 27, 1999) R5.

31. Axelrod, R. *The Evolution of Cooperation.* New York: Basic Books; 1984.

32. Yankelovich, D. Managing a High-Discretion Workplace. *Industry Week* 1988;237(11):64–65.

33. Nault, BR, Vandenbosch MB. Eating Your Own Lunch: Protection through Preemption. In: Ilinitch AY, Lewin AY, D'Aveni RD, editors. *Managing in Times of Disorder: Hypercompetitive Organizational Responses.* Thousand Oaks, CA: Sage Publications; 1998. p. 171–206.

34. International Institute for Management Development. *The World Competitiveness Yearbook 1997.* Lausanne, Switzerland: International Institute for Management Development; 1997.

35. D'Aveni, RA, Gunther R. *Hypercompetitive Rivalries: Competing in Highly Dynamic Environments.* New York: Free Press; 1995.

36. Meehan, EJ. *Social Inquiry: Needs, Possibilities, Limits.* Chatham, NJ: Chatham House Publishers; 1994.

37. Thurow, LC. *The Future of Capitalism: How Today's Economic Forces Shape Tomorrow's World.* New York: William Morrow and Company; 1996.

38. Culbertson, JM. *Competition, Constructive and Destructive.* Madison, WI: Twenty-First Century Press; 1985.

39. Johnson, DW, Johnson RT. *Learning Together and Alone: Cooperative, Competitive, and Individualistic Learning.* 4th ed. Boston: Allyn & Bacon; 1994.

40. Rosenau, PV, Linder S. Two Decades of Research Comparing For-Profit and Nonprofit Health Provider Performance in the U.S. *Social Science Quarterly* 2003;84(2).

41. Fletcher, RH. Who Is Responsible for the Common Good in a Competitive Market? *Journal of the American Medical Association* 1999;281(12):1127–28.

42. Cunningham, PJ, Grossman JM, St. Peter RF, Lesser CS. Managed Care and Physicians' Provision of Charity Care. *Journal of the American Medical Association* 1999;281(12):1087–92.

43. Preston, J. Hospitals Look on Charity Care as Unaffordable Option of Past. *New York Times* (April 14, 1996) A1, A15.

44. Moy, E, Mazzaschi AJ, Levin RJ, Blake DA, Griner PF. Relationship between National Institutes of Health Research Awards to US Medical Schools and Managed Care Market Penetration. *Journal of the American Medical Association* 1997;278(3):217–21.

45. Weissman, JS, Saglam D, Campbell EG, Causino N, Blumenthal D. Market Forces and Unsponsored Research in Academic Health Centers. *Journal of the American Medical Association* 1999;281(12):1093–98.

46. Etzioni, A, et. al. The Responsive Communitarian Platform: Rights and Responsibilities. *The Responsive Community* 1991–1992(Winter):4–18.

47. Anonymous. Teaching Hospitals Facing Financial Crisis. CNN Interactive; 1999.

48. Campbell, EG, Weissman JS, Blumenthal D. Relationship between Market Competition and the Activities and Attitudes of Medical School Faculty. *Journal of the American Medical Association* 1997;278(3):222–26.

49. Meehan, E. *Economics and Policy Making.* Westport, CT: Greenwood Press; 1986.

50. Sachs, JD, Warner AM. Executive Summary. World Economic Forum; 1999; at www.weforum.org/publications/repository/gcr98.pdf (accessed July 27, 1999).

51. Sachs, J. Sachs on Development: Helping the World's Poorest. *The Economist* (August 14,1999) 17–20.

52. Schlesinger, JM. U.S. Economy Shows Foreign Nations Ways to Grow Much Faster: By Looking at Denver, They Can See the Flexibility in Capital, Labor Markets. *Wall Street Journal* (June 19, 1997) A1, A12.

53. Steckel, RH, Floud R, editors. *Health and Welfare during Industrialization.* Chicago: University of Chicago Press; 1997.

54. Stevens, WK. Warmer, Wetter, Sicker: Linking Climate to Health. *New York Times* (August 10, 1998) A1, A12.

55. Bloom, DE, Canning D. The Health and Wealth of Nations. *Science* 2000;287(5456):1207–9.

56. Lohr, S. Computer Age Gains Respect of Economists. *New York Times* (April 14, 1999) A1, C14.

57. *The Economist.* Private Profit, Public Service. *The Economist* (December 9, 1995) 66–67.

58. Burke, T, Genn-Bash A, Haines B. *Competition in Theory and Practice.* London: Routledge; 1991.

59. Diamond, J. *Guns, Germs, and Steel: The Fates of Human Societies.* New York: W. W. Norton & Company; 1999.

60. Harvard Institute. *Emerging Asia.* Manila: Asian Development Bank; 1997.

61. McNeil, DG. That Whining Sound of Lost Money and Lives. *New York Times* (April 30, 2000) sec. 4, p. 2, col. 1.

62. Landes, DS. *The Wealth and Poverty of Nations: Why Some Are Rich and Some So Poor.* New York: W. W. Norton & Company; 1999.

63. Inglehart, R. Culture and Democracy. In: Harrison LE, Huntington SP, editors. *Culture Matters: How Values Shape Human Progress.* New York: Basic Books; 2001.

64. Stille, A. An Old Key to Why Countries Get Rich: It's the Culture That Matters, Some Argue Anew. *New York Times* (January 13, 2001) A17.

65. Stiglitz, JE. The Roaring Nineties. *The Atlantic Monthly* 2002(October):75–89.

66. Public Broadcasting System. The News Hour with Jim Lehrer: "The 'New' Economy." January 13, 2000.

67. Wallerstein, I. The Eagle Has Crash Landed. *Foreign Policy: The Magazine of Global Politics, Economics, and Ideas* (July/August 2002) 60–68.

68. Schmitt, J, Mishel L. The United States and Europe: Who's Really Ahead? In: Madrick J, editor. *Unconventional Wisdom: Alternative Perspectives on the New Economy.* New York: Century Foundation Press; 2000.

69. Stevenson, RW. Dollar Hits a 2-Year Low against Euro. *New York Times* (June 21, 2002) C1.

70. *The Economist.* Trade: Bush the Anti-Globaliser. *The Economist* (May 11, 2002) 14.

71. Cummings, J, Boston W. Bush Faces Widening Gap with Europe. *Wall Street Journal* (May 21, 2002) A15.

72. Crossette, B. Washington Is Criticized for Growing Reluctance to Sign Treaties. *New York Times* (April 4, 2002) A5.

73. Schmemann, S. U.S. vs. U.N. Court: Two Worldviews. *New York Times* (July 2, 2002) A8.

74. Crossette, B. U.S. Fails in Effort to Block Vote on U.N. Convention on Torture. *New York Times* (July 25, 2002) A7.

75. Council on Foreign Relations. *Public Diplomacy: A Strategy for Reform.* New York: Council on Foreign Relations; 2002. p. 28.

76. Hwang, S. Feeling Blah at Work? It May Be Your Job, Not Your Prescription. *Wall Street Journal* (September 18, 2002) B1.

77. Turner, JC. Anthropological and Cross-Cultural Perspectives. In: Colman AM, editor. *Cooperation and Competition in Human and Animals.* Wokingham, U.K.: Van Nostrand Reinhold; 1982. p. 219–49.

78. Kohn, A. *No Contest: The Case against Competition.* Boston: Houghton Mifflin Company; 1992.

79. Kelley, HH, Stahelski AJ. Errors in Perception of Intentions in a Mixed-Motive Game. *Journal of Experimental Social Psychology* 1970;6:379–400.

80. Chatman, JA, Barsade SG. Personality, Organizational Culture, and Cooperation: Evidence from a Business Simulation. *Administrative Science Quarterly* 1995;40(September):423–43.

81. French, DC, Brownell CA, Graziano WG, Hartup WW. Effects of Cooperative, Competitive, and Individualistic Sets on Performance in Children's Groups. *Journal of Experimental Child Psychology* 1977;24(1):1–10.

82. Acheson, SD. Independent Inquiry into Inequalities in Health Report. London: The Stationery Office; 1998.

83. Flynn, R, Williams G, Pickard S. *Markets and Networks: Contracting in Community Health Services.* Buckingham, U.K.: Open University Press; 1996.

84. Sherif, M, Harvey OJ, White BJ, Hood WR, Sherif CW. *Intergroup Conflict and Cooperation: The Robbers Cave Experiment.* Norman: Institute of Group Relations, University of Oklahoma; 1961.

85. Deutsch, MA. A Theory of Co-operation and Competition. *Human Relations* 1949; 2(April):129–51.

86. Worchel, S, Andreoli VA, Folger R. Intergroup Cooperation and Intergroup Attraction: The Effect of Previous Interaction and Outcome of Combined Effort. *Journal of Experimental Social Psychology* 1977;13:131–40.

87. Gilpin, R, Gilpin JMG. *The Challenge of Global Capitalism: The World Economy in the 21st Century.* Princeton, NJ: Princeton University Press; 2000.

88. Group of Lisbon. *Limits to Competition.* Cambridge, MA: MIT Press; 1995.

89. Soros, G. *The Crisis of Global Capitalism: Open Society Endangered.* 1st ed. New York: Public Affairs; 1998.

90. Wallerstein, I. Judge, Jury, and Cavalry. Commentary No. 93. Binghamton: Fernaud Braudel Center, State University of New York at Binghamton; at http://fbc.binghamton.edu/93en.htm (accessed July 15, 2002).

91. Deutsch, M. *The Resolution of Conflict: Constructive and Destructive Processes.* New Haven, CT: Yale University Press; 1973.

92. Hirsch, F. *Social Limits to Growth.* Cambridge, MA: Harvard University Press; 1976.

93. Hicks, A, Kenworthy L. Cooperation and Political Economic Performance in Affluent Democratic Capitalism. *American Journal of Sociology* 1998;103(6):1631–72.

94. Paltrow, SJ. Mutual Insurer Found Way to "Demutualize" That's Fast and Cheap. *Wall Street Journal* (December 1, 1998) A1, A8.

95. Rapoport, A, Chammah AM. *Prisoner's Dilemma: A Study in Conflict and Cooperation.* Ann Arbor: University of Michigan Press; 1965.

96. Axelrod, R. *The Complexity of Cooperation: Agent-Based Models of Competition and Collaboration.* Princeton, NJ: Princeton University Press; 1997.

97. Kramer, RM, Wei J, Bendor J. Golden Rules and Leaden Worlds: Exploring the Limitations of Tit-for-Tat as a Social Decision Rule. In: Darley JM, Messick DM, Tyler TR, editors. *Social Influences on Ethical Behavior in Organizations.* Mahwah, NJ: Lawrence Erlbaum Associates; 2001. p. 177–200.

98. Erdal, D, Whiten A. On Human Egalitarianism: An Evolutionary Product of Machiavellian Status Escalation? *Current Anthropology* 1994;35(2):175–83.

99. Fehr, E, Gachter S. Altruistic Punishment in Humans. *Nature* 2002;415:137–40.

100. Bowles, S, Gintis H. Reciprocity, Self-Interest, and the Welfare State. *Nordic Journal of Political Economy* 2000;26(1):33–53.

101. Fischbacher, U, Gatchter S, Fehr E. Are People Conditionally Cooperative? Evidence from a Public Goods Experiment. *Economics Letter* 2001;71:397–404.

102. Sigmund, K, Fehr E, Nowak MA. The Economics of Fair Play. *Scientific American* (January 2002) 83–87.

103. Henrich, J, Boyd R, Bowles S, Camerer C, Fehr E, Gintis H, et al. In Search of Homo Economicus: Behavioral Experiments in 15 Small-Scale Societies. *American Economic Review* 2001;91(2):73–78.

8

Changing the Competition Paradigm
and Restoring Balance

MAINTAINING BALANCE REGARDING COMPETITION IS no easy task, but it is a reasonable goal. Balance means reserving a place for constructive competition and cooperation. Revising the competition paradigm, or simply attaining a better balance, does not mean ceasing to compete. It means striving for constructive forms of competition, emphasizing appropriate competition. It means designing markets that are both profit producing and socially constructive.[1] Constructive competition almost never exists in the absence of some degree of cooperation.[2] As Robert Frank and Phillip Cook put it in their book *The Winner-Take-All Society,* "Between the extremes lies a prudent middle ground—one that preserves the vibrancy of market forces and at the same time acknowledges that, in matters of culture, our collective interests often differ profoundly from our individual interests."[3, p. 229]

In this chapter, attention turns to policy and regulation to correct some of the problems arising from a too-enthusiastic acceptance of the competition paradigm. If the vulnerability problem outlined in chapter 7 can be solved, then substantive policy is one way to manage the degree and intensity of competition, to bring discourse about competition in line with how we behave, and to contain the self-reinforcing spiral of increasing competition. Policy may encourage constructive forms of competition and offer incentives for moderating destructive competition.[4] In this regard, knowledge-based policies are effective, as are best-for-all policies. Regulation is part of the problem, but it is also essential to any solution. There are good reasons to be suspicious of regulation but no reason to adopt the view central to the competition paradigm, namely, that regulation is inherently objectionable in the abstract. Regulation can be pro-competition as well as anticompetition, and it can favor business interests or hinder them. But it is central to constructive competition and essential to responsible stewardship.

The final sections of this chapter discuss the need to make provision for that substantial portion of the population that cannot effectively produce to capacity within an excessively competitive environment. The competition paradigm and the self-reinforcing spiral of competition foster exclusion. But inclusion works better, as research across the past century shows over and over again. In the end, the competition paradigm is not destiny; it is a diversion.

Public and Private Policy for Constructive and Appropriate Competition

Integrated into the competition paradigm is the belief that there is little need for policy of any kind, private or public. What is best is assumed to happen naturally if the market is given free rein, if individuals have the freedom to pursue their self-interest. This is the market fundamentalism described in chapter 1, and the opposite is just as likely to be true. But advocating no policy is itself a conscious policy choice with now-known consequences.

Policy for Appropriate and Effective Competition

Six types of policies that encourage appropriate and constructive competition are proposed here as an alternative.[5, 6] These policies are not entirely new, nor are they necessarily more expensive than their opposites. Neither are they obviously politically partisan in one direction or the other. All can be employed to structure incentives for better performance without individual failure, whether the "individual" be defined as a person, a corporation, or a country. Constructive competition incorporates incentives that improve individual performance, increase productivity, and enhance efficiency.

First, policy that encourages goal-oriented competition rather than interpersonal competition is desirable and constructive. Health maintenance organizations that offer incentives for reaching specific practitioner goals are an example of such policy. All physicians and physician groups attaining a specific goal regarding quality measures and patient satisfaction are awarded a 10 percent bonus by Blue Cross of California.[7]

Second, policies that encourage zero-sum, winner-take-all results should be avoided. For example, if an incentive pool is set up with a fixed amount of money distributed to employees at the end of the year on the basis of measured individual productivity, then destructive competition is increased. What one employee gains, another loses. If, however, a bonus of a specific amount or percentage of salary is offered to all employees who attain a certain level of productivity or degree of improvement, then overall performance may increase while destructive competition between employees does not. Giving a single large prize to the child who wins a footrace is another example, especially if other participants win nothing at all.

Third, policy should discourage forms of competition that provoke levels of anxiety so high that it interferes with performance. A lot is known about the relationship between anxiety and stress levels and what is optimal for individual and society.[8] This was discussed in chapter 2. Communicating as much information as possible about the competition-related situation in advance may, in some situations, reduce anxiety for many people. Taking steps to enhance individual control in competitive situations works the same way. Permitting participant input and involvement in establishing the context of competition may similarly reduce isolation and anxiety. Private policies along these lines would include "trying forms of worker cooperatives, elected directors, employee share ownership, or almost any other forms of democratic decision-making."[9, p. 538] As mentioned in chapter 4, such innovations have been found to increase productivity in many different situations.[10]

Fourth, policies to encourage constructive competition need to be structured so that everyone has a fair chance of, if not winning, at least gaining something they value from participating. Examples from the sports world are discussed in this chapter. Such competition is structured to offer an advantage to those who have not won in the recent past in order to keep everyone trying. For example, limiting past winners from being considered for awards for a certain period of time gives others a chance to win.

Fifth, policies for constructive and appropriate competition encourage rules that are agreed on in advance, that seem fair to all, that indicate appropriate behavior, and that outline unacceptable activity. Gaming the rules as well as explicit cheating may be human nature, but policy needs to discourage them if constructive competition is to be assured.

Sixth, policies are best if they organize the competitive encounter so that individuals, organizations, and nations receive constant feedback and can tell how they are doing, where they can improve, and where they are meeting expectations. Total quality improvement techniques, for example, are based on these principles. In this situation, each individual competes with him- or herself, striving to develop new and useful skills, sharpen performance, and boost productivity, all the while enhancing what has already been accomplished.

Private policy is as important as public policy in moderating the effects of the competition paradigm and encouraging constructive versus destructive forms of competition.[11] Private policy is policy established by the private sector, largely internal to an organization that affects the normal, routine functioning of that organization. In this case, the goal is to implement policies that encourage constructive competition within an organization, designed along the lines indicated previously. Corporate policy, private policy, as well as public policy could bring balance to the competition paradigm by pursuing appropriate and constructive competition wherever possible. In the end, these six types of policies that assist in controlling destructive competition will not solve all problems. No claim is made that they constitute anything more than part of the answer to the dilemmas faced by societies around the world today. They do, however, constitute a beginning, and they are hardly likely to make things worse.

Prioritizing Policy Change: Fundamental, Ameliorative, or Reinforcing Policy

Policymakers can attempt to balance competition in several ways. Direct intervention involves fundamental policy change. Ameliorative policies are another option; they leave the basic difficulties unchanged but redress some of the worst problems associated with destructive competition. Ironically, the absence of any new policy is, in fact, reinforcing policy. This is because no policy means no change, and the competition paradigm continues on the same course. Finally, policymakers can choose measures to strengthen the competition paradigm, though there is no support for such intervention within the terms of the competition paradigm itself. Public intervention to shore up a paradigm that opposes government involvement is a contradiction.

Fundamental, ameliorative, or reinforcing policy approaches imply a clearly different course of action.[12] The division in the business community as to how to react to some of the most dysfunctional consequences of competition-associated inequality among nations illustrates these differences. Ameliorative policy is proposed by those fearing the disruption of civil society and of the peaceful exchange of goods and services. Debt forgiveness for very poor countries is an example of ameliorative policy designed to moderate the effects of the growing inequality that results as the competition paradigm plays out at the international level. Reinforcing policy—in line with the competition paradigm—is advocated by those who require recipient countries to make substantial internal reforms before receiving foreign aid. Debtor nations must make investors feel more secure in ways outlined in chapter 1. For example, proponents of this view argue that property rights must be ensured.[13] Further policy intervention is considered unnecessary. Fundamental policy change would seek to reverse completely the evolving relationship between inequality and competitiveness at the global level; there are few viable proposals along these lines today.

Ameliorative policy moderates the direct or indirect impact of destructive competition. In the United States, reducing substance abuse and providing health insurance are examples of such ameliorative policies that actually save resources if they reduce the cost of police, prison incarceration, and emergency-room visits.[14] These policy approaches conserve taxpayer dollars and improve overall societal productivity, even though they do not fundamentally decrease destructive competition or change the competition paradigm. Rewarding social skills that bring people together to reach common goals or encouraging cooperation or appropriate competition are other examples. The goals of ameliorative policies can be achieved, for example, by improving compensation for the cooperative-oriented professionals, such as social workers and teachers, who are undervalued compared to other professionals who have similar levels of schooling and skills.[15, 16] California's policy to make schoolteachers' wages exempt from state taxes is an example.[17]

Sometimes, policy can be both ameliorative in the short term and fundamental in the long term in an effort to counteract the excesses of the competition paradigm. An example is educational policy that seeks to change values, to foster a more qualified perspective on destructive competition, and to move toward an appreciation of the difference between destructive and constructive competition. Schools and universities that teach respect for fair constructive competition and cooperation and an understanding that achievements need not result only from competitive success are pursuing such policies. They could foster an understanding that not all individuals, organizations, and societies thrive in conditions of rampant competition.

Knowledge-Based Policy

Policy that is sure to be effective deserves priority attention when the goal is to encourage constructive competition and to avoid destructive competition. This is the case where a relevant knowledge base already exists. Basing policy on evidence to achieve specific normative societal choices is more common in Europe than the United States. For example, WHO-Europe sponsored the preparation of "Social Determinants of Health: The Solid Facts" in 1998.[18] This document links specific policies to research designed to reduce inequality. It consciously sets out to formulate policies on the basis of evidence.

If a specific policy has been studied and found to be effective, it makes sense to employ that information immediately. For example, studies indicate that short-term "crowding," working in high spatial density and close physical proximity, can predispose children from the fourth through eleventh grades to be competitive rather than cooperative.[19] Because more learning takes place in a cooperative environment, policy to reduce such density could change the level of competition and enhance learning.[20] Crowding in the workplace has a similar effect of reducing productivity, yet the number of square feet of office space per employee appears to be declining.[20] The consequences of crowding are known to be negative, but private-sector policymakers largely ignore this research. In the very short term, it appears that these research results can be disregarded with impunity. But what of the long term?

A second example of knowledge-based policies relevant for the problems related to the competition paradigm has to do with geographic mobility. Encouraging residential and employment stability in the United States could reduce the ill effects of destructive competition and increase social capital. Stable, long-term human social interaction moderates competition and encourages cooperative behavior to some extent.[21] This is because cooperation is based on a record of reliability and reciprocity. "The expectation of an indefinite number of future meetings means deception is a much less attractive option."[21, p. 28] Similarly, stable organizations share goals and desired outcomes.[22] Residential and employment stability are also related to the maintenance of social capital.[23] If this is the case, then societies with lower levels of residential and employment mobility might be more inclined toward constructive competition and suffer fewer effects from destructive competition than those with higher mobility.

Policies to encourage residential stability are more amenable to public sector intervention than to private-sector efforts. Possibilities include tax incentives to buy a home and stay in a neighborhood. Such incentives already exist to encourage Americans to buy and hold stocks and bonds in return for a reduction in the taxes owed on the capital gains that result. The same types of tax mechanisms are already in place in the housing sector, but they need to be expanded. Capital gains up to $250,000 on home sales are forgiven when specific conditions are met. One is that the home owner resides for at least two years in the home. These types of incentives could be developed and expanded.

Policy That Is Best for All: Who Is the All?

Policies that are best for all are optimal for bringing balance to the competition paradigm. In some cases, what constitutes best-for-all policy is clear, while in other cases it is far more controversial. In each case, the definition is straightforward. Best-for-all policy is policy that yields positive effects for all members of society no matter what their race, religion, gender, ethnic minority identity, and so on. It works for rich and poor alike.[24] This type of policy is the low-hanging fruit—cost effective, benefiting the many, harming the few, and blessedly uncontroversial. It is the place to look in times of economic contraction and political polarization.

Best-for-all policy implies a unit of analysis, a constituency, so to speak. This is so because the term "best for all" refers to "all," and that "all" implies a group of people. Such a group might be a family, neighborhood, city, state, nation, or geographic region. Within the framework of the competition paradigm, individuals strive for maximization of gain, and each individual is on his or her own. This is a substantial departure from the historical case of the subsistence economy where shortages recurred and survival was never guaranteed, where reciprocity and intragroup and interfamily support systems were required for survival.[25, 26] The definition of "all" expands when the sense of community and the perceived overlap between self and other is enlarged.[27] This sense of a broader "all" may also be envisioned as "layered loyalties" of various communities in constant interaction.[28]

Ultimately, and in the very long term, "all" is a planetary term, though a best-for-all policy focus on this unit of analysis is in its infancy, provoked to this level by global environmental concerns more than anything else. It is in this area of environment politics that global interconnectedness and the need for best-for-all policy that is environmentally friendly become clear for both the political left and the political right.[29, 30] An environmental sustainability agenda goes beyond domestic national policy efforts because the environmental "all" is global.[31] Most important, projects that protect the environment are best for all in the sense that they bring economic benefit (new revenue streams) to the companies that implement them.[32] They need not hinder economic progress or jeopardize national competitiveness.[33]

Education is another area where best-for-all policy is global in scope. The benefits of increased access to education at the level of each individual in the developing nations indirectly benefits the trading partners of these countries and the global economy as a whole.[34] Much has been learned from pilot projects about the policy incentives needed to ensure accountability and the ultimate success of such projects.[35]

The view that helping the poor because it is good for everyone, best for all, has taken on an increased importance as claims of equity and fairness for the poor on the basis of justice have faded.[36] Arguing for redistributing societal wealth from the point of view of moral obligation is more compelling if it is combined with the argument that helping the poor is best for all. This is "altruism" combined with self-interest. If the poor are better off, then economic productivity increases, and the poor become consumers. At the national level, if employed, the poor pay taxes, and crime rates are reduced. At the global level, mutual advantage[37] can be related to public health concerns.[38]

Best-for-all policy to manage competition by leveling the playing field involves redistribution. What makes this type of policy different from other forms is the argument that it is best for all because everyone gains in some respect. This may seem counterintuitive. How can it be that the better off would gain from redistribution? For example, everyone may be better off in a society with lower inequality because reduced inequality improves health and longevity for all, the rich and the poor alike.[39] "Health inequalities are not simply a matter of the poor versus everyone else. . . . Living in a more equal society is also good for your health."[40, p. 1] The health of an entire society is better if inequality is reduced. Comparing health inequality in Britain, Wales, and Sweden suggests that death rates for men are lower for all social classes, from the poorest to the richest, where differences in income are smallest.[41] If policy were implemented to make income distribution in Britain as equal as it is in other western European countries, life expectancy would increase by about two years.[42, 43] The same policy, if applied in the United States, is likely to yield even greater gains, though mostly for the poor and middle-level income groups.[44] Other research confirms that the sociophysical environment may have an impact on the health of everyone living in a specific geographic area.[43] This effect is independent of individual health practices—in short, there is a community effect regarding poverty areas.[45]

Why do the better-off sectors of society oppose redistribution policies? After all, they gain years of extended life and would surely welcome increased longevity. One explanation is that the linkages between the price and the payoff are distant, remote, and complex. The end result is easy to overlook, ignore, or dismiss. Finally, denial is at work as well. Those better off might reason that the research does not apply to everyone and certainly not to them in particular. This argument, based on exception, holds that while the research may be true, one's own case is different, and the results do not apply. One will escape the consequences of reduced life expectancy, for example, if one lives in a highly unequal society because of some mysterious special circumstances that remain to be understood and explained.

An Example: Using Knowledge-Based Policy That Is Best for All to Control Competition-Related Inequality

Knowledge-based, best-for-all policies can alleviate many of the negative effects of destructive competition, such as the inequality.[46] These policies range from improving the socioeconomic status of the poorest segment of the population to specific programs to prepare individuals for life in a highly competitive culture. For example, housing policies increase inequality when they result in some people living in gated communities and paying thousands of dollars each year to send their children to safe schools while others live in the opposite circumstances. It may well be worst-for-all policy if the poor live in despair in the crime-ridden inner cities and must send their children to school worrying about whether they will get there without injury because of neighborhood crime and violence.[47] Life in such neighborhoods is unhealthy, and community-level improvements could be expected to reduce health hazards in many ways.[48, 49]

Asset-based redistribution policies to give every child a fair start in life by paying a higher social wage are similarly knowledge based and best for all.[50] The social wage is defined as guaranteed, universal, nonmarket benefits. Related policies with the same effect involve investing in home visiting after birth, early childhood development, basic education, nutrition programs, and housing.[51] Norman Daniels, Ichiro Kawachi, Bruce Kennedy, and Alvin Tarlov point out that reducing income differentials and workplace command hierarchies are additional policy tools to achieve such goals.[52] Policies, they propose, that aim to "reduce material deprivation; invest in infrastructure; lower social gradients; and enhance security" all appear to improve population health, though they do not change the level of competition. In the same way, investment "in education, transport, communication, job creation and training, improved conditions of work, environmental cleanliness, and health care" would concurrently improve societal well-being and improve productivity.[53, p. 88] Because programs to further early child development reduce social inequality,[54] they too have an ameliorative effect. They moderate inequality-increasing destructive competition. A broad array of support services for the working poor has been found to be helpful in leveling the playing field for competition in this respect. Still, not all states in the United States are equally committed to employing such knowledge-based policies.[55] In other countries (Canada, for example) investment in subsidized high-quality early childhood centers is being expanded because this benefits workers, employers and the children who are a resource for the future.[56]

While policies that reduce competition-related inequality are known and can be very effective, they are politically difficult to implement because they go counter to terms central to the competition paradigm. Programs that transfer resources from the wealthy to the poor are politically controversial but terribly effective in reducing social inequality and thus moderating the effects of destructive competition. The United States is less effective than any other industrialized country in eliminating poverty through its posttax and transfer policies.[57, 58] Through such transfers, the percentage of the population living below the poverty level has been reduced to about 9 percent in Sweden, about 14 percent in Canada, and about 19 percent in the United States. All three countries had pretransfer poverty rates of around 22 percent.[59, p. 17] Government policies to reduce the depth, duration, and recurrence of poverty across a decade were found to be highly effective in comparative studies of Germany, the Netherlands, and the United States.[60] The same is true in a comparative analysis of the United States and Canada.[61, 62]

Studies indicate that reducing relative income inequality can best control the negative effects of too much competition in industrial countries.[63, 64] Those who live in competitive countries and who are the relative "winners" in that competitive environment are happier,[65] richer, and healthier.[66] But these benefits are at a price because, by definition, those who land at the bottom in the competitive race are less happy, poorer, and less healthy.[67] Redistribution policies, such as income support in the form of guaranteed annual income, is a device to reduce the income gap between the rich and the poor. But it does not eliminate relative inequality. There are many other policy approaches, each research based and tested for effectiveness.[68, p. 318] In the United States, the earned income tax credit (EITC)is one available policy tool. Like a wage subsidy, it is a credit against federal personal income tax liability for the working poor. Its effect is to increase the income of these families moving them above the poverty line.[69] The earned income tax credit has already been judged effective and could be expanded to further reduce income inequality.[69-71] Minimum-wage legislation is another example of policy to reduce relative inequality.[72]

In developing countries, policies that reduce absolute inequality or that reduce relative inequality all improve the health of the population. Policies to diminish absolute inequality increase overall gross national product. In the developing countries, a rising tide does in fact lift all boats. In other words, if the wealth of the developing country increases, everyone is better off in the long run, no matter who initially receives the increased wealth. Specific policy initiatives within this approach include stimulating the economy, lowering inflation, reducing unemployment, encouraging full factory capacity, and so on. These types of ameliorative policy approaches to reduce the effects of competition are useful in improving health statistics whether or not they are initially redistributive.[73] The same is not always true for the industrialized countries, where only those policies that reduce relative inequality seem to have the effect of improving health.

Policy is not a magic bullet, and its inherent limits need to be appreciated. Sometimes the appropriate knowledge base does not exist. In other instances, the known relationship between competition and social events is not amenable to policy intervention. But overall, where policy provides the means to revise the competition paradigm and restore balance, it should be employed. Public policy depends on regulation for its implementation. Here the competition paradigm comes into play, for it includes a deep suspicion regarding regulation. But regulation is too complex to be as easily dismissed as the competition paradigm suggests. It deserves a more sophisticated consideration, and it is the topic of the next section.

Regulation to Manage Destructive Competition

The competition paradigm does not appeal to the conscience of the winning competitors for restraint. To do so would not matter much anyway because the vulnerability problem, discussed in chapter 7, ironically sets up what Garrett Hardin calls in his now famous article "The Tragedy of the Commons" a "selective system that works toward the elimination of conscience from the race."[74] It simply does not work to depend on the human conscience to solve the problems that result from the competition paradigm, such as those involving the tragedy-of-the-commons type of situation. If those with a conscience refrain from grazing more sheep on the commons, those without such ethical qualms profit. They are enriched and thrive at the expense of their more ethical neighbors, at least in the short term.

If conscience by itself will not work to protect the commons in the form of less intense competition or cooperation, then inducements of a different sort are the only alternative. A carefully constructed system of incentives is likely to be persuasive. Regulation is about exactly this: the necessity of mutual, consensual compulsion to protect the commons, to escape the horror involved in the destruction of the commons, defined in its largest sense. Efficient, carefully designed, and fairly administered regulation is part of the solution. The risks associated with the tragedy of the commons, in its larger, generic sense, makes this so.

The goal of competition is not to be fair, to redistribute, or to ensure that everyone has an equal chance in life. That is why in the absence of outside intervention, the spiral of competition works as it does, to produce repeat winners and repeat losers. Regulation in the form of government intervention appears to be an effective tool in the longer term to reduce the negative effects of the spiral of unimpeded competition.[60] There is no telling whether private–public partnerships might achieve similar accomplishments.[75] But there is no reason that government need be the only source of regulation to encourage constructive competition.

The competition paradigm includes an element of deep and justifiable wariness of regulation. Regulation in the United States has not come to have a bad name without reason. In many instances, regulation has been misconceived. Sometimes it has been imposed when it was not even needed. It has often been poorly formulated and unfairly administered.

No wonder, then, that there is substantial opposition to using regulation as a means to manage the competition paradigm. Regulation is said to be unfeasible and unenforceable. Critics of regulation argue that the free market itself has internal mechanisms that constitute appropriate solutions to problems. For example, it was assumed that investors would stop purchasing stock in companies that did not respect acceptable accounting practices. Only companies that were conscientious in their accounting would survive.[76]

No matter what the sector, the discussions about regulation are much the same. Critics who oppose it suggest that sufficient regulation is already in place in the United States and that such directives, rules, or guidelines need only be respected or enforced. Others propose that while more regulation is needed, it should be self-regulation, for example, by industry itself.[77-79] Self-regulation, however, has not always been sufficient in the U.S. context. But in many cases, it was all that remained in the wake of deregulation in the late 1990s. Deregulation of the utilities, telephone companies, airlines, banking, and cable television did not always save customers money.[80-82] In some cases, the costs of deregulation created substantial inconvenience for consumers.[83, 84] It was seldom an unequivocal success.[85-87]

Where serious problems developed, the urge to reregulate gained greater acceptance and even bipartisan support.[88-90] The fear is that destructive competition in the absence of some regulation might itself undermine capitalism.[91] Terrorism also gave rise to a call for a larger role for government and more regulation.[92-94] In the case of Europe, increasing competition was never viewed as a simple matter of government withdrawal and deregulation. It was something to be carefully managed and even reconsidered from time to time.[95, 96]

In this section, we will see, in sum, that public opinion often supports, even demands, regulation to control competition and that regulation need not be the opponent of competition in every instance. In fact, regulation may be essential for the continued existence of constructive competition, to level the playing field for fair commerce, and to permit value priorities to be protected. It is central to effective stewardship. Competition is already regulated in any case, sometimes in ways that are so taken for granted by consumers and the business community that they escape notice. Finally, the dynamics associated with regulation in the global context suggest why paradigm change is likely whether or not the United States is enthusiastic about it.

Public Support for Regulation

While critical of government intervention in the abstract, public opinion is supportive of regulation in specific, known situations. This is the case even if the result is to reduce competition.[97] Regulation to protect the public, especially in emergencies such as a terrorist attack, is overwhelmingly high.[98] Pro-regulation sentiment is supported if it involves a commodity that is scarce and essential for life. Regulation is more likely to be acceptable if the number of people affected by any shortage is large, the duration of the scarcity is expected to be long, and the producer or supplier has a monopoly.[99] These conditions apply to some of life's most important situations. People compete for scarce resources, and this is where public backing of regulation is highest. On the other hand, people are more likely to cooperate when their goals pertain to abundant resources.[100, 101] Regulation receives less public support in these cases.[102]

Unrestrained competition itself often generates public demand for government intervention in the form of regulation. When competition, even constructive competition, creates problems, it focuses public attention on these specific competition-related issues and forces government action. When specific groups suffer, various types of reregulation are also demanded.[103] According to a 1999 Peter Hart poll, 60 percent of Americans believe that it is more important for children to learn to cooperate with others than it is for them to learn the value of competition.[104]

Regulation as Authentically Competition-Neutral

Regulation is neither inherently pro-competition nor anticompetition in the abstract because the forms it takes and its actual substance determine its effects. Regulation need not be inherently pro-business or antibusiness. Though it may restrain destructive competition, regulation can at the same time benefit organizations, businesses, and individuals. Singapore, for example, ranked as the most competitive country in the world by the World Economic Forum for close to a decade, has a very high level of regulation. Most of its regulations are, however, quite advantageous to the business community.[105] In the United States, the dairy and liquor industries derive major benefits from regulation and go to great expense lobbying to retain these laws.

Regulation, depending on its character, can successfully manage the worst types of destructive competition that threaten to supplant constructive competition and cooperation. This can be accomplished without reducing all differences, handicapping the already highly productive, or unfairly advantaging the less successful. Regulation need not impose the power of Soviet-style state planning, coercive bureaucracy, and authoritarian top-down rules. It can be organized to be less intrusive and yet still prevent breakdown, collapse, and violence. This is the case when it preserves appropriate competition by reducing the negative externalities of unrestrained destructive competition. Regulation, when properly structured, can protect constructive competition from being undermined by the negative practices that so often accompany destructive competition, such as fraud, crime, pollution, price wars, and so on. It can ensure that competition does not become so intense that it gives rise to political instability or threatens democracy.[106] Regulation is one important means to adjust, circumscribe, and discipline destructive competition.

In many situations, regulation is not so much an alternative to competition as it is a complement to it. That the two sometimes go together is not always apparent. Appropriate competition requires a degree of cooperation. For example, in sports, competition depends on a certain amount of cooperation between competitors.[107] "Competition cannot exist if there is no underlying cooperation concerning rules, procedures, time, place, and criteria for determining the winner. Without this underlying cooperative system, no competition can take place. Most competitions have referees, umpires, judges, and teachers present to ensure that the basic cooperation over rules and procedures does not break down."[108, p. 16] Without regulation, sports events would become "aimless activities, lawless conflict, destructive competition. . . . Even wars usually are fought within some rules."[109, pp. 2, 7]

The competition paradigm views regulation as interfering with an idealized process of market competition that is best left on its own. But here, too, as with competition at other levels and in different circumstances, a more balanced view would suggest that regulation is essential to ensure a just and reasonable process of exchange. Many experts conclude that some regulation is required to have effective competition in the business world—if only to guarantee respect for the fair rules of commerce.[110–114]

Part of the regulatory function is to provide the context and culture for safe and fair competition. Regulatory intervention is less controversial in these instances. Such intervention takes place all the time, though the competition paradigm makes no allowance for it and we do not think of it as "regulation." Horse racing is an example, for races are "handicapped" and the competition is closely regulated. The weight a horse carries is "adjusted" to give an advantage to the "underdog" horses. In other cases, designated weights are assigned according to past performances (so much additional weight for three past wins, so much for two, and so much for wins in the past three months, in the last year, in the year to date, and so on) with the objective of equalizing performance. Mares and fillies (females) carry less weight than stallions and geldings in a sweepstakes race such as the Kentucky Derby. No one makes an argument against it because without these "regulations," the outcome would be so predetermined as to bring the sport itself to an end. Where results are a forgone conclusion, things can be very boring, even though the terms of the competition paradigm are respected to the letter. Regulated competition is what keeps the horses running races.

Regulation to make competition fair works the same in other sporting events. "Drafts" for professional players have a regulated lottery system to give the worst team in a league the best chance of getting top players from an eligible field of new players. Why is this done? It is done because it seems fair and makes competing worthwhile—everyone keeps trying because the process makes it possible for all to expect to be on a winning team eventually. Fans keep watching and cheering for their favorite because the outcome is not a forgone conclusion.

Regulation is a means to overcome imperfect market competition in specific economic sectors.[4, 115, p. 644] Markets are almost never perfect, and imperfect markets give rise to great waste. For example, the rapid diffusion of untested, inefficient, and often-harmful medical technology is most likely to occur in unrestricted markets with unsophisticated customers.[116] In this situation, government's regulatory role is to smooth over the basic market structures and remove the worst abuses. This is a role overlooked and forgotten by the competition paradigm.

Regulation to provide consumers with full information about a product is another example. Those producing products often agree among themselves to avoid making full information available to their customers. Yet economists have long agreed that without it, consumers cannot make the informed choices required of them by the market model of commercial exchange. Regulation is a means to approximate perfect competition at least regarding full information for consumers. However, when regulation is unduly influenced or even drafted by those it is, in theory, designed to monitor, it fails to meet these objectives.[117]

In the best of circumstances, regulation contributes to the healthy functioning of the U.S. economy. The Federal Reserve Board sets interest rates and attempts to control inflation—this type of government regulation is essential for continued economic growth, innovation, and fair competition. Regulation is also a tool for controlling the monopoly power that results from the inevitably imperfect nature of market competition and organizational efforts to avoid competition altogether. This was discussed in chapter 5.

Regulating destructive competition (for example, ensuring a fair market) does not necessarily reduce the size of government. Instead, it may, in the long term, mean that government's role must be expanded. But there may be, ironically, no choice either way. Experience indicates that in the health sector, for example, the greater the reliance on market mechanisms, the greater the need for government regulation.[118, p. 102] The free play of the market itself seems to generate a demand for regulation of the dysfunctions that develop from the market itself over time. The competition paradigm suggests that in the real world, competition happens by accident and that it can be sustained without regulation. Wishing it to be so, regrettably, does not make it happen.

Responsible Regulation and the Role of Stewardship: Creating the Conditions for Constructive Competition

Regulations serve another function that is especially important in a period when the competition paradigm is so influential. Regulations are a primary tool of responsible stewardship, protective of social returns that cannot be the basis for profit and private gain. Stewardship requires using regulations to ensure performance accountability, economic responsibility, organizational efficiency, and trust-based authority exercised for the common good.[119] Regulations are the means to make certain that the competition paradigm does not generate a business environment in which it is difficult to fulfill social functions altogether. The competition paradigm neglects stewardship, but such stewardship is essential for managing basic functions, such as achieving social investment and the benefits of education, research, defense, and transportation (roads and airports).[120] Regulation grounded in stewardship is the only alternative where the costs of programs outweigh what any single individual or organization could possibly hope to gain from the provision of such services. It is best for all to provide public goods, yet the incentive to do so is too low to guarantee that they will be carried out.

Stewardship sometimes means employing regulations to protect society when competition fails to achieve the desired goals. For example, competition pushes firms to sell the most product at the lowest price. But this is self-defeating, for example, when the product is electricity, when the supply is inadequate, or when one of the "costs" of production include global warming.[121, 122] In the absence of regulation, private producers must encourage consumption and try to keep prices low to attract customers.[123] Stewardship in the form of regulations is a means to encourage incentives to conserve electricity. Stewardship and regulation may be paternalistic, but they are essential if there is any content at all to the concept of public goods and if the commons is to be protected.[124]

In an unregulated environment, encouraged by the competition paradigm, nonprofit institutions that are designed to fulfill social functions may fail to accomplish their mission. For example, in a highly competitive business atmosphere, nonprofit health providers must behave much the same as for-profit health enterprises. Access to health services for the poor and uninsured in the United States is reduced.[125] Marginally profitable health services, even if needed by society, cease to be provided.[126] A blurring takes place between government, for-profit companies, and nonprofit entities. Too much competition means a reduction in the probability that anyone is paying attention to what is best for all.

Stewardship requires regulation to protect public interest.[119] Public health regulation falls in this category. Requiring vitamin and minerals be added to common foods is not a commercial concern of the market, but it is part of a public interest responsibility worldwide.[127] Government need not always carry out such activities itself, but it must assume responsibility for seeing to it that they are accomplished. However, in many cases, such as ensuring the safety of the water supply, there may be substantial security risk associated with outsourcing and privatization.[128]

Regulation: A Multidimensional View in a Global Environment

Outside the United States, regulation to control destructive competition and policy to moderate its effects are viewed as advisable on the basis of justice and fairness.[129] There is a feeling that action is required where the "activities of one economic unit affect the well-being of another and no compensation is paid for benefits or costs created externally."[130, p. 57] Regulation is the means to preserve societal values that destructive competition places in jeopardy, such as the balance between the interests of society and those of the individual.

Countries such as Denmark, Belgium, Norway, and Sweden have not unequivocally embraced the competition paradigm. As Peter Hall and David Soskice indicate, these are coordinated market economies, and they depend on "non-market relationships to coordinate their endeavors with other actors and to construct their core competencies."[131, p. 8] They choose regulation as a means to protect equality and culturally associated values that are in jeopardy when competition is without restraint.

Even countries in Europe, solidly committed to what Hall and Soskice designate as more liberal market economies, differ from the United States regarding regulation. For example, Great Britain is a liberal market economy with a Third Way approach. It employs regulation to control destructive competition without giving up a pro-competition commitment to a balanced budget, to equal opportunity combined with personal responsibility, and to government in service to business and industry. Third Way regulatory activity is not viewed as inherently incompatible with seeking a robust and competitive market framework.[132] The Third Way approach aims to enhance national competitiveness while at the same time defending the environment, devolving power to the lowest level possible, encouraging public/private partnerships, improving the labor supply, investing in human development, and protecting social capital.[133]

Regulation to level the playing field of commerce and monitor competition among countries at the global level is at an embryonic stage. It is much needed but unlikely to be given much systemic attention soon.[134–136] In the absence of a system of global regulation, destructive competition cannot be managed. Without such coordination, projects such as the social protection of the world's poor, proposed by the World Bank,[137] will be very difficult to implement.

Still, globalization presses forward. The rules of commercial exchange similarly evolve, often in ways entirely unexpected. First, country-level regulations are coming to dominate international exchange. Ironically, the toughest large-market national regulatory product standards or those established by regional trading blocs end up being applied to all countries, even those such as the United States that consciously seek to avoid regulation. This is an ironic twist because while the United States has no competitors on the military level, its future economic competitors (the European Union, Japan, and China[138]) may well, without consultation, be setting the regulatory standards that U.S.-based multinational companies must respect if they are to participate in the global economy. In short, those countries that choose not to regulate or to underregulate are simply being left without much of a say as to the rules that apply in the global marketplace. Brandon Mitchener of the *Wall Street Journal* puts it this way: "Americans may not realize it, but rules governing the food they eat, the software they use and the cars they drive increasingly are set in Brussels, the unofficial capital of the E.U. and the home of its executive body, the European Commission."[139, p. A1]

Second, in the absence of global regulation, destructive competition holds sway. Exporting dangerous and toxic products is not in the interest of the global society.[140] For example, the already industrialized countries export outdated computer equipment to Third World countries. But these products are a source of environmental problems and health hazards.[141] And another example: Cheaper production costs may result from each self-interested multinational corporation neglecting pollution considerations whenever and wherever possible. Regulations prohibited using livestock carcass material in cattle feed in Britain once it was feared that the practice contributed to the spread of "mad cow disease." But British feed manufacturers, facing reduced demand for their product in the European Union and the need to remain competitive, continued to add this cheap source of protein to the products they exported throughout the world. Only after eight years, in 1996, did British authorities prohibit such exports.[142] It is not what competition should be about.

Third, sometimes a multicountry or regional effort to formulate collective regulation of competition ends up pushing standards in a few of the member countries to a lower level. This is the case with social and welfare functions. For example, when Sweden joined the European Common Market, it found it could no longer enforce regulations designed to discourage excessive and unsafe alcohol consumption.[143]

Fourth, diverse country-level attempts to manage destructive competition by way of regulation are illegally circumvented because national borders are so porous. For example, Quebec tried to heavily tax cigarettes to discourage youth smoking. But such regulations failed when cigarettes were smuggled into Quebec from Vermont and New Hampshire, where taxes were lower. To be effective, regulation to manage competition must be coordinated between states, nations, and even regions.

Make Provision for Exceptions

The competition paradigm emphasizes the skills required to survive in a highly competitive environment. Those needed to ensure success in instances that require cooperation are less likely to be appreciated. The innovation and creativity that result from cooperative human exchange are overlooked. Competitors, those who excel when challenged to do their best by comparing themselves to others, make a contribution. But society benefits from having cooperators as well, as discussed in chapter 7.

If all members of society are to be allowed to work to their greatest potential, to maximize their personal contribution to society, then provision must be made for those who work hard but do not function at their best in competitive circumstances, for those who do better and are more productive in a cooperative incentive setting. Overall, Daniel Keating and Clyde Hertzman suggest, "the larger the proportion of the population able to participate productively . . . the greater the likelihood of increased economic prosperity."[144, p. 15] Those who produce superior results in a cooperative situation need to be not just accommodated but also rewarded for superior performance, even when this is not produced through a competitive process.

People vary. One size may not fit all. Some people certainly excel under conditions of competition. The thrill of winning can be positively reinforcing, especially if it happens repeatedly to the same individual. While competition generates stress, this stress may be experienced and interpreted as excitement and stimulation of a positive nature, especially if it is associated with winning. In short, some individuals, probably a minority, may actually thrive on competition despite, for example, its potential long-term negative health effects.[145] There are very few studies of addiction to competition. In the context of the competition paradigm, such an addiction may even be viewed as an asset rather than a liability. But to adopt this uncritical view would be a mistake. When competition is addictive, withdrawal leads to depression, at least if what is known from competitive sports is true of other areas of life.[146]

The literature reviewed in the first few chapters of this book indicates that there are wide individual differences in response to competition at the biological, psychological, and social levels. Sometimes such differences become clear only in certain situations. For example, group-oriented individuals gain satisfaction from group accomplishments and from cooperation. They expect that all members of the group will similarly appreciate such group achievements. Those more individualistically oriented expect to be rewarded as a function of their own performance. Self-interest is a strong motive, and in the absence of such individualistic incentives, they are more inclined to exhibit social loafing than to compete to the best of their ability. "Social loafing refers to the reduced performance of individuals who act as part of a group rather than alone." In general, individualists perform best when working alone, while the collectively oriented do better in groups. Group-oriented individuals do not "demonstrate any social loafing effect . . . regardless of the level of accountability. Research on this topic suggests that, in fact, performance is highest for collectivists when they perform in [a] high shared-responsibility setting. Individualists, however, perform much better if they are held personally accountable. Their performance drops off when they work in an environment of shared responsibility without high accountability.[147, p. 571, 577]

Research, then, suggests a need for flexibility and new innovative efforts to construct a win–win workplace and to ensure that each individual is as productive as possible. It makes sense to permit each individual to work in an optimal environment, be that cooperative or competitive. Ensuring a cooperative work environment for those who perform best in this situation is not a recommendation to return to blanket welfare programs or unrealistic unemployment benefits that set up the wrong incentives. It simply means that at least some of those who fail at competing may be more productive in a cooperative work environment. Performing better in a cooperative situation does not mean that all cooperatively oriented individuals will fail if they are forced to compete by the context, culture, and incentives available. It simply recognizes that some people just do not do as well and will be less productive in a competitive situation.

Research is needed to ensure that all individuals, organizations, and societies can be fully productive. The skills required to succeed in activities that require cooperation receive little attention. In what conditions and for which individuals do the benefits of competition outweigh the costs? What would be the price of providing the opportunity for those who do not work effectively in a competitive environment to work in a more cooperative setting? What would be the expense associated with not doing so?

Competition Paradigm as Destiny or Diversion

"Competition" has two dictionary definitions. By far, the most common is the zero-sum version, destructive competition, discussed at the beginning of this book. It is central to the competition paradigm, indicating that competition is a condition in which what one individual, group, organization, or society attains, another loses.[148, 149] It "implies an opposition in the goals of the interdependent parties such that the probability of goal attainment for one decreases as the probability for the other increases."[150, p. 50]

A fitting conclusion to this book looks back to where it all first began: to definition. Competition's second, often overlooked, characterization is, ironically, unintentionally uncomplimentary. Implicit in it is a warning as to the limits of competition. Competition in this second sense signifies a distraction from the task at hand. It refers to something that occurs peripherally, adjacent to the principal focus, and that hinders or impairs the processing of essential information.[151, p. 1] For example, the child's crying in the backseat of the car distracts the mother's attention from the approaching traffic control signal.

This second definition takes on increased significance in light of the basic research reviewed in the preceding chapters. The competition paradigm may well be a distraction, diverting attention from important problems that need action. It seems to encourage Americans to ignore the costs of destructive competition, to trivialize the damage and injury incurred along the way. It could, in the long term, undermine U.S. strength and superiority and upset the balance and social support systems that have permitted the United States to succeed up to the end of the twentieth century. It is ironic that, because of its unqualified commitment to competition in every sector, the United States may lose out in the future to other countries that have pursued more balanced policies regarding competition.

An unequivocal national commitment to the competition paradigm is unwarranted. There is little or no evidence of a causal relationship between intense and destructive levels of competition and improved performance, broadly defined. It makes no sense to insist on destructive competition in settings where no competition is required, where it does not produce superior results, or where other approaches give better outcomes. The competition paradigm may, in the long term, turn out to be a liability, not an asset. America's commitment to the competition paradigm and its ongoing, often successful efforts to convince other nations of the paradigm's validity could be one of the biggest mistakes of recent history.

Notes

1. McMillan, J. *Reinventing the Bazaar: A Natural History of Markets*. New York: W. W. Norton & Company; 2002.

2. Bethlehem, DW. Anthropological and Cross-Cultural Perspectives. In: Colman AM, editor. *Cooperation and Competition in Humans and Animals*. Wokingham, U.K.: Van Nostrand Reinhold; 1982.

3. Frank, RH, Cook PJ. *The Winner-Take-All Society: Why the Few at the Top Get So Much More Than the Rest of Us*. New York: Free Press; 1995.

4. Etzioni, A. *The Moral Dimension; Toward a New Economics*. New York: Free Press; 1988.

5. Johnson, DW, Johnson RT. Instructional Goal Structure: Cooperative, Competitive or Individualistic. *Review of Educational Research* 1974;4(2):213–40.

6. Johnson, DW, Johnson RT. *Cooperation and Competition: Theory and Research.* Edina, MN: Interaction Book Company; 1989.

7. Gellene, D. Blue Cross Tells Doctors: Stress Care, Not Costs. *Los Angeles Times* (July 10, 2001) A1.

8. Boswell, WR, Olson-Buchanan JB, LePine MA. Investigation of the Relationship between Work-Related Stress and Work Outcomes: The Role of Felt-Challenge, Psychological Strain, and Job Control. Paper presented at the Academy of Management Meetings, 2000; Toronto, Canada.

9. Wilkinson, RG. Income Inequality, Social Cohesion, and Health: Clarifying the Theory—A Reply to Muntaner and Lynch. *International Journal of Health Services* 1999;29(3):525–43.

10. Baker, T. *Doing Well by Doing Good: The Bottom Line on Workplace Practices.* Washington, DC: Economic Policy Institute; 1999.

11. Rosenau, PV, editor. *Public-Private Policy Partnerships.* Cambridge, MA: MIT Press; 2000.

12. Tarlov, AR. Inequalities in Health: Causes and Policy Implications. In: Tarlov AR, St. Peter RF, editors. *The Society and Population Health Reader: Volume II. A State and Community Perspective.* New York: New Press; 2000.

13. Sachs, J. Sachs on Development: Helping the World's Poorest. *The Economist* (August 14, 1999) 17–20.

14. Starr, P. The Homeless and the Public Household. *New England Journal of Medicine* 1998;338(24):1761–63.

15. Steinberg, J. Salary Gap Still Plaguing Teachers. *New York Times* (January 13, 2000) A20.

16. England, P, Folbre N. Capitalism and the Erosion of Care. In: Madrick J, editor. *Unconventional Wisdom: Alternative Perspectives on the New Economy.* New York: Century Foundation Press; 2000.

17. Purdum, TS. Teachers Offered a Tax Exemption: California's Governor Would Waive Levies on Income. *New York Times* (May 14, 2000) A1, A23.

18. Wilkinson, R, Marmot M, editors. *The Solid Facts: Social Determinants of Health.* Copenhagen: World Health Organization Regional Office for Europe and London International Centre for Health and Society, University of London; 1998.

19. Aiello, JR, Nicosia G, Thompson DE. Physiological, Social, and Behavioral Consequences of Crowding on Children and Adolescents. *Child Development* 1979;50:195–202.

20. Costello, D. Incidents of "Desk Rage" Disrupt America's Offices. *Wall Street Journal* (January 16, 2001) B1.

21. Bateson, P. The Biological Evolution of Cooperation and Trust. In: Gambetta D, editor. *Trust: Making and Breaking Cooperative Relations.* Cambridge, MA: Basil Blackwell; 1988. p. 14–30.

22. Olson, M, editor. *The Logic of Collective Action.* Cambridge, MA: Harvard University Press; 1971.

23. Putnam, RD. *Bowling Alone: The Collapse and Revival of American Community.* New York: Simon & Schuster; 2000.

24. Nagel, SS. Introduction: Bridging Theory and Practice in Policy/Program Evaluation. In: Nagel SS, editor. *Policy Theory and Policy Evaluation.* New York: Greenwood Press; 1990.

25. Crook, JH, Osmaston H, editors. *Himalayan Buddhist Villages: Environment, Resources, Society and Religious Life in Zangskar, Ladakh.* Bristol, U.K.: University of Bristol; 1994.

26. Crook, JH. *Himalayan Buddhist Villages: A Study of Communities in Zangskar, Ladakh.* Warminster, U.K.: Aris & Phillips; 1990.

27. Cialdini, RB, Brown SL, Lewis BP, Luce C. Reinterpreting the Empathy-Altruism Relationship: When One into One Equals Oneness. *Journal of Personality & Social Psychology* 1997;73(3):481–94.

28. Etzioni, A. The Responsive Community: A Communitarian Perspective. *American Sociological Review* 1996;61:1–11.

29. Mills, J, Mitchell A. *Back to the Future: Collectivism in the Twenty-First Century.* London: Catalyst; 2002.

30. Nussbaum, MC, Cohen J, editors. *For Love of Country: Debating the Limits of Patriotism.* Boston: Beacon Press; 1996.

31. Paehlke, R. Environment, Equity and Globalization: Beyond Resistance. *Global Environmental Politics* 2001;1(1):1–10.

32. Deutsch, CH. Together at Last: Cutting Pollution and Making Money. *New York Times* (September 9, 2001) sec. 3, col. 1.

33. Esty, DC, Porter ME. Ranking National Environmental Regulation and Performance: A Leading Indicator of Future Competitiveness? In: Schwab K, Porter ME, Sachs JD, editors. *The Global Competitiveness Report 2001–2002.* New York: Oxford University Press; 2002. p. 78–97.

34. Sperling, GB. Toward Universal Education. *Foreign Affairs* 2001;80(5):7–13.

35. Krueger, AB. Putting Development Dollars to Use, South of the Border. *New York Times* (May 2, 2002) C2.

36. *The Economist.* Does Inequality Matter? *The Economist* (June 16, 2001) 9–10.

37. Gauthier, D. *Morals by Agreement.* Oxford, U.K.: Oxford University Press; 1987.

38. Yach, D, Bettcher D. The Globalization of Public Health, II: The Convergence of Self-Interest and Altruism. *American Journal of Public Health* 1998;88(5):738–41.

39. Wilkinson, R. *Mind the Gap.* New Haven, CT: Yale University Press; 2001.

40. Daniels, N, Kennedy B, Kawachi I. Daniels, Kennedy, and Kawachi Respond. *Boston Review* 2000;25(1):18–19.

41. Vagero, D, Lundberg O. Health Inequalities in Britain and Sweden. *The Lancet* 1989(July 1):35–36.

42. Lavis, J, Sullivan T. Governing Health. In: Drache D, Sullivan T, editors. *Market Limits in Health Reform: Public Success, Private Failure.* London: Routledge; 1999. p. 312–28.

43. Mitchell, R, Dorling D, Shaw M. *Inequalities in Life and Death: What if Britain Were More Equal?* Bristol, U.K.: The Policy Press; 2000.

44. Kennedy, BP, Kawachi I, Glass R, Prothrow-Stith D. Income Distribution, Socioeconomic Status, and Self Rated Health in the United States: Multilevel Analysis. *British Medical Journal* 1998;317:917–21.

45. Haan, M, Kaplan GA, Camacho T. Poverty and Health: Prospective Evidence from the Alameda County Study. *American Journal of Epidemiology* 1987;125:989–98.

46. Kunst, AE. *Cross-National Comparisons of Socio-Economic Differences in Mortality.* The Hague: cip-gegevens Koninklijke Bibliotheek; 1997.

47. Lewis, SJ. Advancing the Population Health Agenda: Uniting Altruism and Self-Interest. *Canadian Journal of Public Health* 1999;90(Suppl.):S66–S67.

48. Roux, AVD, Merkin SS, Arnett D, Chambless L, Massing M, Nieto FJ, et al. Neighborhood of Residence and Incidence of Coronary Heart Disease. *New England Journal of Medicine* 2001;345(2):99–106.

49. Marmot, M. Inequalities in Health. *New England Journal of Medicine* 2001;345(2):134–36.

50. Freeman, RB, Cohen J, Rogers J. *The New Inequality: Creating Solutions for Poor America (The New Democracy Forum).* Boston: Beacon Press; 1999.

51. Daniels, N, Kennedy B, Kawachi I. Justice Is Good for Our Health. *Boston Review* 2000;25(1):1–10.

52. Kawachi, I, Kennedy BP. Health and Social Cohesion: Why Care about Income Inequality? *British Medical Journal* 1997;314(April 5):1037–40.

53. Tarlov, AR. Social Determinants of Health: The Sociobiological Translation. In: Blane D, Brunner E, Wilkinson R, editors. *Health and Social Organization: Towards a Health Policy for the Twenty-First Century.* London: Routledge; 1996.

54. Hertzman, C. Early Child Development in the Context of Population Health. In: Tarlov AR, St. Peter RF, editors. *The Society and Population Health Reader: Volume II. A State and Community Perspective.* New York: New Press; 2000.

55. Bernstein, J, McNichol EC, Mishel L, Zahradnik R. Pulling Apart: A State-by-State Analysis of Income Trends. Washington, DC: Center on Budget and Policy Priorities and Economic Policy Institute; 2000.

56. Hanes, A. 20,000 New Daycare Spots: $50 Million Set Aside to Build Centres. *Montreal Gazette* (November 2, 2001); at www.childcarecanada.org/ccin/2001/ccin11_02_01.html.

57. Solow, RM. Welfare: The Cheapest Country. *New York Review of Books* (March 23, 2000) 20–23.

58. Wolff, EN. The Rich Get Richer: And Why the Poor Don't. *The American Prospect* 2001;12(3):15–17.

59. Auerbach, JA, Krimgold BK, Lefkowitz B. Improving Health: It Doesn't Take a Revolution. Washington, DC: National Policy Association, Academy for Health Services Research and Health Policy; 2000. p. 30.

60. Goodin, RE, Headey B, Muffels R, Dirven H-J. *The Real Worlds of Welfare Capitalism.* Cambridge, U.K.: Cambridge University Press; 1999.

61. Ross, NA, Wolfson MC, Dunn JR, Berthelot J-M, Kaplan GA, Lynch JW. Relation between Income Inequality and Mortality in Canada and in the United States: Cross-Sectional Assessment Using Census Data and Vital Statistics. *British Medical Journal* 2000;320:898–902.

62. Wolfson, M, Murphy B. Income Inequality in North America: Does the 49th Parallel Still Matter? *Canadian Economic Observer* 2000;15(6):3.1–3.24.

63. Wilkinson, RG. Inequality and the Social Environment: A Reply to Lynch et al. *Journal of Epidemiological Community Health* 2000;54:411–13.

64. Daniels, N, Kennedy B, Kawachi I. *Is Inequality Bad for Our Health?* Boston: Beacon Press; 2000.

65. Easterlin, RA. Does Economic Growth Improve the Human Lot? Some Empirical Evidence. In: David PA, Reder MW, editors. *Nations and Households in Economic Growth: Essays in Honour of Moses Abramovitz.* New York: Academic Press; 1974. p. 89–125.

66. Wilkinson, RG. Income Distribution and Life Expectancy. *British Medical Journal* 1992;304(January):165–68.

67. Chiang, T-l. Economic Transition and Changing Relation between Income Inequality and Mortality in Taiwan: Regression Analysis. *British Medical Journal* 1999;319:1162–65.

68. Tarlov, AR. Public Policy Frameworks for Improving Population Health. In: Adler NE, Marmot M, S. MB, Stewart J, editors. *Socioeconomic Status and Health in Industrial Nations: Social, Psychological, and Biological Pathways.* New York: New York Academy of Sciences; 1999. p. 281–93.

69. Cherry, R, Sawicky MB. Giving Tax Credit Where Credit Is Due: A "Universal Unified Child Credit" That Expands the EITC and Cuts Taxes for Working Families. Washington, DC: Economic Policy Institute; 2000. p. 23.

70. Scholz, J-K. The Earned Income Tax Credit: Participation, Compliance, and Antipoverty Effectiveness. *National Tax Journal* 1994;47(1):59–81.

71. Greenstein, R, Shapiro I. New Research Findings on the Effects of the Earned Income Tax Credit. Washington, DC: Center on Budget and Policy Priorities; 1998.

72. Marmot, M, Wilkinson RG, editors. *Social Determinants of Health.* Oxford, U.K.: Oxford University Press; 1999.

73. Hales, S, Howden-Chapman P, Salmond C, Woodward A, Mackenbach J. National Infant Mortality Rates in Relation to Gross National Product and Distribution of Income. *The Lancet* 1999;354(9195):2047.

74. Hardin, G. The Tragedy of the Commons. *Science* 1968;162(December 13):1243–48.

75. Rosenau, PV. The Strengths and Weaknesses of Public-Private Policy Partnerships. In: Rosenau PV, editor. *Public-Private Policy Partnerships.* Cambridge, MA: MIT Press; 2000. p. 218–41.

76. Stevenson, RW. Greenspan Says Enron Cure Is in Market, Not Regulation. *New York Times* (March 27, 2002) C5.

77. Weil, J. Andersen Retains Volcker in Effort to Boost Its Image. *Wall Street Journal* (February 4, 2002) A8.

78. Uchitelle, L. Volcker Will Continue His Push for Change in Auditing Standards. *New York Times* (March 15, 2002) C7.

79. Greenhouse, S. Bush Plan to Avert Work Injuries Seeks Voluntary Steps by Industry. *New York Times* (April 6, 2002) A1, A12.

80. Elder, R, Jr. Who's Exempt from Deregulation of Electric Industry—and Why? *Wall Street Journal* (March 10, 1999) T1, Texas Journal.

81. Oppel, RA, Jr., Gerth J. Enron Forced up California Energy Prices, Documents Show. *New York Times* (May 7, 2002) A1.

82. Consumer Reports. Deregulation Was Supposed to Cut Prices, Expand Choice, Enhance Service—Improve Your Life. So How Come You're Not Smiling? *Consumer Reports* (July 7, 2002) 30.

83. Smith, R, Fialka JJ. Juice Squeeze: Electricity Firms Play Many Power Games That Jolt Consumers. *Wall Street Journal* (August 4, 2000) A1.

84. Egan, T. Once Braced for a Power Shortage, California Now Finds Itself with a Surplus. *New York Times* (November 4, 2001) sec. 1, p. 29, col. 1.

85. Coffee, JC, Jr. Guarding the Gatekeepers. *New York Times* (May 13, 2002) A17.

86. Liesman, S, Weil J, Schroeder M. Dirty Books? Accounting Debacles Spark Calls for Change: Here's the Rundown. *Wall Street Journal* (February 6, 2002) A1, A8.

87. Schroeder, M. Enron Collapse Has Congress Backing Off Deregulation. *Wall Street Journal* (January 29, 2002) A22.

88. Power, S, Schlesinger JM. Bush's Regulatory Czar Brings "Smarter" Style to Pivotal Office. *Wall Street Journal* (June 12, 2002).

89. Reuters. California Moving toward Reregulating Energy. *New York Times* (September 21, 2001) A16.

90. Leonhardt, D. How Will Washington Read the Signs? *New York Times* (February 10, 2002) sec. 3, p. 1, 13.

91. Rohatyn, FG. The Betrayal of Capitalism. *New York Review of Books* (February 28, 2002) 6–10.

92. Toner, R. Now, Government Is the Solution, Not the Problem. *New York Times* (September 30, 2001) sec. 4, p. 14.

93. Ip, G. Mood Swings in Favor of Regulation. *Wall Street Journal* (March 29, 2002) A14.

94. Donahue, JD. Is Government the Good Guy? *New York Times* (December 13, 2001) Op-ed.

95. Organization for Economic Cooperation and Development. The Role of the Competition Agency in Regulatory Reform. Paris: OECD; 1998. p. 92.

96. Rhoads, C. Europe's Tender Equity Culture; As Stocks Slump, Continent Retreats from Market-Focused Model. *Wall Street Journal* (September 18, 2002) A17.

97. Frey, BS. *Economics as a Science of Human Behaviour: Towards a New Social Science Paradigm.* Boston: Kluwer Academic Publishers; 1992.

98. *Washington Post.* Washington Post Poll: War on Terrorism. *Washington Post* (September 28, 2001); at www.washingtonpost.com/wp-srv/politics/polls/vault/stories/data092801.htm.

99. Kemp, S. Preferences for Distributing Goods in Times of Shortage. *Journal of Economic Psychology* 1996;17:615–27.

100. May, MA, Doob LW. Competition and Cooperation. New York: Social Science Research Council, Committee on Personality and Culture, Subcommittee on Competitive-Cooperative Habits.; 1937.

101. May, M. A Research Note on Co-operative and Competitive Behavior. *American Journal of Sociology* 1937;42:887–91.

102. Turner, JC. Anthropological and Cross-Cultural Perspectives. In: Colman AM, editor. *Cooperation and Competition in Human and Animals.* Wokingham, U.K.: Van Nostrand Reinhold; 1982. p. 219–49.

103. Belzer, MH. *Paying the Toll.* Washington, DC: Economic Policy Institute; 1994.

104. Peter D. Hart Research Associates. Public Opinion Online. Storrs, CT: Roper Center at University of Connecticut and Shell Oil Company; 1999.

105. Hilsenrath, JE. Time to Ease Up: Singapore Has Thrived with a Government That Is Both Hands-On and Business-Friendly. But the Formula May Be Wearing Thin. *Asian Wall Street Journal* (September 27, 1999) S8, World Business.

106. Garelli, S. The Fundamentals of World Competitiveness. *World Competitiveness Yearbook 1996.* Lausanne, Switzerland: International Institute for Management Development; 1996. p. 10–17.

107. Albert, E. Riding a Line: Competition and Cooperation in the Sport of Bicycle Racing. *Sociology of Sport Journal* 1991;8(4):341–61.

108. Johnson, DW, Johnson RT. *Learning Together and Alone: Cooperative, Competitive, and Individualistic Learning.* 4th ed. Boston: Allyn & Bacon; 1994.

109. Culbertson, JM. *Competition, Constructive and Destructive.* Madison, WI: Twenty-First Century Press; 1985.

110. Osborne, D, Gaebler T. *Reinventing Government: How the Entrepreneurial Spirit Is Transforming the Public Sector.* New York: Addison-Wesley Publishing Company; 1992.

111. Sanger, DE. Look Who's Carping Most about Capitalism. *New York Times* (April 6, 1997) A1 A5.

112. Greider, W. *One World, Ready or Not.* New York: Simon & Schuster; 1997.

113. Lie, J. Sociology of Markets. *Annual Review of Sociology* 1997;23:341–60.

114. Gambetta, D, editor. *Trust: Making and Breaking Cooperative Relations.* Cambridge, MA: Basil Blackwell; 1988.

115. Emanuel, EJ, Goldman L. Protecting Patient Welfare in Managed Care: Six Safeguards. *Journal of Health Politics, Policy and Law* 1998;23(4):635–59.

116. Guillemin, J. Experiment and Illusion in Reproductive Medicine. *Human Nature* 1994;5(1):1–22.

117. Simpson, GR. Deals That Took Enron Under Had Many Supporters; Big-Name Lobbying Stymied FASB Push to Disclose Off-Balance-Sheet Entities. *Wall Street Journal* (April 10, 2002) A1.

118. Saltman, RB, Figueras J. Analyzing the Evidence on European Health Care Reform. *Health Affairs* 1998;17(2):85–108.

119. Saltman, RB, Ferroussier-Davis O. The Concept of Stewardship in Health Policy. *Bulletin of the World Health Organization* 2000;78(6):732–38.

120. Kettl, DF. *The Global Public Management Revolution.* Washington, DC: Brookings Institution Press; 2000.

121. Krugman, P. Power and Profits. *New York Times* (January 24, 2001) A23.

122. Berenson, A. Does Energy Deregulation Still Make Sense? *New York Times* (May 12, 2002) sec. 4, p. 4.

123. Johnson, K. Why Cost of Power Hasn't Dropped. *New York Times* (September 26, 2000) A23.

124. Baldwin, R, Scott C, Hood C, editors. *A Reader on Regulation.* Oxford, U.K.: Oxford University Press; 1998.

125. Stiles, PG, Culhane DP, Hadley TR. For-Profit versus Non-Profit Freestanding Psychiatric Inpatient Facilities: An Update. *Administration and Policy in Mental Health* 1997;24(3):191–204.

126. Schlesinger, M, Dorwart R, Hoover C, Epstein S. Competition Ownership, and Access to Hospital Services: Evidence from Psychiatric Hospitals. *Medical Care* 1997;35:974–92.

127. Chang, L. Saline Solution: China Uses Monopoly and Central Planning to Battle Iodine Ills. *Wall Street Journal* (June 20, 2001) A1, A6.

128. Dreazen, YJ, Caffrey A. Private Concerns: Now, Public Works Seem Too Precious for the Free Market. *Wall Street Journal* (November 19, 2001) A1, A10.

129. Silk, L, Silk M. *Making Capitalism Work.* New York: New York University Press; 1996.

130. Peters, G. *American Public Policy.* New York: Chatham House Publishers; 1996.

131. Hall, PA, Soskice DW, editors. *Varieties of Capitalism: The Institutional Foundations of Comparative Advantage.* Oxford, U.K.: Oxford University Press; 2001.

132. Blair, T, Schroeder G. Europe: The Third Way/Die Neue Mitte. June 11, 1999 ed: *Amsterdam Post*—Irregular Daily; 1999.

133. Dahrendorf, R. The Third Way and Liberty. *Foreign Affairs* 1999;78(5):13–17.

134. *The Economist.* Capitalism and Its Troubles: A Survey of International Finance. *The Economist* (May 18, 2002) 3–28.

135. Olson, E. Global Trade Harmony? Yeah, Right: W.T.O. Nations Can't Even Agree on Framework for Negotiations. *New York Times* (November 13, 1999) C2.

136. Soros, G. *Open Society: Reforming Global Capitalism.* New York: Public Affairs; 2000.

137. World Bank. Social Protection Sector Strategy: From Safety Net to Springboard. Washington, DC: World Bank; 2000.

138. Nye, J. The New Rome Meets the New Barbarians. *The Economist* (March 23, 2002), 23–25.

139. Mitchener, B. Standard Bearers: Increasingly, Rules of Global Economy Are Set in Brussels. *Wall Street Journal* (April 23, 2002) A1, A10.

140. Frank, RH. *Luxury Fever: Why Money Fails to Satisfy in an Era of Excess.* New York: Free Press; 1999.

141. Markoff, J. Technology's Toxic Trash Is Sent to Poor Nations. *New York Times* (February 25, 2002) C1, C4.

142. Stecklow, S. Hazardous Trade: Britain's Feed Exports Extended the Risks of "Mad Cow" Disease. *Wall Street Journal* (January 23, 2001) A1.

143. Daley, S. Europe Making Sweden Ease Alcohol Rules. *New York Times* (March 28, 2001) A1, A8.

144. Keating, DP, Hertzman C. Modernity's Paradox. In: Keating DP, Hertzman C, editors. *Developmental Health and the Wealth of Nations.* New York: Guilford Press; 1999.

145. Richerson, PJ, Boyd R, Paciotti B. An Evolutionary Theory of Commons Management. In: Ostrom E, Dietz T, Dolsak N, Stern PC, Stonich S, Weber EU, editors. *The Drama of the Commons.* Washington, DC: National Academy Press; 2002. p. 403–42.

146. Tarkan, L. Athletes' Injuries Go beyond the Physical. *New York Times* (September 26, 2000) D7.

147. Earley, PC. Social Loafing and Collectivism: A Comparison of the United States and the People's Republic of China. *Administrative Science Quarterly* 1989;34:565–81.

148. Scott, WE, Jr., Cherrington DJ. Effects of Competitive, Cooperative, and Individualistic Reinforcement Contingencies. *Journal of Personality and Social Psychology* 1974;30(6):748–58.

149. Johnson, DW, Maruyama G, Johnson R, Nelson D, Skon L. Effects of Cooperative, Competitive, and Individualistic Goals Structures on Achievement: A Meta-Analysis. *Psychological Bulletin* 1981;89(1):47–62.

150. Deutsch, M. Toward an Understanding of Conflict. *International Journal of Group Tensions* 1971;1(1):42–54.

151. Stankov, L. *The Role of Competition in Human Abilities Revealed through Auditory Test.* Sydney, Australia: Society of Multivariate Experimental Psychology; 1983.

Appendix 1: Data for Figure 6.2.: Change Score Calculations for Each Country

Country	GINI Change Score*	Base Years for GINI Difference Calculation	Change in WEF Competitiveness Ranking, 1996–2001
Australia	0.019	1985 vs. 1994	+7
Austria	0.05	1987 vs. 1995	+1
Belgium	0.028	1985 vs. 1997	+6
Canada	0.022	1987 vs. 1998	+5
Czech Republic	0.052	1992 vs. 1996	−2
Denmark	0.003	1987 vs. 1997	−3
Finland	0.017	1987 vs. 1995	+15
France	−0.007	1984** vs. 1994	+3
Germany	0.012	1984 vs. 1994	+5
Hungary	0.04	1991 vs. 1994	+18
Italy	0.036	1986 vs. 1995	+15
Mexico	0.027	1989 vs. 1998	−9
Netherlands	−0.005	1985*** vs. 1994	+9
Norway	0.005	1986 vs. 1995	+1
Poland	0.047	1986 vs. 1995	+3
Sweden	0.003	1987 vs. 1995	+12
Switzerland	−0.002	1982 vs. 1992	−9
United Kingdom	0.041	1986 vs. 1995	+3
United States	0.037	1986 vs. 1997	+2

* GINI change score based on data accessed from www.lisproject.org/keyfigures/ineqtable.htm, May 23, 2002.
** Average of 1984(a) and 1984(b) data.
*** Average of 1983 and 1987 data.

Appendix 2: Methodology

A S THIS STUDY OF COMPETITION moved from the biological to the societal level, evidence became more difficult to find and sources became more subjective. Chapter 2 reports on studies that are, for the most part, randomized clinical trials, case-central observations, cohort observations, laboratory experiments, and epidemiological studies. The research in chapter 3 includes several types of studies employing widely different methodologies. Though recent inquiries are given most attention, some of the research on this topic was done long ago. Of greatest relevance are the carefully defined experiments undertaken in a laboratory setting, often using college psychology students as subjects. Other studies involve individual subjects in their naturally occurring daily life surroundings. The advantage of the latter is that they are closer to real-world experience than the laboratory experiments. But in the real-world context, researchers are not able to manage the variables of interest involving competition to the same extent as in the laboratory. Small-group research, motivational studies, as well as bargaining and mixed-motive game theory also contribute to an understanding of competition.[1,2] Each methodology or approach has its own weaknesses and strengths.

The nature of evidence and the information available about competition in organizations, the topic covered in chapters 4 and 5, is of a different order than that regarding competition and biology, individuals, and groups. Organizations are an area where the direct effect of competition has been extensively studied, though not always in a strictly systematic or scientific manner. "Rigorous experimental control and manipulation are not always possible. . . . The analytic problem is exacerbated by the lack of sufficient aggregate units and by political constraints on random assignment."[3, p. 296] Naturally occurring experiments involving organizations are infrequent.

Data for evaluating the relationship between competition and productivity at the organizational level are difficult to come by.[4] But in addition, the data that do exist may be proprietary. Organizations often legitimately argue that to make that data public would be to jeopardize an organization's advantage over competitors.

Most of what is known about competition and how it influences organizations is based on expert opinions, intuitive insights, or illustrative examples. In the field of business and management, for example, the case study of a firm, corporation, department, organization, and so on is the classic form of information gathering. Investigations that refer to a limited number of cases are common, and it may not be possible to generalize from them. Anecdotal accounts of organizational success or failure based on single-case studies are considered an important source of learning.[5] Examples are common in the *Harvard Business Review* and the Kennedy School's online "Case Studies in Public Policy and Management."[6] In addition, investigative journalism from the *Wall Street Journal* and the *New York Times* is informative and of value for this topic. While scientifically weak, these forms of information are rich in substantive detail consisting of interviews with experts, synthesis, and observational insight. Even though not technically representative, they point to sentinel events and serve as sources of information that adopt a broader view than that usually taken by academics.[7]

The methodology used to research competition and culture, nation, or society, the topic of chapter 6, is sometimes based on comparative studies of individuals from the various countries of interest. Some of these studies employ the research tools of sociology and psychology just as those reviewed and synthesized in preceding chapters. Others are grounded in economics, employing national statistics from around the world and from international agencies that collect and archive such data. Social scientists have some empirical data about countries and cultures, but their most important tools are analytical, including interpretation to uncover the hidden meaning beneath superficial appearances. The problem with this methodology is that there is no necessary agreement among observers as to how to interpret indicators of what is really going on beneath the surface. Still, in some cases, one interpretation is considered more plausible than the alternatives by most observers. In the end, social analysis, at the level of society and nation, sometimes leaves many questions unanswered. More rigorous methods are desirable, and there are substantial efforts under way to develop them.[3] But until they are available, the only alternative to more subjective social analysis and expert opinion is often no analysis. This is why scholars analyzing phenomena at this level sometimes base their judgments as much on opinion as anything else.

Notes

1. Gerald, HB, Miller N. Group Dynamics. In Fransworth PR, NcNemar O, McNemar Q, editors. *Annual Review of Psychology.* Palo Alto, CA: Annual Reviews Inc.; 1967. p. 287–329.

2. Wrightsman, LS, O'Connor J, Baker NJ, editors. *Cooperation and Competition: Readings in Mixed Motive Games.* Belmont, CA: Brooks/Cole Publishing Company; 1972.

3. McKinlay, JB, Marceau LD. A Tale of 3 Tails. *American Journal of Public Health* 1999;89(3):295–98.

4. Nickell, SJ. Competition and Corporate Performance. *Journal of Political Economy* 1996;104(4):724–46.

5. Rochefort, DA. The Role of Anecdotes in Regulating Managed Care. *Health Affairs* 1998;17(6):142–49.

6. John F. Kennedy School of Government. The Case Program: Case Studies in Public Policy and Management. Cambridge, MA: Harvard University; 2002.

7. Aldrich, TE, Leaverton PE. Sentinel Event Strategies in Environmental Health. *Annual Review of Public Health* 1993;14:205–17.

Index

About the Author

Pauline Vaillancourt Rosenau, Ph.D., is professor at the School of Public Health, University of Texas, Houston Health Science Center. She edited *Public/Private Policy Partnerships* (2000) and *Health Reform in the Nineties* (1994). She is the author of several other books, including *Post-Modernism in the Social Sciences* (1992), which has been translated into Chinese, Korean, and Turkish. Two of her books received Choice Magazine's Annual Outstanding Academic Books Awards (1992, 1994). She has published articles in the fields of health administration, psychology, sociology, law, medicine, policy, psychiatry, social work, technology assessment, international relations, and comparative politics.